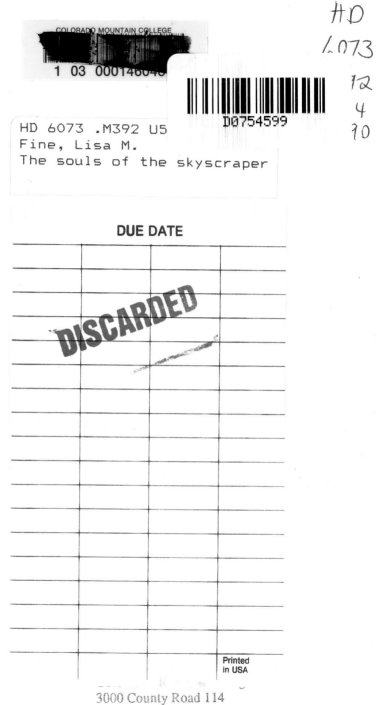

THE *Souls*
OF THE *Skyscraper*

In the series

Women in the Political Economy

edited by Ronnie J. Steinberg

THE
Souls
OF THE
Skyscraper

Female Clerical Workers
in Chicago, 1870–1930

LISA M. FINE

 Temple University Press • Philadelphia

Temple University Press, Philadelphia 19122
Copyright © 1990 by Temple University. All rights reserved
Published 1990
Printed in the United States of America

34,95

Library of Congress Cataloging-in-Publication Data
Fine, Lisa M.
   The souls of the skyscraper : female clerical workers in Chicago,
1870–1930 / Lisa M. Fine.
      p. cm. — (Women in the political economy)
   Includes bibliographical references.
   ISBN 0-87722-674-1 (alk. paper)
      1. Women clerks—Illinois—Chicago—History. 2. Clerks—Illinois—
Chicago—History. I. Title. II. Series.
HD6073.M392U524 1990
331.4'8165137'0977311—dc20   89-5165
                                                               CIP

Excerpt from "Skyscraper" in *Chicago Poems* by Carl Sandburg,
copyright 1916 by Holt, Rinehart and Winston, Inc. and renewed 1944
by Carl Sandburg, reprinted by permission of Harcourt Brace
Jovanovich, Inc.

Cover photo: Civil service exam for stenographers,
Chicago, 1909. Photo courtesy of the Chicago
Historical Society, DN 7016.

To

Shirley Haas Fine, Albert Fine,
and Tina Fine

"Skyscraper"

Behind the signs on the doors they work and the walls tell
nothing from room to room.

Ten-dollar-a-week stenographers take letters from corporation officers, lawyers, efficiency engineers, and tons
of letters go bundled from the building to all ends of the
earth.

Smiles and tears of each office girl go into the soul of the
building just the same as the master-men who rule the
building.

CARL SANDBURG

Contents

Tables

Illustrations

Preface

*T*HIS BOOK explains how women came to be clerical workers and describes the meaning that clerical employment had for women. There has always been a small group of clerical workers in the American labor force; until 1860, these positions were exclusively men's. During the Civil War, women broke through some barriers and became clerks in the federal civil service in Washington, D.C.[1] The first significant influx of women into clerical occupations, however, did not occur until the 1880s.[2] Women's participation in the clerical work force increased until 1930, when they constituted a majority of clerical workers in the United States.[3] As women increasingly dominated clerical positions, the gender association of clerical work changed from an occupation associated with male workers to a job in which the worker was presumed to be a female. Two transformations occurred, therefore, from 1870 to 1930: a simple shift in the sex engaging in clerical work, and a changing gender definition of clerical work.[4]

The industrial and urban growth experienced in the United States during this period certainly instigated and contributed to this labor force transformation.[5] Women's entrance into clerical work was also related to the increased supply of young, single, and trained women. During this period, women's labor force participation increased in every decade. The plight of the small farmer and entrepreneur during this time, and the increased use of labor-saving devices in the home and on the farm, rendered the contributions of daughters less useful.[6] Young women from small towns and rural areas in the Midwest began to migrate to cities such as Chicago for work opportunities.[7] In addition, during the late nineteenth century, women tended to remain in high school longer than men. Women, therefore, were more qualified for the jobs that were becoming available in the clerical sector.[8]

Explaining the growth of the demand for clerical workers, however, does not necessarily explain why women increasingly dominated these occupations. In addition, the increasing availability of young women in the labor force does not necessarily explain why many of those women chose clerical work. Except for those few female clerks employed by the civil service during the Civil War, there was little precedent for women's employment in the world of business and commerce. Clerical work was fundamentally different from other types of women's employment in the nineteenth century because its functions could not, at least initially, be defended as "naturally" extending from women's roles in her separate, domestic sphere. There was nothing inherently feminine in filing, typing, or taking stenographic copy, as there was in the "inherently" feminine occupations of nursing, teaching, domestic service, and sewing. We think of clerical work as inherently feminine today because, as women increasingly took clerical jobs, office work was socially reconstructed to mean a female task.

Women's entrance into clerical work is the story of the breaking of barriers and the redefining of rules governing the behavior of the two sexes. Although women entered clerical jobs as early as 1870, it was not until the early twentieth century that clerical work was generally considered "women's work." The story of women's entrance into and conquest of clerical work is, in one sense, a success story. Women's actions contributed to adding a new and relatively well-paid position to the limited list of occupational opportunities available to women at this time. Whenever a dramatic change occurs, such as the shift in the gender association of a series of jobs, there is always the potential for progress. Whenever one barrier of occupational segregation, or racial or ethnic segregation, for that matter, falls, those benefiting from the increased opportunities perceive a betterment of their condition.

Many women took advantage of this new opportunity. The organization and methodology of this monograph is designed to emphasize the importance of women themselves in shaping their own historical destinies. Female workers did not deterministically react to economic forces, although the changes in the economy certainly affected the occupational opportunities available; female clerical workers were not directed into clerical work by reform-minded groups, although the efforts of these groups certainly facilitated women's choosing office work. In many cases, women's decisions to train for and engage in clerical jobs prompted organizations to redirect the nature of their services to working women. Finally, female clerical workers did not entirely accept the portrayal of their own public images. Even when clerical work became "women's work" by the 1920s, the experience of engaging in this sort of employment did not always "validate conventional life choices."[9] Despite the overwhelming importance of economic changes, I believe that clerical work could not have become "women's work" without the decision of a significant number of women in the late nineteenth century that a clerical job was a good job for them.[10]

Even as women were taking advantage of this new occupational opportunity, they carried their own devaluation in the office with them in the form of their sex. Even when men and women performed the same clerical job, the sex of the worker determined the pay, and perhaps more significantly, the "promotability" of the positions. Significant rationalization, routinization, and mechanization of clerical jobs occurred only after women had completely dominated certain clerical positions.

That clerical work held promise for women before 1929 is often difficult for us to imagine today because of the job's ongoing devaluation, a process that began as soon as women entered the office. This was not a devaluation intimately linked to or corresponding with any fundamental degradation in the skill level in the day-to-day functioning of individual clerical workers. A minority of managers in the largest firms did adopt rationalization, generally, and scientific management techniques, specifically, in their office forces. Nevertheless, these managers did not simply have increased profits and efficiency on their minds; they could expect, in many instances, that the workers they were affecting would be women. Therefore, the exigencies of industrial capitalism alone did not influence the formation of the typing pool; patriarchy fixed women's positions within the occupational scheme of the firm and affected the texture of these positions throughout the twentieth century.[11]

The demographic characteristics of this group of workers reveal the power of patriarchy in even greater relief. Female clerical workers hired between 1870 and 1930 were overwhelmingly white, young, single, and native born. Particularly in the nineteenth century, they tended to come from some level within the "middling classes." Employers believed that clerical work required a certain facility with the language and the codes of middle-class decorum. In fact, significant numbers of black and married women did not enter clerical work until after World War II. Before World War I, however, employers and potential female clerical workers themselves only needed to bring the qualities required for clerical work into accord with the dominant cultural conceptions of white, middle-class womanhood.

This shift of the gender association of clerical work is also an important part of this book. Understanding the social construction of clerical work as a female occupation reveals the importance and plasticity of gender roles. In this book, I have focused on four settings where the gender definition of clerical work was debated, discussed, and negotiated: the world of technical experts concerned with the clerical field and office management; the popular culture and its expression in the popular media of the day; the prescriptions and actions of reformers, politicians, and city administrations, as well as other concerned public citizens in the city of Chicago; and, finally, the private worlds of clerical workers themselves. *The Souls of the Skyscraper* describes the lives and the experiences of a group of women defined by their occupation, but it is not confined to their activities at work. I am interested in the entire meaning of clerical work, from the personal meaning of occupational choice to the structural ramifications this myriad of decisions had within the economy.

Clerical work has always been either directly or indirectly a part of my life. Researching and writing about this occupation seemed natural. My first occupational choice was to be a clerical worker. In grade school, becoming an executive's private secretary was the most exciting, glamorous, and interesting job that I could think of. This was undoubtedly the result of the many stories my mother told about her tenure as a clerical worker before and shortly after she married my father. One of the stock tales in my family was how my grandfather, a barely literate working-class Jewish immigrant from the Carpathian mountains of northern Roumania, had urged my mother to go to business college after high school because he believed "that's what American girls do." I subsequently spent many unglamorous years, through college and graduate school, behind a typewriter to support myself.

My efforts to tell the story of female clerical workers in Chicago have received much assistance, both personal and professional. My work has been supported as a dissertation by a Lena Lake Forrest Fellowship from the Business and Professional Women's Foundation, by an Alice E. Smith Award from the Wisconsin State Historical Society, and by the Department of History at the University of Wisconsin–Madison. For the monograph, I received an All University Research Initiation Grant from

PREFACE xix

Michigan State University for release time, travel expenses, and supplies.

Librarians at a variety of institutions have helped my effort. Mary Ann Bamberger at the Manuscript Division of the University of Illinois, Chicago Circle Campus, Linda Evans and Archie Motley at the Chicago Historical Society as well as librarians at the Newberry Library, the Regenstein Library at the University of Chicago, Sears, Roebuck, and Company, the Library of Congress, the Wisconsin State Historical Society, the Labor Management Documentation Center at Cornell University's School of Industrial and Labor Relations, and the New York Public Library helped me find many rich and important sources.

I owe a special note of gratitude and thanks to the women of the Eleanor Association, now called the Parkway Eleanor Association of Chicago. Both Meg Madsen and Jill Goranson provided me with free access to their rare and wonderfully rich materials. Some of my most pleasant memories of researching this project are of the weeks I spent in their rooms.

Carl Kaestle, my dissertation advisor, who provided help and guidance during all phases of this project, has been a model of how a professor can be both an intellectual mentor and a friend. Thomas McCormick, Gerda Lerner, Barbara Melosh, Anne Meyering, Stanley Chojnacki, Maureen Flanagan, and Cathy Davidson have read all or parts of this project at some stage of completion and provided valuable assistance. Peter Levine has applied his critical and proofreading skills several times to this work, rendering it infinitely better. Three Cornell University professors, Gerd Korman, John Weiss, and Clive Holmes, not only inspired my interest in history, but also gave me the confidence to become an historian. Ronnie Steinberg, Michael Ames, and Terri Kettering of Temple University Press have been skilled and patient editors.

I have profited immeasurably from all of the women who have recently or are now researching and writing about female clerical workers in U.S. history. I am honored to be a part of this work and would like to acknowledge my comrades in this effort, some of whom I have had the pleasure to meet: Margery Davies, Elyce J. Rotella, Anita Rapone, Carole Srole, Sharon Strom, Cindy Sondik Aron, Roslyn Feldberg, Priscilla Murolo, Ileen DeVault, M. Christine Anderson, Angela Kwolek-Folland, and my friend Margaret Hedstrom.

Many fellow graduate students at the University of Wisconsin shared

their ideas and companionship. I would like to thank Margaret Hedstrom, Mary Neth, Mary Lee Muller, Charlotte Borst, Tyler Stovall, Bob
Frost, Ed Agran, and Kathy Alaimo. Personal thanks go to Jennifer and
Stephen Gessner, who gave me a warm home in Chicago. Finally, I
would like to express boundless gratitude to my partner, Peter Iversen
Berg, who, even though he minimizes its importance, never fails to
make me smile.

As I write this introduction, the Clerical and Technical Union at
Michigan State University is on strike. The struggle of these women to
receive fair and just compensation for their labors reminds us of the
importance of understanding the historical roots of these difficulties. I
hope that some of my work will comfort them in their struggle and help
them and other clerical workers develop new ways to bring equity into
the workplace.

PART I

Clerical Work as Men's Work, 1870–1890

CHAPTER 1

Clerical Work as Men's Work

*I*N HER 1873 book *Work: A Story of Experience,* Louisa May Alcott described ten years in the life of Christie Devon. At the age of twenty-one, during the mid-1850s, Christie left her only guardians, an aunt and uncle, to become an independent working woman. Through suitable, respectable, interesting, and remunerative employment, Christie dreamed, she would not only achieve fame and fortune but also contribute something to society. Most of her many work experiences offered neither satisfaction nor good pay, but boredom, danger, harassment, indifference, and exploitation. As a domestic servant, an actress, a governess, a companion to an invalid girl, a seamstress, a home textile worker, a housekeeper, a secretary to a minister, and a nurse and cook during the Civil War, Christie not only depicted the occupational choices available to young, white, native-born single women, but also the advantages and limitations inherent in each of these endeavors.

The fictional circumstances surrounding Christie's entrance into the wage labor force and her opportunities and experiences within the world of work were characteristic of many real women who entered the wage labor force during this period. The difficulty that many native-born women of farm or middle-class families encountered was reconciling their desire for "respectable" woman's work with their usually pressing need to support themselves and, sometimes, dependents. Christie clearly favored work that did not come into conflict with the prescribed role of women at that time, and yet she also took other factors into account as she journeyed from job to job. At the outset of Christie's work life, she brazenly declared that she would not teach because she did not wish to "wear [her]self out in a district school for the mean sum they give a woman."[1] Although she fell upon hard times trying to make ends meet as a home embroidery worker, she refused to take a menial position in a factory. Her inability to support herself was a source of constant torment, and she perceived her options all too clearly: marriage, spinsterhood, or prostitution.

After the Civil War, however, certain aspects of this scenario changed. If Louisa May Alcott had written her book twenty years later, family misfortune and a desire for fame, fortune, and independence would have probably thrust Christie into a different world of work. After becoming dissatisfied with standard types of female employment, Christie might have decided to take a series of courageous steps into a foreign, masculine world of business and commerce. Since she was a white, native-born, high-school-educated, young, single woman, she might have decided to move to a larger urban area to take advantage of the kind of training provided by private business colleges. Fending for herself in this environment would have been fraught with difficulties: the perils of the train station, the difficulty of finding safe, respectable, affordable housing, the challenge of making ends meet, the necessity of establishing a fulfilling social life. Migrating to a large city, attending a private business college, registering at an employment service, and procuring employment as a clerical worker in an office were all actions that required women to cross into worlds dominated by men. In a society in which respectable behavior required the strict separation of men's public sphere outside the home and women's private sphere within it, these actions were truly courageous. And yet, between the years 1870 and 1890, an increasing number of women took these steps, from home to school to office, usually against the backdrop of the burgeoning American city.

These steps might have seemed especially daunting for women in a city like Chicago. During the twenty-two years between the great Chicago fire and the World's Columbian Exposition, Chicago mushroomed into the second largest city in the United States. Between 1870 and 1890 its population increased from 298,977 to 1,098,570, while its area increased from 35.2 square miles to 178.1 square miles.[2] Important economic changes during these years accounted for this growth. Because of her advantageous location, her rich hinterland, and her connections to eastern capital, Chicago became the commercial center of the Midwest by the 1860s,[3] and by the 1890s, a national manufacturing center. Before the Civil War, the manufacturing done in Chicago was small-scale, crude, and oriented to a local market.[4] The most important manufacturing enterprises included blacksmithing, wagon making, farm implement manufacturing, meat slaughtering, saw mills, and flour mills.[5] By the

1880s this had changed, and Chicagoans themselves took note of the transformation of their city. In 1884, the *Chicago Tribune* commented on Chicago's "metamorphosis from a city of commerce to a city of manufacturing."[6] In 1880, Chicago hosted 3,519 manufacturing establishments that employed 79,414 wage workers. By 1890, both of these figures had more than doubled.[7] In both 1880 and 1890, Chicago ranked third in the United States in the average number of employees in manufacturing, the total wages paid in a year to wage workers, the capital invested in manufacturing establishments, and the value added by manufacture.[8] In 1890, Chicago ranked second in the United States in the gross value of products produced.[9]

The burgeoning manufacturing base of the city found its workforce from the ever-increasing pool of foreigners and migrants. Chicago's growth coincided with the major waves of European immigration. Young men and women from small towns and rural areas in the region also gravitated to Chicago in search of job opportunities and a more exciting life in the city. Before the Civil War, New England Yankees and a few Southerners had peopled the city.[10] The dominance of native-born Americans was short lived, however. From 1870 to 1910, the proportion of foreign-born in Chicago remained above the mean percentage of foreign-born in the nation's cities as a whole.[11] Southern and eastern Europeans replaced Germans, Irish, and Scandinavians as the dominant ethnic groups in Chicago as the nineteenth century came to a close. When the World's Columbian Exposition opened its doors, Chicago was not only an ethnically diverse metropolis, but also a preeminent national and international industrial center.

The boosterism, economic and ethnic diversity, and energy of its inhabitants were the stuff of Chicago's emerging reputation as a city on the make, a city in pursuit of the almighty dollar. Observers depicted Chicago as a hard and impersonal city, a city filled with "darkness, smoke, clouds, dirt, and an extraordinary number of sad and grieved persons."[12] In the business districts, "it seems there as if the men would run over the horses if the drivers were not careful. Everyone is in such a hurry and going at such a pace. . . . The whole business of life is carried on at high pressure and the pithy part of Chicago is like three hundred acres of New York Stock Exchange when trading is active."[13]

Throughout the period, observers persistently commented upon one of Chicago's most distinctive features—the stockyards and the coolness, efficiency, and profitability of the slaughter that occurred there. Rudyard Kipling found the stockyard a powerful symbol of the city. He was struck, upon his visit, by the carriage and reaction of a young female visitor. "She was well and healthy and alive, and she was dressed in flaming red and black, and her feet . . . were cased in red leather shoes. She stood in a patch of sunlight, the red blood under her shoes, the vivid carcasses stacked round her, a bullock bleeding its life away not six feet from her, and the death factory roaring around her. She looked curiously, with hard, bold eyes, and was not ashamed."[14] Chicagoans, in their relentless quest for survival and profit, were also unashamed, or so it seemed.

Kipling's brazen and worldly woman in black and red, however, more accurately symbolized Chicago than Chicago's womanhood. The world of the slaughterhouses, like the jobbing houses, banks, financial institutions, railroad offices, retail and wholesale houses, and the entire business district, except for the large department stores and fancy hotels and restaurants, was a world of men. Within this masculine domain, clerical work was a small but consistent component. The clerks and bookkeepers listed in the city directories between the years 1839 and 1880 made up between 7 percent and 8 percent of the labor force, and they were found in the insurance companies, retail and wholesale establishments, financial establishments, real estate firms, and the earliest manufacturing and railroad companies.[15]

Throughout the nineteenth century, clerical work was an almost exclusively male occupation. Although women first took positions in offices during these years, quantitative and qualitative evidence suggests that managers, fellow employees, and the larger society considered office work men's work and assumed that men would fill clerical positions. The office and the business district in the city had almost no accommodations for women. Many employers believed that men possessed the qualities necessary to succeed in office jobs. Men could find appropriate clerical jobs at all stages of their lives: lower-level office jobs were stepping-stones to careers within a firm, while higher-level office positions promised the possibility of earning a family wage.

Throughout the nineteenth century, men generally occupied four types of clerical jobs within a business office: bookkeepers, office boys, copyists, and clerks.[16] The nature of these positions varied greatly from firm to firm. Those men listed as clerks in the Chicago city directories until the 1870s, for example, engaged in a wide variety of activities. A clerk in a small firm might be expected to perform a large number of tasks; a clerk in a larger establishment might be expected to perform a discrete function. Sometimes the directory specified a type of clerk, for example, a cashier, a postal clerk, a billing clerk, a shipping clerk, a hotel clerk, and clerks to individual entrepreneurs. In addition, clerks in different establishments performed different duties. A clerk in a wholesale lumber store, a clerk in a bank, and a private clerk to the president of a company would undoubtedly have had different work experiences and may have also had different access to positions of power in the firm.

Office positions were also often considered entry-level apprenticeships to advancement in the firm. A young man starting out in life would choose his position by the type of establishment, or by the possibility of advancement, not because of the specific skills involved in office work. Except for some copyists, workers in the early office had access to general knowledge of the working of the firm and were given a certain degree of autonomy and independence in carrying out their tasks.[17] A good hand, a good head for figures, loyalty, enthusiasm, and the proper clothes and manners were probably sufficient qualifications for these positions. For many male clerical workers throughout the nineteenth century, the goal in engaging in this type of work was to gain experience for a better job, or wages to pay for further training.

A small number of men also dominated another type of clerical job that was not defined by the kind of establishment in which it was performed, but by its distinctive skill—shorthand writing. As early as 1830, the American Stenographic Academy of Philadelphia advertised for students of shorthand.[18] Throughout the century, the number of shorthand styles and their advocates multiplied. The shorthand expert found employment as a transcriber of court testimony, as a verbatim reporter of important speeches, as a correspondent for businessmen, as an employee of a newspaper, or as a self-employed businessman, selling his services wherever or whenever needed.[19] Self-employed stenographers often rented offices in downtown buildings that contained either governmental agencies or private businesses requiring stenographic and transcribing services. The *Edward's Annual Directory of the City of Chicago, 1868–1869* contained two listings under the heading "Shorthand Writers and Reporters": one was the firm of Ely, Burnham, and Bartlett, the official reporters of the courts of Chicago; the other was a

John Richie, with his room and office listed. By 1890, there were sixty-four listings of either individual male or female stenographers, or stenographic firms.

The types of men who engaged in clerical work throughout the last half of the nineteenth century were as diverse as the types of jobs they occupied. The demographic characteristics of the male clerical labor force in Chicago in 1890 suggest that some clerical work was not simply a first job for a young man starting out in his career. Almost a third of the male clerical labor force in Chicago in 1890 was married, and 42.9 percent was between the ages of twenty-five and forty-four.[20] During the nineteenth century, the position of clerk, for example, was a broad occupational category that included men of different ages as well as different family situations. One possible indication of this diversity was the residential patterns of clerks. For example, in *D. B. Cooke and Company's City Directory, 1859–1860,* 31.4 percent of all clerks lived in their own homes, while 62.3 percent boarded either with a relative, an employer, or in a lodging house or hotel. (Some 6.2 percent of the clerks in the 1859–1860 directory had no residence given.)[21] In the middle-class neighborhood of Union Park in 1880, 22 percent of the work force engaged in clerical work, and many of these clerical workers were heads of households.[22] It is probable that those clerks who boarded were single, young men starting their careers as clerks. Those clerks living with employers were clearly following the classic apprenticeship model, both living and working with their bosses. Those clerks who owned their own homes had either inherited a house or were older and married and had established themselves in careers as clerks. Therefore, some men were not promoted into management's ranks, but remained clerks after settling down with families of their own. Since many of these early firms were small and family-run, and since there were inevitably more clerks and bookkeepers than managers, some male office workers spent a significant part of their working lives as clerks or bookkeepers.

During this period, as well, clerks increasingly came from diverse ethnic and class backgrounds. Richard Sennett's study of the occupations of fathers and sons in the Union Park neighborhood of Chicago in 1880 reveals that clerical work was the most important occupation for sons of all classes of workers, except unskilled workers, and even 27 percent of sons of unskilled workers were clerical workers. In 1880, clerical work "was a kind of second-generation melting pot," "tending to expose a young man to a diversity of people."[23] In comparison with other cities in the United States, Chicago's male clerical labor force in 1890 drew more heavily from the ranks of the foreign and first-generation workers. Twenty-nine percent of the male clerks listed in the 1890 census were from predominantly northern and western European countries, and almost 36 percent had foreign parents.[24]

The stories of two immigrants to Chicago illustrate the promise that clerical positions held for the foreign-born man. Christian H. Jevne immigrated to Chicago in 1864, and through family connections obtained work as a clerk with a coffee and spice merchant. In a letter home, Jevne explained that he "attends school in the evenings from 7 to 9, namely at a commercial institute, in order to learn English, bookkeeping, banking, and brokerage." Just one year later, Jevne and his former employer's brother-in-law established what would become a thriving retail business of their own.[25] One of the most respected and successful male stenographers during this period was Charles L. Driesslein. Driesslein was born in Bavaria in 1832, came to Chicago in 1863, and began advertising his services as a court stenographer in the Chicago city directory in 1873. By 1880, Driesslein lived in the western Chicago suburb of Maywood with his wife, six children, and a live-in female servant. Clearly, he had achieved a moderate degree of success. Because of his background, Driesslein had the "rare facility of reporting a proceeding in German and rendering the same in English." He published two books, one of some specimens of his reporting work, and the other a German phonography textbook. When Charles Driesslein died in 1888, the most popular national typewriting and stenographic journal, then called *The Typewriter and Phonographic World,* contained an obituary for this one of their own, "held in high esteem by his professional brethren."[26]

Throughout the nineteenth century, men still sought these jobs, as their numbers in the increasingly popular private business schools suggest. Until around 1900, most men and women in Chicago who desired commercial education had no choice but to attend a private business college.[27] Early on, business colleges recruited among soldiers returning from the Civil War, boys who had migrated to cities in search of work, and adults who wished to continue their educations.[28] The first private business college in Chicago opened in 1848. The Jones and Company Commercial School advertised for young men "wishing to become practically and scientifically acquainted with the art of double entry bookkeeping, with commercial calculations, and business penmanship."[29] In 1871, almost 95 percent of the student body in private business colleges in Chicago were men. Although this percentage declined to almost 68 percent by 1892, the absolute number of men enrolled in private business colleges did increase and men still dominated the private business colleges during this period, particularly the commercial course, which provided the student with general training in office practices.[30]

Clerical positions remained popular with men because they were still considered "men's work." Throughout the nineteenth century, clerical positions appeared to fulfill a variety of occupational and domestic strategies for men. The positions on the lower end of the hierarchy of a firm were considered entry-level or transitional positions. It is unlikely that a young man starting as an office boy or a clerk wished to remain in this position throughout his work life. Cindy Sondik Aron describes how many government clerks saw their tenure as time to gain experience, receive training, or launch into a more high-level government position.[31] Those men seeking positions as clerical workers seemed to assume that promotions leading to a family wage would be their reward for hard work, initiative, and luck. Ileen DeVault, in her dissertation on Pittsburgh's clerical workers during the late nineteenth century, claims that "male clerical workers focused on their promotional opportunities and job stability. Interested in these two features of their jobs, they sought identification with (and entry into) managerial ranks."[32]

The men who occupied these positions worked in what was a male space: the office. During these early years, most single-sexed offices contained relatively undifferentiated space. "With the exception of distinctions among the president or company head, bookkeeper, cashier, and the clerks, the work done in the offices was not marked by stratification," and, in fact, "the small spaces of the pre-corporate office reinforced personal relations within the firm."[33] Such relations would have been extremely problematic in the presence of female workers (see Illustration 1).

There is also some evidence to suggest that some male clerical workers had established their own distinctive work culture, in many ways similar to the work cultures of skilled workers and artisans. Patronizing saloons and drinking in general seems to have been a part of the work life of some male clerical workers. Perry Duis, in his examination of the saloon in Chicago, claims that "many skyscraper office buildings contained drinking spots, but these were usually small, stand-up places that drew their patronage from the young male clerks and secretaries who worked in the nearby financial district." An important feature of down-town saloons was the free lunch that was offered to anyone who pur-chased a drink. Apparently, clerks did not confine their patronage of these saloons simply to lunch hour. "[A] clerk found ways to sneak a drink during a lull in business. The *Chicago Tribune* in 1889 even went so far as to blame drinking for the excessive speculation on the Board of Trade."[34] Although speaking primarily of copyists for the theater world, one writer in *The Phonographic World* claimed that "indeed beer was as essential a fluid to the professional copyist as ink. He was, as a rule, a decidedly snuffy and grubby person, given to chronic alcoholism, and as careless in his attire as he was irregular in his habits."[35]

Young, single, male clerks who lived and worked in the city also had a rich variety of alternatives with respect to housing and leisure. The choices for housing ranged from a "respectable" Young Men's Christian Association dormitory room to a furnished room in the "bohemian" boarding-house district. Young men had an equally varied array of leisure activities from which to choose. While they were young, and still making their way in the world, young, single, male office workers could certainly partake of the variety of city amusements, both the more "legitimate" leisure of the white-collar world and the "alternative" culture of the working classes.[36]

Between 1870 and 1890, however, changes in the economy would begin to alter this masculine world forever. Clerical work, a service occupation, was growing along with industrial capitalism. During the industrialization of the second half of the nineteenth century, firms not only increased in size, but also differentiated in function. Many histo-rians of American capitalism describe how large firms developed plan-ning and managerial departments at this time, and physically separated these functions from their production departments.[37] Regardless of the firm, the work of the clerical worker was not directly involved in either the productive or planning functions of the firm. The "output" of a clerical worker, however, serviced both the "brain" and the "hands" of a firm and often connected these two functions.[38] The growth of clerical occupations was related to the differentiation and growth of these two functions. In a manufacturing establishment, the demand for what is produced is called final demand.[39] Clerical workers do not produce the good demanded, but they produce an intermediate good that economists call clerical output. When, during the late nineteenth century, technological advances in production and transportation broadened the market for goods and helped to increase demand, the demand for clerical labor increased as well.

Because the 1870 and 1880 city censuses do not contain accurate figures on the percentage of the labor force engaged in clerical work during these early years, an exact assessment of this increase for Chicago is not possible. Nevertheless, the figures that do exist are suggestive. Between 1870 and 1890, the percentage of Chicago's labor force engaged in clerical work rose from less than 0.1 percent to 9 percent. In 1870, clerical work occupied a negligible percentage of both the male and female labor forces. By 1890, male clerical workers constituted 9 percent of the male labor force and female clerical workers constituted 9.8 percent of the female labor force.[40] Although this large increase may be somewhat overstated, one scholar cognizant of the difficulties of using the 1870 and 1880 censuses believed that "it is a safe guess, however, supported by some scattered items, that a more than two fold increase in manufacturing and mechanical activities was accompanied by an equivalent, if not greater, percentage increase in the employment of persons engaged in the associated recording and accounting tasks."[41]

The dramatic increase in demand for clerical work, the enlargement in office forces in individual firms, and the persistent upswings and downturns of the late nineteenth-century economy created uncertainty, unemployment, and geographic mobility for some men expecting to move up the ranks within an office. The employment records of twenty-one men who worked as clerical workers at the Deering Harvester Company in Chicago in the late 1890s provide some insights into the difficulties that male workers encountered in the late nineteenth century.[42] These men fell into three general occupational categories, clerks, bookkeepers, and correspondents, with two men in composite jobs, one clerk-correspondent and one clerk-stenographer. Of the fifteen men who listed reasons for leaving their previous positions, eight mentioned either business failure or reduction in force. P. E. Luney, for example, a 35-year-old married man, who worked as a receiving clerk starting on May 28, 1897, began his working life as a telegraph operator in 1877 in

Chicago. He left this position in 1881 to begin a ten-year period when he was self-employed at some unspecified job. Between 1891 and 1892, Luney worked in a real estate office until the head of the company died. Luney then assumed a position as a bill clerk and cashier in a company in Chicago until the depression caused his dismissal. Between 1894 and 1896, Luney worked again in a real estate office until it also failed. During 1896, Luney took a job as a stenographer but again lost his job due to hard economic times. And finally, before his hiring at Deering, Luney labored as a clerk in a company that he considered too far from home. At Deering, Luney made thirty-five dollars a month.

Better paid employees also had checkered work histories, but appeared committed to careers as white-collar workers. Charles Hanson, a thirty-two-year old, married man with four children, who made seventy-five dollars a month as a bookkeeper, began his work life in 1886 as a bookkeeper and general office manager in a lithography company that failed in 1890. Between 1890 and 1895, Hanson left two jobs to "make a change." During the year 1895, Hanson operated his own painting and decorating business. This apparently did not succeed, and Hanson found himself working as a bookkeeper for a company in Racine, Wisconsin, that failed in October 1896.

Those men committed to success in the shorthand profession were also experiencing both legal and economic difficulties because in Chicago, in the 1870s and 1880s, court and newspaper stenography was becoming a more demanding and competitive profession. In 1873, just six years after its passage, the State of Illinois law permitting the appointment of exclusive rights to a stenographic firm was declared unconstitutional. As a result, the stenographic firm of Ely, Burnham, and Bartlett lost its exclusive right to the transcription work of the courts of Cook County, setting many firms and individuals into competition for the patronage of the most successful lawyers and the most lucrative newspaper accounts.

The use of the typewriter in stenographic transcription starting in the 1880s exacerbated the problems of stenographers by quickening the pace and increasing the volume of their work. Before the typewriter came into general use, transcription was done into hand-written text. For conventions, for example, stenographic firms sent six or seven reporters, who each took notes for five minutes at a time, allowing thirty minutes to write out the text in longhand. The copy was then put together and sent to a newspaper office. In the 1880s, a reporter covering a trial would spend about one and a half hours taking notes in the morning, and after an associate relieved him, would return to the office to dictate the text to a typewriter operator. He would then return for more notes in the afternoon, and the two reporters would usually have the transcription of the whole day's testimony completed by 8 P.M. Twenty-four of Chicago's most eminent stenographers, all men, attended the First Annual Dinner of Chicago Stenographers on January 5th, 1878. They proclaimed that they "had not prospered" of late, "for we have inaugurated and carried on a system of competition which has reduced the general profits, and created ill feelings, while it has not increased the amount of business."

As a result of the increased pace of work and the competition among firms, some stenographers wished to reinstitute official stenographers as well as minimum rates. On July 1, 1887, a law was passed in the Illinois legislature allowing judges to appoint an official shorthand reporter for their courts. Minimum fees per folio were included as well. Nevertheless, the majority of court reporters in the city of Chicago were opposed to this law and made their sentiments known. Judges, as a result, refused to appoint under it. Apparently, these court reporters objected to its exclusionary nature. Competition was preferable to oligarchy.[43]

The increasing volatility and competition in the masculine world of the office was not simply a result of new male entrants into the field, but also the result of female entrants. In the late 1870s, the same male court stenographers that were concerned about the increased competitiveness asserted their unique suitability for the profession. At the Second Annual Banquet of Chicago Stenographers, Isaac Dement proclaimed that "the obscenity in many trials and which a lady reporter cannot always foresee and avoid, constitutes a very serious objection, for she must not only listen to it, but write it down, and when called upon, read it, in presence of court, counsel, jury, and the prurient crowd. Besides, the work is too severe and arduous for organisms such as theirs. The constant strain of constant note-taking, the drudgery of transcription at night, the anxieties of soliciting, the foul atmosphere of the courts, will kill the hardiest of them in no time, and will quickly destroy their graces and beauty."[44]

Male clerical workers did recognize that women's assumption of clerical jobs posed a threat to both their status and economic worth. The great competition and difficulties encountered by shorthand reporters did provoke some of Chicago's stenographers to join together into professional associations in an attempt to protect and promote their interests, just as doctors, lawyers, and other male professionals did during this period in the United States. In 1886, Chicago's National Union of Stenographers adopted its rules, regulations, and scales of prices. Having characteristics of both a professional association and a craft union, the union's stated object was to "advance [stenographers'] interests, and elevate the position of the profession in general . . . and protect the craft from sudden and unreasonable fluctuations in their salaries; protect just and honorable employers from annoyance from illiterate, good-for-nothing apprentices, rejected by the union for general incompetency"; and "to encourage conciliation and arbitration in the settlement of differences between employers and employees, and to better the conditions of service by shorter hours and increased privileges." The union perceived that the problem in the stenography profession was caused by "scab schools," "which every three months are turning out swarms of 'rats' " who depressed salaries. This union sought to control the supply of workers through a form of licensing and by establishing something resembling a union hiring hall. The union would endorse competent schools and teachers, and boycott "scab schools." In addition, the union would certify "practical stenographers and machine experts (male and female) known to be competent workers and of good character" and these members would form lodges from which they would receive referrals for employment. The union called for an eight-hour day, no short hours, and double time for Sunday, overwork, and holidays.[45] Similar organizations appeared between the 1880s and 1910s in Chicago.[46]

Despite these efforts, male stenographers never received the salaries or status of professionals or even craft workers. When Mr. Gurtler, the president of Chicago's Law Reporters, pleaded for the just recognition of court reporters in *Chicago Commerce* in 1913, it was really more of a last gasp. "But who is this silent man, the shorthand reporter, this man who quietly records court proceedings? Is he not a man of ability? Is he not a different person than a commercial stenographer? Does he not possess the educational qualifications beyond the scope of the clerical employee? Is it not time that you cease measuring the highly skillful work of the artist by the eight dollar a week stenographer?"[47]

Like craft workers through their unions, and other professionals through their associations, male stenographers attempted to control access to and conditions in their occupation. Unlike many of these male professionals, however, male stenographers would ultimately fail in their attempt to control entrance and quality. Although these efforts would increase by the turn of the century, the reasons for their failure would remain the same. The expanding economy of the city of Chicago required the services of ever-increasing numbers of office workers. It must have been difficult, in light of this relentless demand, to control the activities of those institutions that trained and hired clerical workers. In addition, unlike other craft workers, such as printers, male clerical workers did not have a union or organizational tradition to draw on to assert and maintain their exclusive claim to their jobs.[48] Finally, younger or lower-level male clerical workers probably identified more with the middle class to which they aspired than with clerical workers at their level despite their increasing economic difficulties during this time. The absence of any controls on the occupation of stenography as the demand for workers increased and the nature of the occupation changed probably plunged stenography as a discrete skill and an occupation into a period of transitional status starting sometime in the 1880s. This development contributed to why male workers (and their employers) could not keep women out of these jobs, should women want them.

And women did want clerical jobs. Office work was a new opportunity for safe, relatively well-paid employment amidst extremely limited options. During the 1880s, it appears, the earliest female clerical workers took advantage of a small opening in the large edifice that was the male business world. As far as women were concerned, clerical work seemed to allow them to fulfill some occupational and life strategies of their own.

CHAPTER 2

Venturing into a Masculine World

IN 1885, Isabel Wallace took a temporary position as a copyist in a pension office in Chicago, where her uncle worked. She apparently took the position to supply her mother with some needed cash. In letters to her mother, she described the atmosphere in this office as essentially pleasant, and yet she never enjoyed the experience. Even though "the desks are comfortable, the chairs, etc, light, good, and room well heated," and "there seemed a very pleasant set of ladies," Isabel claimed she "felt like somebody else all day. *Out of my element and sphere somehow. It made me feel less womanly and somehow as if I was doing something I didn't approve of.* I suppose," Isabel continued, "it's because it's in the Court House and in an office" (emphasis added).[1]

Whether out of necessity or desire or both, women did take their first tentative steps into a masculine world during the years between 1870 and 1890. What is important and interesting about this development is precisely that women entered into a realm of work and into a city that many, including some female clerical workers, felt was out of women's proper sphere. Certainly, widowed or single women throughout the seventeenth and eighteenth centuries could and did take over their fathers' or husbands' businesses. Throughout most of the nineteenth century, women left the security of the world of the hearth and home to take jobs as domestic servants, governesses, seamstresses, teachers, or as operatives in textile factories—all considered natural extensions of their traditional female functions inside the home.[2]

Women's entrance into the office, however, posed a number of new challenges. Their presence in the undifferentiated space of the business office jarred the sensibilities of members of a society preoccupied with separate spheres.[3] The previously "personal" relationships among the men in the office were not acceptable models of behavior for a woman in the office. Promiscuous mixing of the sexes was not the only problem.

Entering into an office meant that women would come into contact with men of different classes, ages, and ethnicities.

There were no distinctive or specific spaces for women within the city, either. Art museums, concert halls, public parks and libraries, expensive restaurants, and the World's Columbian Exposition were leisure places for respectable women, but even then they were expected to be with a friend or escort. The female office worker who lived apart from her family also had a more difficult time than her male counterpart in finding suitable and respectable housing.[4] Ina Law Robertson, who arrived in Chicago in 1895 to begin graduate school at the University of Chicago, personally experienced the kinds of problems many women faced in finding decent housing and living a decent life. She believed that the cheap boarding-houses that most working women could afford were undesirable and "there was nowhere an opportunity for any kind of social life."[5]

In Chicago, between 1870 and 1890, a coincidence of extraordinary and ordinary developments prompted women's first steps out of their sphere and into this masculine world. These female pioneers ventured into a variety of male spaces without the comfort of knowing that most of their contemporaries considered that what they were doing was acceptable for women. Until the Civil War, there was no precedent for women working in the office setting. Cindy Sondik Aron, in her valuable study *Ladies and Gentlemen of the Civil Service: Middle Class Workers in Victorian America,* documents the stories of the path-blazing female clerks in the civil service in Washington D.C. In most instances, the women who engaged in this nontraditional labor maintained that they did so to support their families. They used "the language of domesticity to carve out a new role for middle-class women—one that would allow them to enter a previously all-male occupation without feeling that they had forsaken their position as 'true women.'"[6] Their presence and success in government offices was an important precedent and probably began to weaken the prevailing sentiment that the business office was not women's proper sphere.

The woman who took office jobs during the 1870s in Chicago were an elusive group. The want-ads in the *Chicago Tribune,* which, as was the custom, differentiated "Help Wanted" and "Situation Wanted" by sex, provide a valuable insight into these early female clerical workers. Throughout the 1870s, these advertisements suggest that most women

desired office positions that required skills that many of them undoubtedly already had—the ability to read, write, and do arithmetic.[7] Only
approximately 5 percent of the "Situations Wanted—Female" advertisements in the 1870s specified amanuensis [shorthand and transcription],
shorthand, or typewriting skills; the vast majority of a sample of 144
women who advertised their willingness to engage in clerical work
desired "to do copying at her home or at an office," while a majority of
the thirty-eight employers who requested female clerical help wanted "a
smart, intelligent young lady to keep office open 10–5, and at times to do
writing."[8]

The numbers of advertisements may not depict larger labor market
trends; however, there are several striking qualitative features of the
listings put in by women seeking clerical work during the 1870s. A few
of the women who were desperate, courageous, or ambitious enough to
place an advertisement in the newspaper already considered writing,
copying, or keeping a set of books in an office to be an appropriate
woman's job. They included these types of office positions in lists of
desired jobs that included traditional women's jobs. Miss Rena Mon-
tague, for example, put an advertisement in the *Chicago Tribune* on
February 18, 1872, requesting a position, "as a copyist, clerk, lady's
companion, or governess for small children or housekeeper in a refined
family." On May 6, 1877, Miss Ora Lee placed an advertisement in the
paper desiring positions for "two young ladies; writing, dressmaking, or
any respectable employment where they can earn reasonable wages."[9]

The women who wrote these advertisements sometimes revealed the
reasons why they wanted clerical work. Of course one cannot generalize
these experiences to the entire population; nevertheless, the advertisements do provide us with a list, albeit an incomplete one, of reasons why
women wanted clerical work during the 1870s. Some women considered
writing in an office as a form of "light employment." Like many others
during the decade, Mrs. L. requested some "light employment, either to
write in an office or some desirable situation."[10] Various types of office
positions seemed not only to offer women self-support, but also the
possibility of supporting dependents. In 1872, "a lady, thirty years old,
well educated, refined, used to literary work, a first-class correspondent,
a good and rapid writer [desired] a situation as a correspondent in a
publishing, insurance or any business house, or as a private secretary or
clerk for a gentleman, or in any capacity where she [could] earn her

bread." And one woman, "who ha[d] two children to support," desired copying and writing, assuring her potential employer that "all work done shall give entire satisfaction."[11] Women also stated that they wanted copying work because, apparently, in some instances, it could be done at home. For example, in the July 25, 1875, newspaper, a young lady "who [was] a good penman" desired "to do copying or other writing at home," and in the April 20, 1879, newspaper, a "widow woman" advertised her willingness to work "as a governess, or as cashier, or to do writing at home."[12]

These early forays into office work in the 1870s provided an important precedent for the developments of the 1880s, when clerical work began to change. One significant change for women was the appearance of a new clerical job, the stenographer-typist, sometimes referred to as the business or commercial stenographer, or simply the stenographer. Obviously, the widespread production, availability, and use of the typewriter was crucial to this development. The stenographer-typist held a very specific position in the office setting and in the context of women's employment opportunities at the time, with her own status position, as well as her own skill and function. Although the day-to-day work and volume of individual stenographer-typists varied from firm to firm and even from boss to boss, stenographer-typists engaged in the same basic activities. The stenographer-typist took dictation of correspondence, meetings, reports, telegrams, and memos. After transcribing the dictation on the typewriter, the stenographer-typist submitted the finished product to his or her employer for signature and approval. He or she made appropriate records of all paperwork and then filed it or sent it out. In addition, the stenographer was often responsible for keeping his or her desk area clean, the typewriter in good repair, and supplies plentiful. The term stenographer-typist, therefore, refers to the two main functions of the occupation. Most women entering into these new positions during these early years performed both functions.

The vast majority of women who entered the office between 1880 and 1910 did so as stenographer-typists, and stenography-typing was the first clerical job completely dominated by women. It is extremely difficult to date exactly when women entered stenography-typing before 1890. The city census schedule did not provide figures for female or male stenographer-typists in 1870 or 1880, and in 1890, it contained figures only for females. Nevertheless, the appearance in the 1890 city census of a listing for female stenographer-typists is certainly significant in itself. Of the female clerical workers listed in the 1890 census, 55.8 percent worked as clerks and copyists, 21.7 percent were bookkeepers and accountants, and 22.6 percent had jobs as stenographer-typists. In addition, in 1887, the *Chicago Tribune* began listing two new categories under its "Help Wanted—Female" and "Situations Wanted—Female" columns: Book-keepers and Clerks, and Stenographers. While these two headings had existed under "Help Wanted—Male" and "Situations Wanted—Male" before 1887, women seeking clerical work or employers seeking female help needed to use the "Other" category in the female employment section. That newspapers and census compilers created categories spe-cifically for female clerical workers in 1887 and 1890 certainly marks a critical change in the nature of clerical work and clerical workers. Understanding why and how women entered these positions in the 1880s, therefore, is crucial for explaining the transformation of clerical work from a male to a female occupation.

Women may have entered the office because of the introduction of the typewriter. There is some evidence to suggest that the typewriter may have been associated with female operators even before its widespread commercial use. Typewriter companies chose women to demonstrate their new machines. Margery Davies reports that "when Mark Twain bought his first typewriter in early 1875, the salesman had a 'type-girl' on hand to demonstrate the machine to prospective customers."[13] The choice of female typewriter demonstrators was apparently deliberate. Typewriter salesmen, companies, and even typing schools believed that most educated, middle-class women, in particular, possessed a skill that would enable them to effectively learn and demonstrate this new machine—piano playing. The first manufacturers of typewriters sent out "little circulars calling the attention of educated women, particularly those skilled in pianoforte playing to a new opportunity," demonstrating typewriting.[14] One of the first "type-girls" was Mrs. A. M. Saunders of New York City. A widow looking for employment, she answered just such an advertisement from the Remington Company, "A bright educated woman wanted to take a remunerative and pleasant position. Musician preferred."[15] The Bryant and Stratton Business College of Chicago advertised their new typing courses as being particularly suited to women. An 1880 catalogue stated that "ordinarily one who has the ability to play well upon the piano and especially one who has practical knowledge of phonography may become an expert typist. This department of industry is exactly suited to women. Requires none of the physical exhaustion which causes the sewing machine to be dreaded."[16] An advertisement in *System* magazine in 1920 for a Royal typewriter revived the identification between pianos and typewriters (see Illustration 2). Even before typewriting machines came into general use in offices, these machines may have been associated with female operators.[17]

Typing, however, was just one skill required of stenographer-typists. The other necessary skill was shorthand, stenography, or phonography, as it was called, and this skill was considered men's work. During the 1880s, the profession of stenography was undergoing a crisis and male practitioners were unsuccessful in their attempts to curtail competition, in part from female entrants. In addition, these female entrants might have had a easier time defending their presence in the business office as stenographer-typists. The newness of the job and its technology may have reduced the possibility of accusations that women were stealing men's jobs.[18]

The evolution of the private business college during the last half of the nineteenth century also contributed to women's ability to take clerical jobs. Women's participation in these private schools was limited at first, but their increasing enrollment throughout the period contributed to altering the colleges' offerings and focus. These institutions were, after all, businesses, as interested in profit as in educational ideals. It mattered little to most of the administrators of these institutions who paid the fee. When women considered office work as an occupational alternative, they discovered ever-increasing opportunities for training and proprietors of business colleges profited.

Starting in the 1880s, the number of private business colleges in Chicago began to increase, and the curricula of these schools became more varied. In 1880, only five business colleges operated in Chicago; this number increased to twenty-eight in 1890, and to forty in 1910. Like most small businesses, private business colleges were highly speculative ventures and individual colleges did not last long.[19] To capture as much business as possible, business schools of the 1880s and 1890s offered students a wide variety of choices in types and lengths of courses. For example, when the Chicago Athenaeum Business School began its tenth year in 1882, it offered courses in phonography, telegraphy, German, French, Spanish, business correspondence and business English, penmanship, drawing, bookkeeping, mathematics, surveying, banking, commercial law, political economy, and life insurance. A course that included stenography and typing was called an amanuensis course. A course lasted for forty weeks and cost sixty-five dollars. Students could enter at any time and attend from one to four terms in a year. Of the 3,020 students attending during the 1882–1883 year, almost 70 percent were men, and their ages ranged between twelve and forty-five years.[20] Specialized shorthand and typing schools began to appear in the 1880s. For example, in 1886, just two years after it was founded, Kimball's Short-Hand and Typewriting Training School had thirty-three male and fifty-eight female students whose average age was twenty years. The four-month day course and the six-month night course cost forty dollars. Over the years, correspondence, corporation, and denominational schools, and schools affiliated with a particular typewriter brand or shorthand procedure, also added to the diversity of private business schools.[21]

The blossoming of the number and diversity of these schools both reflected and hastened women's interest in engaging in clerical work during these early years, particularly for stenography-typing. Some colleges advertised their new typing or amanuensis courses as being particularly suited to women. Indeed, women began to dominate the amanuensis courses during this period. By the 1892–1893 year, 90 percent of those enrolled in the amaneunsis course at the Metropolitan Business College in Chicago were women. (Women constituted only 25 percent of the more general commercial course.)[22] As more and more women made the decision to attend private business colleges, these amanuensis courses increased in importance in those schools.

As business colleges changed their focus and clientele, businessmen in the United States began to express concern over the lack of professional business training available to young men. This concern was exacerbated by the increasing reluctance of business houses to take on young men in apprenticeship positions. In 1886, the American Bankers' Association appointed a committee to investigate business training in higher institutions. When the committee found that only the Wharton School of Finance was adequate, the U.S. Commissioner of Education printed the aims and method of this exemplary school in his annual report. This became the model for the next two collegiate schools of business to open in the United States, at the University of Chicago and the University of California. The College of Commerce and Administration opened at the University of Chicago during the summer of 1897.[23] From its inception, this professional school was designed to train young men for positions in trade and industry, for charitable and philanthropic work, for public service, for commercial teaching, and in secretarial practice.

Even as private business colleges reached their peak in numbers and attendance, they had lost their monopoly on business training as the professional, collegiate business school achieved legitimacy. One effect of this development was immediately clear. Men dominated the more comprehensive, professional collegiate business schools, while women remained in the more technical, lower grade of private business college. Like the stenography-typing position itself during these early years, the private business colleges were also transformed into institutions increasingly dominated by women.

Many women who entered the private business colleges and business office during the 1870s and 1880s, however, undoubtedly profited from this education and used the training they received to carry out a variety of occupational and domestic strategies. Throughout the period the relationship between clerical work and the family economy was remarkably varied. The story of Annie Ball demonstrates most clearly the potential value of a business education for women at this time.[24] Annie Ball was born in 1844 in Holland. When she was twenty-five years old, Annie worked as a clerk in Chicago at Mason and Company. The next year, in 1870, she enrolled as a student in the Bryant and Stratton Business College and for three years she was not listed in the Chicago business directory. In 1874, she reappeared in the directory, working at 92 Market Street as a bookkeeper, and she remained at this job until 1880. In this year, Annie Ball either started or bought her own company, A. Ball and Brother, a playing-card company. She lived with her brother, William, a sister four years her junior, and a seventy-year-old, widowed mother. By 1910, she headed a different household. Her family was gone, but she lived with two female boarders and a female servant. She owned her house and still owned her company. It is quite possible that what Annie Ball learned at business college helped her to succeed.

Seven female students at Chicago's Bryant and Stratton Business College in 1880 had more conventional life stories than Annie Ball's.[25] All seven women were single and lived in a family as a daughter or sister of the head of the household. Of the three who had started working in

1880, two were shorthand reporters and one was a typist. Six of the seven women were between the ages of sixteen and nineteen. The one woman who was considerably older than that, forty-two years of age, was also the only woman who did not reside with her father. Anna Mitchell lived with her brother, his wife, and their married son.

Even though most of these women came from middle-class families of craftsmen and small-scale merchants and traders, the families were not all in the same economic condition. Anna Mitchell's brother, for example, was a corn merchant. In addition to the family members described above, the household included two servants. Edith Wignall's family included her father, an editor of a local newspaper, her mother, young brother, and an Irish servant. Sixteen-year-old Minnie Drechsler, however, lived with her widowed German mother, who kept two Prussian boarders in their home. And Lottie Dalton, a seventeen-year-old typist, lived with a disabled father, a mother and sister who kept house, and a twenty-five-year-old sister, who was a teacher.

Economic misfortune, then, may have driven some women to business college, but it was certainly not the only reason that women went. Anna Mitchell's work history is illustrative. In 1878, Mitchell was a clerk, but the next year she worked as a teacher. Then in 1880, Mitchell attended business college, and three years later she procured work as a stenographer. Since the household employed two servants, it is unlikely that Mitchell was driven to work out of economic need; rather, like Annie Ball, who had attended the same business college ten years before, Mitchell's decision to attend business college appears to have been a way to train for a better job. For some women, at least, the way to get a better job was to train in a private business college to become a stenographer or typist.

Although the stories of these women as they progressed from home to school to office seem commonplace to a late twentieth century American, they are, in fact, the stories of courageous pioneers. In the 1870s and 1880s, women entered male-dominated offices and business districts to engage in work previously done by men. They did so, in part, because of the overwhelming demand for the services of office employees. The enormous increase in demand associated with the growth of Chicago's manufacturing sector started the process of gender transformation. But this increase in demand alone would probably not have been sufficient to explain this process. The example set by those women who worked in government offices during the Civil War apparently provoked a small number of women to pursue primarily copying positions in the 1870s and early 1880s. These early forays would become increasingly important as the nature of the office and office work began to change in the late 1880s.

The changes in office work brought about as a result of the typewriter had an enormous impact on women's activity in this field. This technological innovation created a new clerical job, the stenographer-typist. Because women were associated from the start with the typewriter, and because male stenographers could not control entrance into their field, women were able to take these new positions. This development was aided by the existence of the private business colleges which, because their owners had profits preeminent in their minds, met the needs of the increasing number of women who sought training for these positions. And finally, clerical positions of all sorts, because they provided women with a new and potentially better job opportunity, offered all sorts of women a solution to their own, distinct domestic or occupational strategies. The young widow with two children to support as well as the middle-aged, single, career woman could look to clerical work as the right job.

Between the 1870s and the 1890s, women's entrance into clerical positions posed a direct challenge to the commonly held belief that not only was the office a male space, and office jobs men's work, but also that all sorts of urban settings—elevators, street cars, restaurants, board-ing-houses—were inappropriate for working women. Women's entrance into these places set in motion a redefinition of women's sphere within the world of work and the city that continued throughout the twentieth century. But during these early years, the outcome was completely uncertain. Once given the opportunity to enter this previously forbidden world, women had to isolate their own space, forge a code of behavior, and legitimize their presence in these male environments. By the late 1880s and early 1890s, much of this work was under way. The social construction of clerical work as an occupation for women had begun.

PART II

"By Right Both of Fitness and
of Conquest": Clerical Work
Becomes "Women's Work,"
1890–World War I

CHAPTER 3

The "Conquering" Female Clerical Worker

*I*N *1892*, a writer for the most popular stenography and typewriting trade journal, *The Phonographic World,* predicted that "if women continue their advancement during the next generation as they have during the last decade of years, male service in shorthand and typewriting will have been relegated to a past which will exist only in history, and these two professions will be her own, by right both of fitness and of conquest."[1] This writer was correct on all counts. During the years between 1890 and World War I, women did enter office jobs in large numbers and they took over the new field of stenography-typing. Although men did not drop out of the clerical labor force, their numbers and percentage within it significantly declined.

Effie Jones, who left her Iowa home for Chicago in 1890, was one of these "conquering" female clerical workers. After finding a place to live and receiving the training she needed to procure work as a stenographer, Effie procured her first position in an import agent's office as a substitute stenographer because the usual male stenographer was on a two-week vacation. Effie wrote to her father that her employers "always had a man, and said that they did not know whether a lady would do or not, but I think I will do just as well."[2] Between 1890 and World War I, the number of women following in Effie's footsteps increased dramatically as the number of office jobs grew. Women's presence in these occupations, in the business office, and in the downtown business district illustrates the popularity these jobs had among women (see Tables 1 and 2).[3]

Who was the female clerical worker during this transitional period, why did she take an office job, and what were the implications of her actions? An important element in women's domination of clerical jobs was the desire of young, single, white, native-born women for this type of employment. Compared with other jobs available to this group of

Table 1. Number and Percentage of Male and Female Clerical Workers in Chicago, 1870–1930

YEAR	TOTAL[a]	NUMBER OF MALES	PERCENT MALE	NUMBER OF FEMALES	PERCENT FEMALE
1870[b]	154	145	94.2	9	5.8
1880[b]	1,120	996	88.9	124	11.1
1890[c]	41,015	32,391	79.0	8,624	21.0
1900[d]	74,866	52,476	70.1	22,390	29.9
1910[e]	105,257	62,539	59.4	42,718	40.6
1920[f]	190,615	93,652	49.1	96,963	50.9
1930[g]	238,124	111,232	46.7	126,892	53.3

Source: U.S. Bureau of the Census, *1870 Census on Population Statistics*, vol. 1, p. 782; U.S. Bureau of the Census, *1880 Census of the Population of the United States*, vol. 1, p. 870; U.S. Bureau of the Census, *1890 Census of Population*, vol. 1, part 2, pps. 650–652; U.S. Bureau of the Census, *Special Report on Occupations, 1900*, pps. 516–523, and 558–560; U.S. Bureau of the Census, *Statistics of Women at Work, Based on Unpublished Information Derived from the Schedules of the 12th Census* (Washington: D.C., U.S. Government Printing Office, 1907), pps. 29, and 228–233; U.S. Bureau of the Census, *Population—Occupational Statistics, 1910*, vol. 4, pps. 165, and 544–547; U.S. Bureau of the Census, *Population—Occupations, 1920*, vol. 4, pps. 149, and 1076–1080; U.S. Bureau of the Census, *Population—Occupations by States, 1930*, vol. 4, pps. 423–429, 447–450, 456–457, and 463–465.

[a]All workers 10 years of age and over.

[b]Only included clerks and bookkeepers in manufacturing establishments and clerks and copyists, not specified. This figure is low because no clerks and bookkeepers in trade, transportation, or professional service, or stenographer-typists, were included.

[c]The 1890 census classified clerical workers by function rather than by type of establishment. The classification is: bookkeepers and accountants, clerical and copyists, and stenographers and typists. The 1890 count of female clerical workers is probably high because census collectors included some saleswomen in the category of clerks and copyists. See U.S. Bureau of the Census, *Statistics of Women at Work*, p. 100.

[d]Same classifications as 1890 census.

[e]The classifications used for 1910 were: bookkeepers, cashiers, and accountants; clerks (not in stores); and stenographers and typists.

[f]The classifications used for 1920 were: accountants and auditors; bookkeepers and cashiers; clerks (except in stores); and stenographers and typists.

[g]The classifications used in 1930 were: bookkeepers, cashiers, and accountants; clerks (except in stores); and stenographers and typists.

women, clerical work was a good occupational opportunity. A job in an office could allow these women to meet a variety of occupational and familial needs. Yet, although this group of women dominated clerical jobs throughout the period, older women, and married, widowed, or divorced women were starting to enter the clerical labor force as well.

Table 2. Number and Percentage of Males and Females Taking New Clerical
Positions, 1880–1930

YEAR	NEW CLERICAL POSITIONS	NUMBER OF MALES	PERCENT MALE	NUMBER OF FEMALES	PERCENT FEMALE
1880	966	851	88.1	115	11.9
1890	39,895	31,395	78.7	8,500	21.3
1900	33,851	20,085	59.3	13,766	40.7
1910	30,391	10,063	33.1	20,328	66.9
1920	85,358	31,113	36.5	54,245	63.5
1930	47,509	17,580	37.0	29,929	63.0

Source: U.S. Bureau of the Census, *1870 Census on Population Statistics*, vol. 1, p. 782; U.S. Bureau of the Census, *1880 Census of the Population of the United States*, vol. 1, p. 870; U.S. Bureau of the Census, *1890 Census of Population*, vol. 1, part 2, pps. 650–652; U.S. Bureau of the Census, *Special Report on Occupations, 1900*, pps. 516–523, and 558–560; U.S. Bureau of the Census, *Statistics of Women at Work, Based on Unpublished Information Derived from the Schedules of the 12th Census* (Washington, D.C.: U.S. Government Printing Office, 1907), pps. 29, and 228–233; U.S. Bureau of the Census, *Population—Occupational Statistics, 1910*, vol. 4, pps. 165, and 544–547; U.S. Bureau of the Census, *Population—Occupations, 1920*, vol. 4, pps. 149, and 1076–1080; U.S. Bureau of the Census, *Population—Occupations by States, 1930*, vol. 4, pps. 423–429, 447–450, 456–457, and 463–465.

This first step in the broadening of the demographic characteristics of the female clerical labor force (although certainly limited before 1930 and not accomplished until the 1960s) was also a sign of the widespread acceptance of clerical work as a job appropriate for all women.

The women who participated in this transformation conformed to what, in the twentieth century, have become the stereotypical characteristics of the female clerical worker. Most clerical workers were white, young, single, native-born, and lived with a family member. Throughout the period and continuing throughout the twentieth century, however, the female clerical labor force did change demographically. Although the majority of female clerical workers in Chicago were less than twenty-five years of age as late as 1930, the percentage of women who were twenty-five to forty-four years old did increase between 1890 and 1930 (see Table 3). In 1890, 21.9 percent of female clerical workers were between twenty-five and forty-four years old. By 1930, 40.4 percent of all female clerical workers were in this age category. Undoubtedly, some women who started work when they were less than twenty-five years old were aging with their jobs, while other women were beginning clerical work

Table 3. Age Distribution of Female Clerical Workers in Chicago, 1890–1930

YEAR	10–24	25–44	45–64	65 AND OVER
1890	76.9	21.9	1.0	0.2[a]
1900	67.4	31.2	1.2	0.2[a]
1910	42.5[b]	55.7[a,c]	1.8[d]	—[d]
1920	63.6	33.4[a]	2.9	0.1
1930	54.4	40.4	4.9	0.3[a]

Source: U.S. Bureau of the Census, *1890 Census of Population*, vol. 1, part 2, pps. 650–652; U.S. Bureau of the Census, *Special Report on Occupations, 1900*, pps. 516–523, and 558–560; U.S. Bureau of the Census, *Statistics of Women at Work, Based on Unpublished Information Derived from the Schedules of the 12th Census* (Washington, D.C.: U.S. Government Printing Office, 1907), pps. 29, and 228–233; U.S. Bureau of the Census, *Population—Occupational Statistics, 1910*, vol. 4, pps. 165, and 544–547; U.S. Bureau of the Census, *Population—Occupations, 1920*, vol. 4, pps. 149, and 1076–1080; U.S. Bureau of the Census, *Population—Occupations by States, 1930*, vol. 4, pps. 423–429, 447–450, 456–457, and 463–465.
[a]includes unknown.
[b]1910 Census category was 10–20.
[c]1910 Census category was 21–44.
[d]1910 Census category was 45 and over.

later in life, perhaps after spending more time in school. Although clerical work would remain primarily a young woman's work experience, older women did enter clerical jobs throughout the period.

The vast majority of female clerical workers were single, but the percentage of married women in the female clerical labor force of Chicago increased dramatically from 3.4 percent in 1890 to 17 percent in 1930. Unfortunately, the city censuses of 1910 and 1920 did not report on marital status, making the dating of the change that did occur extremely problematic. Nationally, the decade between 1920 and 1930 saw the largest increase in the number of married women in the clerical work force. During this decade, 41 percent of all new female clerical workers were married.[4] Whether the largest part of this increase occurred during the 1920s, mirroring national trends, is uncertain. There is no question, however, that as more women took office jobs (and this is true for most of the female labor force throughout the twentieth century), the percentage of married women and women over the age of twenty-four in the female clerical labor force of Chicago increased.

Clerical work was also an important occupational opportunity for

Table 4. Percentages of the Nativity of Female Clerical Workers in Chicago and in the United States, 1890–1930

	NATIVE WHITE, NATIVE PARENTS		NATIVE WHITE, FOREIGN OR MIXED PARENTS		WHITE, FOREIGN-BORN		BLACK AND OTHER	
	CC[a]	CN[b]	CC	CN	CC	CN	CC	CN
1890	30.4	52.7	52.4	38.1	17.1	8.9	0.1	0.4
1900	31.2	50.8	53.8	40.7	14.6	8.2	0.4	0.3
1910	28.2	51.7	62.0	41.0	9.4	6.8	0.4	0.5
1920	30.8	54.8	58.6	38.3	9.4	6.4	1.1	0.5
1930	90.8[c]	93.5[c]	[c]	[c]	8.1	5.7	1.1	0.7

[a]CC stands for female clerical workers in Chicago. The source of this information is census material. U.S. Bureau of the Census, *1890 Census of Population*, vol. 1, part 2, pps. 650–652; U.S. Bureau of the Census, *Special Report on Occupations, 1900*, pps. 516–523, and 558–560; U.S. Bureau of the Census, *Statistics of Women at Work, Based on Unpublished Information Derived from the Schedules of the 12th Census*, Washington, D.C.: U.S. Government Printing Office, 1907, pps. 29, and 228–233; U.S. Bureau of the Census, *Population—Occupational Statistics, 1910*, vol. 4, pps. 165, and 544–547; U.S. Bureau of the Census, *Population—Occupations, 1920*, vol. 4, pps. 149, and 1076–1080; U.S. Bureau of the Census, *Population—Occupations by States, 1930*, vol. 4, pps. 423–429, 447–450, 456–457, and 463–465.

[b]CN stands for female clerical workers nationally. The source of this information is Elyce J. Rotella, *From Home to Office: U.S. Women at Work, 1870–1930* (Ann Arbor: UMI Research Press, 1981), p. 114.

[c]1930 census did not distinguish between native-born of native parents and native-born of foreign stock.

native-born daughters of immigrants. This feature of Chicago's female clerical labor force distinguishes it markedly from the national female clerical labor force. During this period, the majority of female office workers in the United States were native-born women of native parents. In Chicago, the majority of female clerical workers were native-born women of foreign or mixed parentage (see Table 4). That Chicago's female clerical labor force had a larger percentage of children of foreign parents is not surprising, but it is significant. Throughout the late nineteenth and early twentieth century, Chicago was an ethnically diverse city. In the late nineteenth century, Germans, Irish, Scots, English, and Scandinavians were the dominant ethnic groups in the city. Starting at the turn of the century, immigrants from southern and eastern Europe, particularly from Poland and Italy, and Russian Jews increasingly made

Chicago their destination in the United States. Until 1920, it was the daughters of "older" immigrants, those from northern and western Europe, as well as Canada, who were more successful or more interested in procuring clerical jobs. In 1900, 80.5 percent of all female clerical workers in Chicago with foreign parents traced their ancestry to (or came from) Germany, England, Ireland, Scotland, Sweden, Norway, Denmark, or Canada, while only 7.8 percent traced their ancestry to (or came from) Austria-Hungary, Italy, Poland, or Russia.

The implications of immigrant daughters' activity in this type of employment were undoubtedly varied. In her study of clerical workers in Pittsburgh, Pennsylvania, Ileen DeVault suggests that, at the turn of the century, "daughters' clerical employment can be seen as one of many attempts by native-born and 'old' immigrant group workers to define themselves in opposition to the city's new immigrants from Southern and Eastern Europe."[5] Without additional data, it is impossible to test this hypothesis for Chicago, but, in light of the material available, it seems plausible that, as DeVault argues, some "old" immigrant families of the labor aristocracy experiencing threats to their status saw clerical work as a good occupational choice for their daughters. In Chicago, a number of these "old" ethnic groups, particularly through their religious organizations, provided opportunities for their daughters as well as their sons to train for commercial opportunities.[6] The contribution to the family economy and status that a daughter engaging in clerical work brought was beneficial. A clerical job, however, also exposed immigrant daughters to a world quite different from that of her parents. There are no figures listed in the census to give us a clue about how engaging in an office job contributed to "Americanizing" these young women and the effects that this process had on their family life and cultural identity. It seems likely that in certain cases an immigrant daughter's foray into the office and business district during this period provoked some tension in her family.[7]

Most members of Chicago's female clerical labor force lived in a household with kin. In 1900, the percentage of the entire female labor force over the age of sixteen boarding or living with an employer was almost identical to the percentage of female clerical workers over the age of sixteen boarding or living with an employer, 21.1 percent and 20.3 percent, respectively. The percentage of women living away from family, however, could vary widely within the clerical labor force and these variations appear to be associated with nativity and marital status. For

Table 5. Percentage of Female Clerical Workers Who Boarded; by Clerical Occupation and Nativity, 1900

GROUP OF FEMALE CLERICAL WORKER[a]	PERCENTAGE BOARDING
Native-born with native parents Stenographer-typists	40.0
Native-born with native parents Bookkeepers and accountants	34.1
Native-born with native parents Clerks and copyists	29.2
Foreign-born Stenographers-typists	19.3
Native-born with foreign or mixed parents Stenographer-typists	16.5
Foreign-born Bookkeepers and accountants	16.2
Foreign-born Clerks and copyists	15.2
Native-born with foreign or mixed parents Bookkeepers and accountants	11.7
Native-born with foreign or mixed parents Clerks and copyists	8.8

Source: U.S. Bureau of the Census, *Statistics of Women at Work Based on Unpublished Information Derived from Schedules of the 12th Census* (Washington, D.C.: U.S. Government Printing Office, 1907), pp. 228–233.
[a]N=12,041. This includes only white female clerical workers aged sixteen and over.

example, 35.2 percent of native-born clerical workers with native-born parents lived away from home, while only 12.2 percent of native-born clerical workers with foreign parents did, and 16.1 percent of foreign-born female clerical workers did. Variations existed within occupations as well. Table 5 gives the percentages of female clerical workers by nativity and occupational groups in 1900 that boarded. In Chicago in 1900, native-born, female, white stenographers of native-born parents boarded more often than any other group of clerical worker. Not surprisingly, widowed and divorced women also tended to board more than single women. In 1900, for example, 46.2 percent of widowed and divorced stenographer-typists in Chicago boarded away from home.[8]

Native-born white women of various ages, backgrounds, and familial circumstances looked to clerical work to fulfill a variety of domestic and occupational strategies. In an article that appeared in 1900 in *The Phonographic World,* a male typist, Oliver Smith Williams, humorously depicted the four life stages of the female typist in his article, "The Typewriter Girl in Chicago." Stage one in a female typist's life cycle was characterized by the seventeen-year-old "slim girl" who was extremely inexperienced and self-conscious. "When she takes her first position she just knows that everybody in the office and all the people in the houses across the street are watching her . . . but when Saturday night comes and she is dismissed, she wonders if she has really failed to be as nice as she should have been or if the omissions in her notes and blotches on her letters really did figure in the matter." After "studying up her shorthand, brushing up on reading, practicing on the typewriter," lengthening her dress several inches and dispensing with "ribbons, frizzes and colors," she metamorphosed into stage two, "a demure looking maid," who "is rapidly approaching that stage where she will make herself useful." With increasing competence and confidence, she entered the third stage. Even though "she is making more money than Charlie, the bookkeeper in the same office, while Charlie labors twelve hours a day and she only eight," she took pity on him, married him, and ended up supporting him. "Her figure takes on the matronly air of added wisdom, experience, and age . . . as she now wabbles down Madison and steps into the elevator leading to her own office in the big building on LaSalle Street." In the fourth stage, our typewriter girl has "been left alone in the world. She has made her little 'pile' and owns her own home on the North Side, where she keeps two servants, one a maid-of-all-work and a man of the same stripe who drives her back and forth to her office, where from morning till night of everyday she oversees a dozen or more typewriter girls of the species that she herself was thirty years ago."[9]

These stereotyped images of female clerical workers do provide us with an incomplete roster of the relationships possible between a female clerical worker and her kin. Five possibilities existed. Most prevalent was the young, single daughter living at home and contributing to the family economy, usually receiving money back from her parents for expenses and luxuries. The second most common was the wife or sister of the male head of the household who entered the labor force to contribute to the family economy. Third, an older sister or a widowed or

Table 6. Age Distribution of Chicago's Female Clerical Labor Force, Chicago's Stenographer-Typists, and Fifty-Four Female Public Stenographers in Chicago, 1900

AGE RANGE	PERCENTAGE OF ALL CLERICALS[a]	PERCENTAGE OF STENOGRAPHER-TYPISTS[b]	PERCENTAGE OF PUBLIC STENOGRAPHERS[c]
10–24 Years	67.4	63.0	27.8
25–44 Years	31.2	36.0	68.5
45–64 Years	1.2	0.8	3.7

[a]Figures do not add up to 100 percent because 65 and over and unknown are not included. Source: U.S Bureau of the Census, *Special Report on Occupations, 1900,* pps. 516–523, and 558–560. N=22,390.
[b]Figures do not add up to 100 percent because 65 and over and unknown are not included. Source:ibid. N=8113.
[c]Source: Names of stenographers were first located in the business advertising section of the Chicago City Directory of 1900. The fifty-four female stenographers included here were successfully located in the Federal manuscript census. See Appendix A.

divorced woman might head her own household, either to provide solely for or to contribute to the livelihood of elderly parents, young relatives, or children. The fourth variation was a woman who was physically separated from her family, but who still contributed to the family economy, either by her absence or by cash payments home. Finally, a woman, single, widowed, divorced, or separated, might live independently without any ties to a family economy.

Two special populations of female clerical workers can help reveal how an office job fit into various stages and circumstances in a woman's life. The fifty-four public stenographers who advertised in the 1900 Chicago city directory and were linked in the 1900 manuscript census did not conform to many of the demographic characteristics of the majority of female clerical workers in Chicago.[10] This small, elite group of public stenographers advertised their services in Chicago's business directories between 1875 and 1923. Their number never exceeded 265, and by the 1890s, the women listed outnumbered the men. Of the 198 public stenographers listed in the Chicago business directory of 1900, 118, or 59.6 percent, were individual women.

The women who advertised as stenographers in Chicago's business directory of 1900 were remarkably older than the female clerical labor force in general (see Table 6). The percentages in the categories of ten to twenty-four years old and twenty-five to forty-four years old are reversed. The average and median age of the fifty-four public stenographers was 30.5 years. Married, widowed, and divorced stenographers tended to be older. The average age of single stenographers was 29.8 years, and for non-single stenographers it was 36.7 years. In addition, female stenographers who lived without a father present, and who presumably supported or helped to support their mothers, tended to be older. The average age of single women living only with their mothers was 34.8 years, while the average age of single women with both parents present was 22.1 years. Public stenography, therefore, was not necessarily a young woman's occupation, but, as it had been for some men, a middle-aged occupation. In addition, some women were able to help support dependent parents by working at this form of stenography.

Public stenographers tended to be married, widowed, or divorced more often than Chicago's female clerical labor force generally. While 6.7 percent of Chicago's office workers were listed as married, widowed, or divorced in the 1900 census, 12.96 percent (seven out of fifty-four) of these public stenographers were married, widowed, or divorced. Of the 118 female stenographers listed in the business directory for 1900, 18.6 percent listed "Mrs." before their names. Although some of these women may have lied about their marital status, it seems likely that the percentage of married, widowed, or divorced women in this group was higher than in the general female clerical labor force in Chicago.

Public stenographers also lived on their own more often than clerical workers in general. In 1900, while 21.1 percent of the entire female labor force in Chicago over the age of sixteen and 20.3 percent of Chicago's clerical labor force lived apart from kin, 37 percent of public stenographers lived on their own. This percentage of public stenographers who lived away from kin was also higher than the 26 percent of all stenographer-typists in Chicago in 1900 who boarded.[11]

The majority of Chicago's female public stenographers were native-born women of native-born parents (68.5 percent, or thirty-seven women). Of the 29.7 percent with foreign parents (three foreign-born and thirteen native-born with foreign parents), all came from Canadian, German, Irish, English, Scotch, or Scandinavian stock. Ethnically, Chicago's female public stenographers resembled the clerical labor force of the United States more closely than they did Chicago's.

Finally, these stenographers probably stayed in the work force longer than office workers in general. By tracing the fifty-four women located in the 1900 manuscript census in the Chicago city directory between 1885 and 1923, one can estimate how long these women remained in the labor force as stenographers. The average tenure on the job for these women was ten and a half years, with a range of from one to thirty-one years. Almost 60 percent of these women worked for more than five years, and more than 20 percent of these women worked for between twenty-one and thirty-one years during their lifetimes.

A majority of these fifty-four women (thirty-four, or almost 70 percent) lived in a household with kin. Of these, twenty-seven (50 percent) lived with one or both parents or grandparents present; five lived with sisters; and two, both childless, lived with a spouse. Of the remaining twenty women, nineteen lived alone in a variety of arrangements ranging from rooming with a single family to boarding in a home with dozens of other single adults. Only one woman lived in (and headed, according to the census taker) a household completely made up of what appears to be unrelated adults.

One-half of these stenographers contributed significantly to the running of the household. Because of the presence of a retired father or a widowed mother and other working siblings present in the household, it is safe to assume that the wages of the female clerical worker were important to the family economy. Annie M. Adams, a thirty-eight-year-old native-born single stenographer, lived in a household that included her sixty-four-year-old widowed mother and two single sisters. Her sister Helen, who was forty-two, worked as a bookkeeper. Although we do not know what Annie Adams's father did for a living, he must have been relatively comfortable since the family owned its home. Marion Drake, a thirty-five-year-old native-born single stenographer, lived with both parents, a grandmother, and a younger brother. Only Marion and her brother worked, however, as the patriarch of the family, Manley, was retired. Twenty of these public stenographers, in fact, lived as daughters in households with either a widowed mother (or father not present in household), a retired father, or with both parents not working.

Seven stenographers contributed to their households as wives or as sisters. Minnie Patterson, for example, a thirty-four-year-old Scottish woman, lived in a rooming house with her husband Herbert, who was a thirty-five-year-old, Scottish school teacher. They had emigrated to the United States separately when they were in their early twenties (Herbert in 1888 and Minnie in 1886) and married in 1892. The Shaw sisters,

Jenette, thirty, and Mabel, twenty-three, lived in an apartment with another sister, Alice, a twenty-year-old milliner. They were all born in Illinois of parents from New York. Jennette and Mabel not only lived in the same apartment, but also worked in the same office downtown in room 312 at 79 Dearborn Street. These women, like daughters with an unemployed or widowed parent, probably contributed to the economic viability of their household.

Only seven of these women were daughters (in one instance, a granddaughter, and in another suspicious listing, a daughter-in-law) living in "intact" families with fathers working. These women were significantly younger than the group as a whole; their average age was 18.4 years. It is likely that within these households, contributions from the daughter-stenographer were less crucial, but still important, depending on the occupation of the male head of the household and family structure. Evelynn Marquardt, for example, a seventeen-year-old stenographer, lived with her forty-eight-year-old German father, who was a barn foreman, her native-born mother, who stayed at home, her twenty-year-old brother, who was also a stenographer, a young sister, and two boarders. Evelynn probably contributed something to the rent for the house and the food bills in this household. Mabel Snell's contributions may have been less important than Evelynn's. Mabel, twenty-two, lived with her father, Will Snell, a fifty-four-year-old, native-born lawyer of native stock, her mother, who stayed at home, her thirty-year-old brother George, who was a minister, and her fourteen-year-old brother William, who went to school. The Snells owned their own home. Economics and ethnicity could not only affect a young woman's reasons for engaging in clerical work but also the meaning that venturing into the world of work had for her.

Nineteen of these public stenographers lived singly as lodgers, roomers, or boarders in a variety of arrangements ranging from lodging with an unrelated family to renting a furnished room in a hotel that also contained dozens of other adults. Census data do not make it possible to establish the type of relationships these women had with families elsewhere; nevertheless, a number of tentative hypotheses can be asserted. The large number of these public stenographers living on their own certainly suggests that self-support was possible for certain clerical workers. It may have also been possible, although probably extremely problematic, for some women to provide some support for dependents as well. Jessie Holmes, for example, lived in a relatively small household in which she and another divorced working woman boarded with the female head of the household, and her two working brothers. Jessie was a thirty-year-old widow with two living children who apparently did not live with her. Perhaps she contributed to their support and upbringing elsewhere.[12]

Living physically apart from kin, therefore, did not (and does not) necessarily mean that a woman worker was completely detached from some sort of family or domestic economy. Her very absence may have helped the budget of the family she had just left. She may have sent cash payments home; she may have had relations nearby whom she could have helped or relied upon monetarily. Or, obviously, she may have been entirely self-supporting and independent. The second data source reveals specific information about one group of Chicago's female clerical workers who lived apart from family in 1910. These women lived in residences provided by the Eleanor Association of Chicago. This organization was founded in 1898 by Ina Law Robertson, then a graduate student at the University of Chicago, to provide safe, affordable, and respectable living quarters for self-supporting, working women. By 1910, the association had four residences throughout the city.[13] Of the 175 women who lived in these residences in 1910, sixty were clerical workers (including two students of stenography and two teachers of stenography).

The demographic characteristics of the women who lived in the Eleanor residences were similar to those of the clerical labor force in Chicago, generally. The average age of these women was 25.8 years, with 55 percent of these under the age of 25; 90 percent of these women were single. The proportion of foreign-born women and women of foreign stock was higher than in the general population of clerical workers in Chicago, however. Ten out of the eleven foreign women were from Canada, England, Ireland, or Scotland; one was a Russian. Twenty-seven of the twenty-nine second-generation women came from northern or western European stock; the remaining two were from Bohemian and German Jewish stock.

The major difference between these women and most clerical workers in Chicago was that they did not live within a household of kin. Two characteristics of these women, however, suggest the persistence of family ties. The most obvious was the presence of sisters. Five sister groups can be identified among the clerical workers in these residences.

The three Ludwig sisters, Cecilia, twenty-four, Rose, twenty-two, and Margaret, twenty, for example, all lived in an Eleanor residence together. Cecilia worked as a stenographer in a druggist's office; Rose worked as a stenographer in a wholesale house; and Margaret worked as a bookkeeper in a tailor's office. They were born in Iowa of German parents and perhaps the distance from home made this arrangement more appealing or necessary. Some of these sisters may have even worked in the same establishments. Blondina and Millie Strucke, born in Illinois of German parents, both worked as stenographers for a railroad. In addition, most native-born women who lived in the Eleanor residences were born relatively close to Chicago. Out of the forty-eight native-born women (one unknown), twenty-three were born in Illinois and an additional twelve in the adjacent or nearby states of Michigan, Wisconsin, or Indiana. Even if a resident did not have a sister close by, a certain amount of familial contact was certainly possible for many of these women.

Whether a woman lived at home or apart from family, whether she was young or middle-aged, married, widowed, divorced, or single, whether she was the daughter of immigrants or Yankees, whether her family needed her wages or not, she probably considered clerical work a good job. Clerical work fit into a wide variety of domestic arrangements and there were a number of jobs from which to choose. All three job categories of clerical work—bookkeeper, cashier, and accountant; clerk and copyist; and stenographer-typist—were relatively good jobs for women. To speak of the "decline" of office positions during this period is to speak of it from the perspective of a male worker. Certainly, female office workers almost universally made less money than male office workers and their promotional opportunities were extremely limited. Because of the universality of the sexual division of labor, however, it is perhaps more fruitful to compare women's office work with other occupations dominated by women when trying to understand why women took office positions. In terms of the hours, wages, and conditions of work, a clerical position was one of the best occupational opportunities for women at that time.[14]

In 1892, the Illinois Bureau of Labor Statistics released a detailed study of working women in Chicago.[15] Of the 5,099 women and ninety-five establishments included in the survey, 245 women in twenty industries were clerical workers.[16] Except for the small number of forewomen, editors, proofreaders, and administrators, clerical workers

Table 7. Standard of Living of Operatives, Clerks, and Stenographer-Typists, Chicago, 1892

EXPENSES PER YEAR	OPERATIVES[a]	CLERKS[b]	STENO/TYPE[b]
Clothing	$63.00	$90.53	$139.53
Illness	$15.00	$13.83	$22.88
Carfare	$22.00	$27.85	$33.86
Room and Board (or assistance to others)[c]	$179.00	$187.95	$289.57
Dressmaking	$12.22	$16.71	$18.40
Other Expenses	$20.85	$29.67	$41.33
Yearly Wage[d]	$296.92	$389.48	$622.96
Minus Total Expenses	−$312.07	$366.54	$545.57
Difference	−$15.15	+$22.94	+$77.39

Source: Illinois Bureau of Labor Statistics, *Seventh Annual Biennial Report: Part One: Working Women in Chicago* (Springfield, Ill., 1892), pp. v–354.

[a] Average figures on operatives calculated by the statistician of the Illinois Bureau of Labor Statistics and appearing in the introductory summary.

[b] Average figures on clerks and stenographer-typists were calculated from the raw data supplied in Table 1. The number of stenographer-typists was 38 and the number of clerks was 104. Bookkeepers, cashiers, and cash girls were not included because of small size of sample and because some cashiers in the sample ate at their place of employment.

[c] The report gave figures on room and board and support to others. Usually, a woman either lived on her own or surrendered her paycheck to the family and received money for expenses. In some instances, women provided figures for both. I calculated the average of both figures and included the highest in the table.

[d] Calculated by multiplying the average weekly salary by 52 weeks.

uniformly had higher wages than other women workers. Bookkeepers' average wage was eleven dollars and forty-eight cents a week; stenographers and typists averaged eleven dollars and ninety-eight cents per week; clerks averaged seven dollars and forty-nine cents a week; cashiers and cash girls averaged six dollars and forty-one cents a week. The average weekly wage for all clerical workers listed in the survey was eight dollars and seventy-eight cents a week, while the average wage for non-office employees was five dollars and seventy-one cents a week.

Since the Illinois Bureau of Labor Statistics inquired about living expenses, we can estimate the different standards of living of office and factory women (see Table 7). Despite increased expenses for clothing and room and board, office workers, particularly stenographer-typists and the higher-paid bookkeepers, had more income left over after taking care of necessities. Office workers were certainly not well off, but they could feel somewhat more secure and use some of their income on education, entertainment, savings, or to help their families.

Because most female clerical workers during this period were white, native-born, single, and relatively well-educated women, other possible employment options were clerking in a store or teaching. Although some women chose saleswomanship because of its potential for advancement and its glamour, Susan Porter Benson reports that, throughout the period, "clerical workers consistently earned more than saleswomen," and clerical work bestowed more prestige on young women and their parents.[17] Clerical salaries for women in Chicago, however, were lower than for Chicago's female teaching force throughout the period. In 1894, a female high school teacher in the Chicago schools received an average of $1,319 a year, while a clerical worker at the Board of Education got $967 a year.[18] By 1923, the average salary for teachers in Chicago ranged from $2,057 a year for kindergarten teachers to $3,080 a year for high school teachers.[19]

Nevertheless, there were many reasons why women took clerical instead of teaching jobs throughout the period. Although the number of teaching jobs increased, teaching could not absorb the large number of women entering the labor force during the first decades of the twentieth century. Teaching often required more formal training than clerical work did. And the comparison between the wages of Chicago-based teachers and clerical workers may not accurately characterize the choice involved. The teaching positions in Chicago were certainly the most lucrative, if not the most desirable, teaching jobs available in the region. If a young woman procured a position in a rural school, her wages would have been significantly less. For example, in 1924, the average salary for rural teachers in Illinois was $898 a year, while the average yearly salary for elementary school teachers in Chicago was $2,387.[20] Not only did clerical work pay better than rural school teaching jobs, but the city setting of the office job was often preferable to many of these young women.

The hours of office workers, particularly of stenographer-typists, were also favorable. Most office employees worked six days a week, with perhaps a half-day off on Saturday during the summer months. Except in mail order houses and some retail and wholesale establishments, the work was not seasonal. Clerical work was less affected by economic downturns than other employment. And clerical workers did not put in long days relative to other employment opportunities available to women. The average day of the 245 office workers in the Illinois Bureau of Labor Statistics study of 1892 was 8.9 hours per day. Book-keepers averaged 9.1 hours a day; cashiers and cash girls, 9.6 hours a day; clerks, nine hours a day; and stenographer-typists, 8.5 hours a day. And twenty years later, the hours of female clerical workers had improved. A study of more than 100,000 of Chicago's working women done in 1913–1914 reported that 81.6 percent of 5,380 clerical workers examined worked less than nine hours a day. Only employees in neck-wear factories and in the publishing business had higher percentages of female employees working less than nine hours a day.[21]

Even if all clerical jobs were relatively good positions for women, they were not sharing equally in new female entrants. Chicago's potential female clerical workers were increasingly choosing one type of clerical job. Between 1890 and 1920, women made stenography-typing their exclusive domain among office jobs and within offices. In fact, much of the increase in women's labor force participation in clerical work was a result of women's employment in stenography-typist positions. The rapid increase in the number of stenography-typist positions between 1900 and 1910 altered the distribution of the clerical labor force. Of the entire clerical labor force, stenography-typing contributed 13 percent of the total clerical labor force in 1900. By 1910, however, almost 24 percent of the total clerical labor force was stenography-typing positions (see Table 8). Women took an overwhelming majority of these positions. The percentage of female stenographer-typists increased from 83 percent in 1900 to 93.3 percent by 1920 (see Table 9). In 1910, stenography-typing accounted for 50.7 percent of all women in clerical work, a high point for the period between 1890 and 1930 (see Table 10). Some 55 percent of the clerical workers who lived in the Eleanor residences in 1910 were stenographers.

Stenography-typing, the fastest growing clerical job, was attracting a different sort of woman. Stenographer-typists provide the only exception to the aging trend in Chicago's clerical labor force. Just the reverse of the clerical labor force as a whole, between 1900 and 1920, the percentage of ten-year-old to twenty-four-year-old stenographer-typists increased and the percentage of female stenographers from twenty-five to forty-four years old decreased (see Table 11). Without comparable 1910 data,

Table 8. Percentage of Chicago's Clerical Labor Force, Male and Female, in Each Clerical Occupation, 1900–1930

YEAR	STENOGRAPHER-TYPIST	BOOKKEEPER, CASHIER, ACCOUNTANT	CLERK
1900	13.1	22.6	64.3
1910	23.6	24.1	52.3
1920	23.7	19.5	56.8
1930	23.5	17.9	58.6

Source: U.S. Bureau of the Census, *Special Report on Occupations, 1900,* pps. 516–523, and 558–560; U.S. Bureau of the Census, *Statistics of Women at Work, Based on Unpublished Information Derived from the Schedules of the 12th Census* (Washington, D.C.: U.S. Government Printing Office, 1907), pps. 29, and 228–233; U.S. Bureau of the Census, *Population—Occupational Statistics, 1910,* vol. 4, pps. 165, and 544–547; U.S. Bureau of the Census, *Population—Occupations, 1920,* vol. 4, pps. 149, and 1076–1080; U.S. Bureau of the Census, *Population—Occupations by States, 1930,* vol. 4, pps. 423–429, 447–450, 456–457, and 463–465.

Table 9. Percent of Male and Female Clerical Workers in the Three Clerical Occupations in Chicago, 1900–1930

YEAR	CLERKS		BOOKKEEPERS, CASHIERS, AND ACCOUNTANTS		STENOGRAPHERS AND TYPISTS	
	M	F	M	F	M	F
1900	81.0	19.0	69.8	30.2	17.0	83.0
1910	79.9	20.1	60.7	39.3	12.7	87.3
1920	65.0	35.0	54.6	45.4	6.7	93.3
1930	62.1	37.9	53.3	46.7	3.3	96.7

Source: U.S Bureau of the Census, *Special Report on Occupations, 1900,* pps. 516–523, and 558–560; U.S. Bureau of the Census, *Statistics of Women at Work, Based on Unpublished Information Derived from the Schedules of the 12th Census* (Washington, D.C.: U.S. Government Printing Office, 1907), pps. 29, and 228–233; U.S. Bureau of the Census, *Population—Occupational Statistics, 1910,* vol. 4, pps. 165, and 544–547; U.S. Bureau of the Census, *Population—Occupations, 1920,* vol. 4, pps. 149, and 1076–1080; U.S. Bureau of the Census, *Population—Occupations by States, 1930,* vol. 4, pps. 423–429, 447–450, 456–457, and 463–465.

Table 10. Percentage of Chicago's Female Clerical Labor Force in Each Occupational Category and the Percentage of Chicago's Male Clerical Labor Force in Each Occupational Category, 1900–1930

YEAR	STENOGRAPHER-TYPISTS	BOOKKEEPERS, CASHIERS, ACCOUNTANTS	CLERKS
Females			
1890	22.6	21.7	55.7
1900	36.2	22.8	40.9
1910	50.7	23.4	25.9
1920	43.5	17.4	39.2
1930	42.7	15.7	41.6
Males[a]			
1900	3.2	22.5	74.3
1910	5.0	24.6	70.3
1920	3.2	21.6	75.1
1930	1.7	20.4	77.9

Source: U.S. Bureau of the Census, *Special Report on Occupations, 1900,* pps. 516–523, and 558–560; U.S. Bureau of the Census, *Statistics of Women at Work, Based on Unpublished Information Derived from the Schedules of the 12th Census* (Washington, D.C.: U.S. Government Printing Office, 1907), pps. 29, and 228–233; U.S. Bureau of the Census, *Population—Occupational Statistics, 1910,* vol. 4, pps. 165, and 544–547; U.S. Bureau of the Census, *Population—Occupations, 1920,* vol. 4, pps. 149, and 1076–1080; U.S. Bureau of the Census, *Population—Occupations by States, 1930,* vol. 4, pps. 423–429, 447–450, 456–457, and 463–465.
[a]1890 figures not available for men. The census did not differentiate the clerical workforce by occupation.

it is difficult to determine exactly why the percentage of younger stenographer-typists increased while the percentage of this age group decreased in the other clerical categories. This phenomenon does coincide with women's domination of new stenographer-typist positions. Perhaps the first significant group of women to enter this clerical occupation were younger than subsequent entrants. As Elyce J. Rotella states, "younger women may have been more likely to have the daring to flaunt convention by taking clerical jobs."[22] Employers, whether for business or personal reasons, may have preferred younger stenographer-typists. In addition, the increased demand for women's employment during World War I may have pulled younger, previously unemployed women into the clerical work force. Stenography-typing positions may have also been the clerical occupation of choice for new female entrants into the office.

Table 11. Age Distribution of Female Stenographer-Typists in Chicago, 1890–1930

YEAR	10–24	25–44	45–64	65 AND OVER
1890	73.0	26.1	0.5	0.4[a]
1900	63.0	36.0	0.8	0.2[a]
1910	44.8[b]	54.2[a,c]	0.9[d]	—[d]
1920	69.5	28.9[a]	1.6	less than 0.1
1930	62.5	35.0	2.4	0.1[a]

Source: U.S. Bureau of the Census, *1890 Census of Population,* vol. 1, part 2, pps. 650–652; U.S. Bureau of the Census, *Special Report on Occupations, 1900,* pps. 516–523, and 558–560; U.S. Bureau of the Census, *Statistics of Women at Work, Based on Unpublished Information Derived from the Schedules of the 12th Census* (Washington, D.C.: U.S. Government Printing Office, 1907), pps. 29, and 228–233; U.S. Bureau of the Census, *Population—Occupational Statistics, 1910,* vol. 4, pps. 165, and 544–547; U.S. Bureau of the Census, *Population—Occupations, 1920,* vol. 4, pps. 149, and 1076–1080; U.S. Bureau of the Census, *Population—Occupations by States, 1930,* vol. 4, pps. 423–429, 447–450, 456–457, and 463–465.
[a] Includes unknown.
[b] 1910 census category was 10–20.
[c] 1910 census category was 21–44.
[d] 1910 census category was 45 and over.

The women who chose stenography-typing during these years belonged to the ranks of another fast-growing population in Chicago, daughters (and sons) of the foreign-born. In 1890, of the three major clerical jobs, stenography-typing had the highest percentage of native-born women with native-born parents and the lowest percentage of native-born women of foreign or mixed parentage. By 1920, stenography-typing had the largest percentage of second-generation women of the three clerical jobs and the lowest percentage of native-born women with native parents (see Table 12). Between 1890 and World War I, stenography-typing, the fastest growing clerical job, was increasingly the province of younger women of foreign stock.

In Chicago, between 1890 and World War I, women took advantage of a favorable economic climate that demanded their services, a labor market with few institutionalized barriers to entrance, and educational institutions willing to provide training, and entered clerical jobs. Whether a woman needed to support a retired father, a widowed mother, or a young son or daughter, or to contribute to a household economy, or

Table 12. Percentages of White, Native-Born Female Clerical Workers with Native Parents and White, Native-Born Female Clerical Workers with Foreign or Mixed Parents in Each Occupational Category, Chicago, 1890–1920

GROUP	1890	1900	1910	1920
Bookkeepers, Cashiers, and Accountants				
Native-Born, Native Parents	32.2	29.8	27.9	32.2
Native-Born, Mixed or Foreign Parents	53.1	54.9	59.8	56.1
Clerks and Copyists				
Native-Born, Native Parents	22.9	25.5	27.9	31.5
Native-Born, Mixed or Foreign Parents	56.0	56.3	61.5	57.2
Stenographer-Typists				
Native-Born, Native Parents	47.0	38.4	28.5	29.6
Native-Born, Mixed or Foreign Parents	42.7	50.3	63.3	60.9

Source: U.S. Bureau of the Census, *1890 Census of Population,* vol. 1, part 2, pps. 650–652; U.S. Bureau of the Census, *Special Report on Occupations, 1900,* pps. 516–523, and 558–560; U.S. Bureau of the Census, *Statistics of Women at Work, Based on Unpublished Information Derived from the Schedules of the 12th Census* (Washington, D.C.: U.S. Government Printing Office, 1907), pps. 29, and 228–233; U.S. Bureau of the Census, *Population—Occupational Statistics, 1910,* vol. 4, pps. 165, and 544–547; U.S. Bureau of the Census, *Population—Occupations, 1920,* vol. 4, pps. 149, and 1076–1080.

wanted to live independently, clerical work was a viable occupational option. To many of these women, working in an office could not have been simply a way to pass the time between childhood and adult responsibilities to husband and children or a way to meet eligible husbands. A clerical job was a way to support dependents on your own, a way to help out your family, or a way to strike out on your own, and because of this, women, for their own reasons, made clerical work women's work.

Women's early "conquest" of stenography-typing and their entrance into other office positions may have produced what economists and sociologists call "tipping." Social scientists first identified the tipping phenomenon as they tried to understand why the racial characteristics of housing projects and neighborhoods changed when "some recognizable minority group reach[ed] a size that motivate[d] other residents [to] begin to leave." In housing markets, once a critical percentage of blacks, for example, moved into a neighborhood, not only would fewer whites move in, but also those already there would leave.[23] This process of tipping has recently been applied to try to understand gender shifts in occupations. Myra H. Strober and Carolyn L. Arnold, when discussing the gender shift of bank tellers during World War II, claim that "when large numbers of women enter a formerly all-male occupation, the occupation often 'tips' and becomes virtually all female."[24] Women's very presence, therefore, in increasing numbers in certain clerical occupations may have provoked and hastened the process of resegregation of those jobs. Since there was (and still is) a powerful distaste for both sexes working at the same job in near-equal numbers, it follows that the existence of a critical number of women in a particular occupation would set in motion the redefinition of that job, and the concomitant exit (or decreasing entrance) of men and the increasing entrance of women.

While women took advantage of these developments, society tried to catch up. Women's desire for remunerative and respectable employment and economic changes than required more workers cannot by themselves account for women's entrance into a particular line of work. Similarly, equating a supply of qualified female workers ready to join office forces and the increased demand for clerical services does not account for an acceptance of women as clerical workers. The relationship between clerical work and women was worked out through discussions about and depictions of clerical workers in print and visual media. It is to this "reconstruction" of the imagery and language associated with clerical work that we now turn.

CHAPTER 4

The Discourse on "Fitness": Science and Symbols

*A*S WOMEN entered the office, the editors of *The Phonographic World* took note of a new language problem in their profession in an editorial entitled, "New Words Sadly Needed." The editor claimed that "when a person wished to speak of those charming creatures in petticoats who pat the keys of writing machines, he must say, 'girl typewriters,' 'young lady typewriters,' 'women typewriters,' 'girl typewriter operators,' etc., etc." Because of the varied ages of these women, many of these appellations were inappropriate and " 'woman typewriter' or 'female typewriter,' " "would be resented—and 'she-typewriter,' is to say the least, not acceptable." Referring to men who operated the typewriter was fraught with similar problems. The difficulties described were also compounded by the fact that "typewriter" could refer to both the machine and its operator. To alleviate all of these problems, the editor not only proposed to use different words to signify operator (the generic term "typist") and machine (typewriter), but also to make the word signifying the operator gender specific. Therefore a male typist would be a "type" and a female typist a "typess," a male stenographer a "stenographer" and a female stenographer a "stenographess." But, in fact, just as the editor proposed these changes in language, he also acknowledged why these alterations would prove unnecessary. Even by 1896, when this editorial appeared, it was also readily evident to its writer that, "when one speaks of 'typewriters' or 'typewriter operators' usually the hearer first thinks of female typewriter operator because they are in the great majority."[1] What was beginning and emerging out of this gender confusion was the association of at least certain kinds of clerical work with females.[2]

Women's entrance into most clerical jobs and complete domination of stenography-typing positions set in motion a redefinition of the normative characteristics and popular image of clerical work and workers. The descriptions and depictions of the female clerical worker underwent dramatic transformations as the woman office worker changed from an aberration to a commonly recognizable feature of the downtown business district. In the journals concerned with the world of the office, both workers and so-called experts, male and female, discussed and debated the role and appropriateness of the female clerical worker. In the popular media of the day, the image of the female clerical worker was sensational, but evolving into a stock character. It is during this crucial period between 1890 and World War I, within the world of so-called scientific experts and the subjective world of symbols, that the process of "socially reconstructing" clerical work as a female occupation occurred.

This was necessary because women's entrance into offices posed a direct threat to a number of Victorian prescriptions for respectable behavior, not just for women, but between the sexes. The prevailing belief in nineteenth and, at least, early twentieth century society that men and women naturally occupied separate spheres has been well documented.[3] This conception of separate spheres was intimately related to the concept of the sexual division of labor, originally evident in the pre-industrial domestic economy in both agricultural and artisan households, and then translated into an industrial economy with the delineation of men's public sphere, outside the home, and women's private sphere, within the home. Under ideal economic circumstances, men's work would provide all the money necessary to support the family. The ability for the male head of household to make a "family wage" was and is a persistent goal of organized labor specifically, and for all working men in general. Women's proper and natural role, therefore, was to perform the duties necessary within this setting: food production and meal preparation, clothing production and maintenance, household cleaning, child rearing and education, and a variety of support services for family members and sexual services for the husband. Finally, propping up this complementarity of function was the general belief in the complementary characteristics of men and women. Men and women neatly embodied a duality of personality traits, underscoring the importance and naturalness of union in marriage. Women were considered moral, religious, emotional, weaker in physical and emotional strength, aesthetic, private, and intuitive, for example, while men were considered to have more vices and to be more rational, logical, ambitious, forceful, strong, practical, and so forth. These particular qualities were less important than the commonly held assumption that men and women were distinguishable by opposite, complementary, innate gender characteristics.

Women certainly entered the paid labor force well before they entered clerical work, and, as a result, explanations existed to legitimize this activity out of their sphere. Women who worked outside the home could usually rely upon three explanations for their activity. First, women could perform functions outside the home that they had traditionally performed within the home, usually within a closely monitored, "family" setting. The most important occupation for women in the nineteenth century, domestic service, clearly fell within this prescription. Second, women could engage in work outside the home on a temporary basis to help their families. This prescription allowed women to work for wages without posing a threat to the male workers; after all, women were not working for self-support enabling them to exist outside of the family, but for the continuation of the family and the concept of the family wage. Third, women could work outside the home for a limited period of time, usually for a few years before marriage. Like the preceding rationalization, this functioned to substantiate, not threaten, the concept of the family wage provided by the male head of the household. Woman's work outside the home and her natural functions within the home were perceived to be mutually exclusive. A true woman, with the possibility of support as a wife within a family, would reject any self-supporting employment no matter how fulfilling or remunerative.

Within the world of wage work, a number of other implicit rules also seemed to operate based upon these assumptions about women's work. "Respectable" middle-class members of Victorian society believed that it was morally dangerous for unrelated men and women to work together in the same physical space. It was also considered unnatural for a man to work in a position subordinate to a woman and this allowed for restricting women's promotion within firms. Many members of nineteenth (and twentieth) century society saw women workers as secondary workers, providing wages that merely supplemented but did not support their families. It was assumed that women were physically weaker than men and this limited the type of work possible as well as the time and length of shifts. Finally, many employers believed that since a female worker's primary commitment was to her present or future family, she was less willing to move geographically or make a long-term commitment to employment.[4]

Women's presence in clerical occupations posed a threat to many of these assumptions. The office was a male bastion, and clerical work, a male-dominated occupation, was associated with masculine characteristics. In an office, a woman would work closely with men. If no changes were made within the office hierarchy, she could attempt to work her way up through the ranks, posing the possibility of a woman supervising a man or men. If a woman did become a manager, supervisor, or even boss, her earning power would pose a direct threat to the concept of the male family wage. Her success at work might damage her "natural instinct" to abandon work for marriage. And if a woman attempted to succeed within this setting, she would necessarily adopt certain behavior patterns that might "unsex" her or render her more masculine than feminine in the eyes of her co-workers, associates, and family.

Clerical work had to be redefined as an occupation consistent with innate feminine qualities. The skills necessary to engage in clerical work needed to be seen as women's skills; the personality traits necessary to perform in these positions needed to come into correspondence with feminine traits; and, like traditional women's occupations, clerical jobs needed to be described as jobs that provided training for women's "natural" and ultimate job: as a wife and mother in her own family.

Debates in the Realm of Science

The issue of women's entrance into clerical work was part of a larger national debate concerning women's place in society. The period between 1890 and World War I saw an unprecedented increase in women's philanthropic, club, and suffrage activities, and, although this was by no means acceptable to most members of American society, also in women's labor and radical activities. All women's new activities outside the home both provoked and hastened a reassessment of womanhood in the United States. The process by which clerical work was socially constructed as a female occupation would serve as an important precedent as more and more women entered the labor force, increasingly in clerical jobs, throughout the twentieth century. Contributors (including many female clerical workers) to the two important stenographic and typing trade journals of the day, *The Phonographic World* and *Gregg Writer,* as well as other popular and trade journals, participated in this process of reassessing clerical work, specifically, and women's position in society, generally.

For much of the period between 1890 and 1910, a great deal of confusion accompanied the gender associated with, and therefore the characteristics associated with, clerical work (see Illustration 3). During the years 1889 and 1890, the journal *The Phonographic World* engaged in a survey of preachers throughout the country and one of the questions asked was whether men or women were better stenographers. Forty-seven of the eighty-seven asked responded, with nineteen preferring men; sixteen, women; and twelve claiming that either suited. What is more interesting than the diversity of opinion were the reasons given for preferring one sex over the other. Rev. T. DeWitt Peake of Merrill, Wisconsin, claimed that he preferred men because "men, as a rule, make the best and most reliable shorthand reporters," while Rev. Theodore F. Garrett of Covington, Kentucky, claimed that "women make the best and most reliable reporters."[5] According to different preachers, each sex held a monopoly on accuracy, reliability, steadiness, and quickness. Clearly at this early date, the qualities needed to succeed as a stenographer were not yet considered exclusively male or female.

There was nothing inherent in the skills necessary to engage in clerical work that someone living in late nineteenth and early twentieth century American society would have considered particularly female. Except for the identification of the piano and the typewriter there was no aspect of a clerical worker's job that in any way resembled what women traditionally did in the home. Therefore, the skills necessary to engage in clerical work needed to be socially constructed as women's skills. The major obstacle was the claim by various commentators that certain clerical occupations, particularly court reporter jobs, required a degree of physical stamina that women did not possess. Mr. William H. Slocum, the official stenographer of the eighth judicial district in Buffalo, New York, claimed that women do not succeed as court reporters because "after she has suffered the strain to a certain degree, and beyond which she cannot go, she becomes tired and finds that her mind is off wool-gathering, and her lack of concentration of thought has caused her to unconsciously miss a word here and another there."[6] Male court reporters, who were experiencing great uncertainty and a loss of status in their positions as a result of the entrance of women into their profession, used this time-worn reason to attempt, in vain, to exclude women from their ranks.

These objections were overshadowed by assertions that women were innately superior in other areas. The skills that women presumably possessed that made them better office workers have become, over the years, part of the baggage of gender stereotypes. For example, as early as 1886, women were considered "nimbler, neater, and steadier than men," and it was thought that "the broad tipped fingers of a man do not fit him for a very graceful operator on writing machines." That men were also winning speed contests on the typewriter seems to have been irrelevant.[7] One writer, however, unwittingly exposed the subjectiveness of these so-called gender specific skills. In a reprint in *The Phonographic World* from the *New York Sun* the author claimed that "it is a popular error to suppose that a woman can be light fingered and lightning fingered at the same time. The reverse is the fact. Among the watchmakers of Geneva and elsewhere the finest work, requiring extreme delicacy of touch and accuracy of execution is done by fellows with powerful fists. The wabbling [sic] fingers of a woman can never accomplish it."[8] In 1900, the editor of the *Ladies' Home Journal* was also not at all convinced that office work was good or natural for women. The editor baldly stated that it "is a simple fact that women have shown themselves naturally incompetent to fill a great many of the business positions which they have sought to occupy." In addition to an alarming tendency among business girls and women to nervous collapse, the editor also claimed that "the vast majority of women in business to-day have absolutely no taste for it. They are there simply because necessity drove them to it." These women, the editor predicted, will leave the "foreign soil" of the business office and return to their "natural sphere," domestic service, either in homes of their own or of others.[9]

The editor's prediction was obviously wrong, but women's competence in the office was not sufficient to alter the gender association of clerical work; it was also necessary to demonstrate that women's innate personality characteristics were consistent with clerical work. This, it seems, was much more problematic. It would have been entirely inappropriate for women to argue their worthiness in the office because they could perform just like a man, because most nineteenth and early twentieth century Americans believed that women were entirely different from men. Experts and female clerical workers needed to assert that women's special innate characteristics contributed to the smooth and efficient running of the office in ways that men's nature could not.

When women left that private sphere of hearth and home and journeyed into the public world of the office, she posed two problems because of her supposedly innate nature. First, it was not entirely clear whether women would be a moral or an immoral influence in the business office. Would her innate moral superiority extend into the business office and provide a model for behavior to her more raucous male coworkers? Would she find herself in peril as a result of the immorality of the denizens of these commercial brotherhoods? Or, would the promiscuous mingling of the sexes in close quarters make some sort of mischief inevitable, regardless of the best intentions of either party? Second, it was uncertain to many experts and contemporaries whether women had enough of a work ethic to perform adequately within the world of the office. Women, particularly the predominately young, middle-class variety taking clerical jobs, were supposedly unused to time discipline, business etiquette, impersonal interactions, and teamwork. Most women were expected to marry, making employers wary of women's commitment to their jobs.

Hattie A. Shinn, a Chicago clerical worker who contributed to *The Phonographic World,* summed up the problem associated with the reconciliation of women's nature and clerical work in an article from the *Chicago Tribune,* reprinted in *The Phonographic World* in 1889. She stated that "woman as a creature of business is an experiment as yet, but we are trying hard to make the experiment a success, and to prove that woman has abilities which she may so utilize as to become self-supporting and independent, and at the same time lose none of the womanly modesty of her nature—without which womanliness it were better to be dead."[10] Mrs. R. F. Allie believed that even though women possessed "no lack of ability," women should not take positions as court reporters. "There are certain restrictions placed upon the relations of men and women, for which every woman should be grateful and which are really the safeguard of the nation's morality. Let this be once broken down, and it would soon become evident that the tendency of the times would be toward a familiarity of intercourse which all women of true modesty would deprecate."[11]

This concern for women's morality, and hence the nation's, as they entered the business office came from different quarters. The famous Chicago reformer, Jane Addams, was concerned that the work settings and meager wages of many female workers created situations where women accepted money and gifts in exchange for sexual favors. Despite the relatively better wages and working conditions in offices, female clerical workers were not exempted from the temptation to "fall into a vicious life from the sheer lack of social restraint." In 1912, Addams wrote, "perhaps no young woman is more exposed to the temptation of this sort than the one who works in an office where she may be the sole woman employed and where the relation to her employer and to her fellow-clerks is almost on a social basis. . . . The girl is without the wholesome social restraint afforded by the companionship of other working women and her isolation in itself constitutes a danger."[12] Clara E. Laughlin examined this problem in more detail. In her 1913 study of Chicago working girls, she reported that many girls who worked in offices and stores supplemented their wages by receiving the attentions of men. "Many girls who work in offices and stores spend one or two or three nights a week in some 'resort' and earn the difference between shabby insufficiency and the ability to compete with or even dazzle the girls who work beside them."[13] She told of Eugenia, a high school and private business school graduate, who came from a small town to earn her living as a stenographer in the city. She answered an advertisement from the Union Novelty Company. "Inside were two men. The office was scantily furnished. There was a cheap roll-top desk . . . a giant cuspidor, a swivel chair, and two others that look like stray members of an erstwhile dining-room set. Smoking and aiming at the cuspidor seemed to be the only business of the place; and while the smoke was voluminous, the other half of the enterprise evidence some lack of expertness." Eugenia escaped from this unhealthy environment and procured work in a reputable establishment, but before too long, she was fired for refusing to go to dinner with her boss.[14]

Less hysterical but no less concerned were the ideas of Janette Egmont, who claimed that "when she [the stenographer] goes into an office, she burns her bridges behind her. She must be a law unto herself." The stenographer, therefore, had an enormous and difficult responsibility to steer "well between the Scylla of prudery and the Charybdis of familiarity, to raise the standard (and in this generation, even establish the standard) by which men will judge her sex in this profession."[15]

Other writers in the technical journals believed that even if women were not helpless victims, and men hopeless lechers, the proximity between the two sexes made the business-like running of the office almost impossible. As Janette Edgmont implied, the blame for this and the responsibility for changing it lay with women. Women "in an office are disconcerting. They demand more privileges than men." "Whenever a girl happens to be in an office, there is always too much discussion, and when there are two or three girls, the male clerks will compare the blonde with the brunette, and the discussion is apt to last a little too long."[16]

Some felt, in fact, that America's young womanhood was a danger to respectable businessmen, and would disrupt business life. Even though this viewpoint did not receive an enthusiastic airing in the technical and trade journals, the image of the female clerical worker as a corrupting influence did surface. Some contemporary commentators believed that a large number of stenographers were "venturesome butterflies masquerading as stenographers." A gentlemen named Fessenden Chase put together a pamphlet comprised of newspaper articles and illustrations about the stenographer and her boss. The purpose of the pamphlet was apparently to prove that many business offices were no better than brothels and many stenographers no better than prostitutes. He claimed that "in the cozy den or private 'studio' of her employer, temptations and opportunities are constantly arising, and the susceptible employer is easy picking for the girl of brilliant plumage with tender glances that fascinate and lure. It is only a step from the tender glances to the satisfying kiss, and we cannot escape the fact that the 'private-office' girl is generally quite willing to kiss and to be kissed, in order to secure special favors and perhaps an increase in her salary from her susceptible employer." Virtuous stenographers claimed that "no girl can live a consistent Christian life and hold a business position." And of course, many articles in the pamphlet told of how stenographers broke up respectable marriages.[17] In the trade journals, writers of letters and articles voiced their objections to this image of "the pretty typewriter."[18]

What was needed was some explanation of how women's supposedly innate morality could be a positive benefit to the office. Kathryn Chatoid, who briefly wrote a column in *The Phonographic World* called "The Fem-Sten's Retreat," asserted that female stenographers must "never lose sight of the fact that women were not employed because of their superior mentality but because their innate qualities admirably advantage them to certain work and make their presence desirable in an office;" after all, "[i]f a man were needed, employers could secure the genuine article without very much trouble, and not be compelled to accept a poor imitation of masculine gender."[19] Women's "habits, principles, neatness, quiet manner, and carefulness" were considered superior and "possessed in the highest degree by the womanly woman."[20] Not only were women workers free from addiction to "the same habits as men," they also tended to alter the atmosphere of an office by their very presence."[21] Women "bring with them order and refinement, banish tobacco smoke and profanity, and set an example of regularity and decency."[22] The female office worker, one commentator thought, "has been a missionary," rendering offices more like parlors. Men have "modified their habits and dress, and the office has taken on a moral aspect."[23]

The female clerical worker, enjoined to "moralize" the business office, was depicted as a new type of woman, no less feminine, but equipped to deflect threats to her nature. Her behavior and demeanor cast no doubt upon her "womanliness" as she not only "solved her individual part of the woman question," but also "disproved the statement that business unsexes a woman or makes her less worthy of respect."[24] "Womanliness," female clerical workers were counseled, "is their ornament and protection." To preserve both elements, women received advice in the columns of the trade journals concerning all aspects of proper and effective demeanor. Cromwell Childe, the head of a very large stenographers' and typewriters' employment bureau, described the perfect stenographer in an article for *System* magazine called "How to Select a Stenographer." "She is a rather slender but healthful girl, obviously in the early twenties. She is dressed in a black jacket reaching to her hips, and a well-laundered, plain, white shirtwaist. She wears low shoes with patent leather tips, comfortable but a trifle 'dressy' with moderately high heels to poise her well, and small black bow tie, a rather broad turn-over collar, and small black hat, simple and unobtrusive. There is no suggestion of color, not even of a gold chain or ornament to break the effect of black and white. Her face is bright and engaging. It shows quick understanding and appreciation, together with decision and possible concentration. It is a face that looks another clearly in the eye. There is a hint of merriment and tolerance, but, along with these, a decided evidence that bounds may not be overstepped. The slightly parted lips show a complete absence of anything like obstinacy. It is a feminine face throughout, that of a just matured woman who thinks for herself, yet does not expect the world necessarily to agree with her."[25] This detailed description characterized an idealized model of the female clerical worker as she evolved during this period.[26] Even though this is not a Victorian lady, the ideal clerical worker is neither brazen vamp nor helpless victim; she is a new woman, charting a course between pre-scribed female characteristics and the demands of the world of work.

Debate during this period also revolved around whether women possessed a work ethic: did women have enough experience with time discipline, and interactions in an impersonal world, and did they have a serious commitment to their work? In 1887, Miss Jeanette Ballantyne succinctly summarized the case many businessmen made against female stenographer-typists. "Women," she quoted from a women's paper, "are singularly slow to comprehend that their time is worth anything in dollars and cents. . . . This disregard on their part of the value of time is one reason for man's contempt for women's work." Women are also too social; they do not "separate the business from the social life," they are over-sensitive, "expecting the same little delicate attention from a gen-tleman during business hours as [they] are accustomed to receive in the parlor." Finally, women were not committed enough to their careers. They were careless, "flowers in the office," and did not prepare them-selves adequately for the most responsible position for which their potential qualified them.[27] These criticisms were common throughout the period. As late as 1910, a writer in the *Chicago Journal* reported that women were not punctual, spent too much time with their "powder puffs, . . . munching on chocolates, and going to the matinee" and that they were "not ambitious as compared to young men," working for pin money, not for family support or personal advancement.[28]

Even though these questions about women's work ethic continued throughout the period, a distinctively feminine work ethic did emerge in the trade journals to counteract these allegations.[29] Apparently, some female clerical workers were learning to adhere to time discipline and to adjust to business office etiquette. Many a serious office woman had learned to "labor hard with her hands and with her brain"; it was said of her that she "works long hours," and "keeps confidences," winning her "goodwill and respect."[30] Her success in the business office was at-tributed to her "enthusiasm," the "care as to details," "punctuality, attention to business," and her "feminine conscientiousness and the charm of [her] pleasant voice, dress, and manner."[31] In fact, the experience of business could actually benefit women. "It may perhaps have made them more independent and fearless than the damsel who thinks it, 'so queer that people do not have to ring a bell before entering a business office.' " The necessity to work and adhere to the rules of behavior within the office did not have to threaten femininity. Kathryn Chatoid counseled her readers that, "[i]f a business woman desires to be womanly, we know of nothing that will prevent her."[32] The agreement that adhering to a rigorous work ethic did not unsex women was the first step to the development of a distinctively feminine work ethic.

The second step to the development of a feminine work ethic was the reconciliation of women's entrance into clerical work with what were supposedly women's ultimate goals: marriage and motherhood. Some employers considered women inadequate clerical workers because they supposedly did not see these erstwhile entry-level positions as stepping-stones to advancement. This assumption was based upon logic that apparently carried some weight in the nineteenth century. Women were inappropriate for promotable positions because it was taken for granted that they would ultimately marry and leave the workforce, but whenever the possibility of a woman's occupational upward mobility through a company, such as the railroad or the civil service, arose, she either "crowded out" her more worthy brother, overstepped her feminine sphere, or was an inefficient or uncommitted worker because her mind was only on marriage. *The Phonographic World* reported that the government preferred men because "women stenographers have a habit of getting married just about the time they have become familiar with the work in hand," and that the railroads preferred men because "women stenographers are always women stenographers unless they get married . . . ending their business careers where they began them."[33] Charles R. Barrett, the superintendent of one of Chicago's business colleges, the Chicago Athenaeum, encouraged women to enter commercial employment because he believed that they were "just as well qualified . . . as is the average young man," but warned that a female office worker "can never get positions or offices of trust and responsibility, because the business world will always look upon her work as temporary." While to a young man marriage meant "greater responsibilities and larger expenses," making him more ambitious and "more valuable to his employer," marriage for women meant the "occasion of her resignation," because "women's ideal of life is not to be found in the business world."[34] And yet, even if they perceived their stay in the world of work as temporary, they should "be thoroughly mastered and pursued daily with all the attention and diligence that is possible, until attention and diligence become mechanical."[35] A female clerical worker, therefore, found herself in a confusing position; she was supposed to be committed to her job, but not to pose a threat to the male, family wage-earner by rising through an occupational hierarchy. Although she was implored to be diligent and conscientious, there was apparently no reward for this except the satisfaction of a job well done.

To counter the common allegation that women were not committed to their jobs because they had only marriage and motherhood in mind, commentators claimed that this short-term commitment was actually beneficial to the employer and that clerical work was excellent training for women's future role in her own family. Clerical work, therefore, was not just a job suited to women's innate qualities, but a job suited to women's life cycle. By the 1910s, some writers were acknowledging that women's presumed limited commitment to the labor force might actually be an advantage to an employer. An article in the *Chicago Journal* in 1910 stated that "men are no longer acceptable as stenographers, although in reality they are more desirable. Young men advance too rapidly, it is argued, while a girl, once a stenographer, is always one." Ironically, this phrase contained exactly the same words used earlier to argue that men were better clerical workers! A writer in the *Chicago Tribune* concurred that "the mere limitations of the woman in business make her a better stenographer than the man. She does not expect promotion and gives her thought to things as they are. The man, on the other hand, is only on the wing."[36]

I cannot resist ending by quoting from the one voice of reason in this debate. Miss Frances M. Fox of San Francisco wrote a letter to *The Phonographic World* in May 1888, apparently furious about the claim that most women consider their work "merely a bridge to matrimony." She continued, "if they [female clerical workers] were paid adequately for their labor, would they be so ready to resign?" She thought not, adding that "it is scarcely to be wondered at that a girl who has worked unremittingly for several years with the consciousness of having given satisfactory service, and of having received wholly inadequate remuneration therefore, should waver in discouragement, and look with at least relief upon an opportunity to end it forever."[37]

But would women give up work for marriage? Between 1890 and 1910, commentators and experts in the trade journals contemplated the possibility that women would change, and not the jobs they took. If, in fact, women and clerical work were so well suited, would some women become either uninterested in or ineligible for marriage? Cynical "Been There" claimed that working as a stenographer was injurious to young women. "She works and becomes a comparatively expert stenographer, gets eighteen or twenty dollars a week. Along comes a young man getting about the same and wants to marry her. No, she will not. She is doing as well as he. Well, by the time he is getting $150 or more a month she has become cranky about men and an old maid before her time. Her constant contact with men has made her suspicious of them all and she ends her life without knowing the joys of married life."[38]

Many contributors to these journals, however, maintained that clerical work was the perfect training ground for marriage. Although working outside the home cultivated self-reliance and independence and did delay marriage, this exposure to the impersonal, materialistic, male world of commerce would allow women to better understand and help her husband as well as to appreciate her own work in her proper sphere. Within the setting of the business office, men and women (presumably bosses and their stenographer-typists) would get to know each other better, learning to work together in ways that courting couples never did. This type of interaction, many believed, would produce the best marriages, "homes made by men and women who understand each other," where "each is an entity entitled to respect." Many, in fact, came to believe that working as a clerical worker for a while was the best possible training for marriage. "The business girl has her wits sharpened by her training and contact with the world . . . and always scores and readily adapts herself to the new conditions of her life and surroundings." Stenographers made good wives because they were "doubly valuable," "a business companion as well as a wife and a social companion."[39] Mrs. Frank Learned, in an article in the *Gregg Writer*, took this reasoning to its logical conclusion when she asserted that careless clerical workers would make poor wives. "A poor worker is never a good homemaker, and she will be very badly prepared to make home a happy or comfortable place if she is undisciplined or irresponsible."[40] The attempts by experts and commentators in the technical journals between the years 1890 and World War I to reconcile clerical work and women's "natural" life cycle produced one of the most enduring cultural stereotypes of the twentieth century, the office wife. It is in the pages of these journals that she first appears. And, within these trade journals, she also appears not only as a "social problem" or "social evolution," but also as a cultural symbol.

Debates in the Realm of Symbols[41]

By the beginning of the twentieth century, writers in *The Phonographic World* noted how the female clerical workers' appearance had become more respectable over the years. Female clerical workers had been the "butt of jokes . . . receiving the fond caresses of her elderly employer; . . . a successful adventuress," who "used rouge, bleached her hair; she winked at strange drummers who came into her boss's office to sell dime bills of codfish or pig iron; she flirted outrageously with the bald-headed bookkeeper; she accepted caramels from the office-boy, the janitor, the letter-carrier, and the elevator man." According to one writer, this sensational depiction, however, was thankfully changing to a proper image of the female clerical worker as "Americanism in skirts!"[42]

The main characters of short stories about female clerical workers that appeared in *The Phonographic World* between 1887 and 1907 were "Americanism in skirts." The male editors of the journal included these stories, many written by women, for the enjoyment and profit of their readers. The depictions of the female clerical workers and their situations were in many ways consistent with the concerns expressed by commentators in the journals. These stories were presumably written with a specific and more empathic readership in mind, primarily female, but also male stenographer-typists, and presented a complicated and serious depiction of the situation of the female clerical worker.[43]

The majority of the twenty-four short stories about female clerical workers that appeared between 1887 and 1907 suggest an enormous amount of optimism regarding women's potential in office work.[44] The plots of fifteen of these stories are *not* resolved with the marriage of the female clerical worker to the boss or some other desirable or appropriate man. Although the main characters of these stories do not start out in dire poverty and do not end as the president of the company or excessively rich or powerful, they do succeed within the office setting. These are, in effect, distinctively feminine Horatio Alger tales. What makes these tales feminine is not just that the main characters were women, but the kinds of qualities that were shown as necessary for women to succeed and the measure of that success.

The heroines of these short stories saw clerical work as a unique opportunity to make their way in the world. Lou, the twenty-year-old main character in "Women and Their Work," "had grown weary of idle dreams and dependence, and had learned stenography and typewriting, not because she must work, but because she wished to make her own way, to see what the world was really like, to be free and of use." Through hard work, initiative, and business acumen Lou succeeded in owning a stenographic agency. In stenographer Hattie Sutton's story, "The 'Air' of Meggy," little Meggy, "busy, contented, the drudge of the office," became the head of the stenographic department and "came into her great good fortune." And in Edith Azalia Adams's "Her Independent Touch," the main character, Louisa James, capitalized on her ability to touch-type to earn five dollars a week more than she had when she started working at the Smith-Jones Company. These fifteen stories end after the main character has achieved success in her work.

Hard work and skill were not the only reasons for success, however. In language strikingly similar to that of the experts who appeared on the pages of this same journal, the main characters of these stories also achieved recognition and fortune because they embodied certain personality characteristics. These stories contributed to the social construction of clerical work as a female occupation because they associated the success of the main character with what readers perceived as distinctively feminine characteristics, thus presenting a female work ethic. The examples are numerous. In the Adams story, "Her Independent Touch," Louisa distinguished herself from the other stenographers not only because she had mastered the touch method but also because of her willingness to work late. "She often stayed over-time and did it, if it was not required, for the sake of feeling that her work was done. If she was asked to get out a letter that would keep her late, she did it with an obliging grace that won favor." In Anne Mahon's "A Stenographer's Compensation," Miss Gray, the busy stenographer, left her pile of work to wait on some customers even though this was the counter clerk's job. This same clerk had just finished tantalizing Miss Gray with opera tickets that Miss Gray could never hope to afford. But, late that day, the very customers she had taken the time to help sent her season tickets to the opera as thanks for her patient service. In Jennie Cook's "True Blue," the younger stenographer supporting several siblings resists the temptation of more money for information about her boss's business dealings from her boss's rival. She is rewarded for her faithfulness with a raise and a job for her younger brother. And finally, in Anne Mahon's "The Too Obliging Miss Blake," the stenographer, Miss Blake, types a letter for an old woman during her lunch break out of kindness and pity over the objections of her co-workers. She is rewarded the next day when it is discovered that the old woman had left Miss Blake $30,000 in her will.

Success was not always measured in dollars and cents. The happy ending was often the acceptance of the female clerical worker or the resolution of her role within the office. Lillian M. Gowdy, who apparently worked at the Chamber of Commerce in Minneapolis, Minnesota, wrote "The Amanuensis Girl: Being a Truthful Narrative of How She Brought Order, Neatness, Efficiency, and Comfort in Her Train," for *The Phonographic World*. Mr. Warde hired the extremely neat, refined, quiet, and dignified Miss Allison, claiming that his business "required the services of a man," but he gave her a trial. She proved so satisfactory, "neat and correct," that "long before the trial month was at an end the girl amanuensis was recognized as a very important, a necessary adjunct to Manager Warde's office." And in Hattie Witherington's "The Will and the Way," Mr. Gresham and his stenographer Miss Weldon got into a fight. He had spoken harshly to her for no reason. Miss Weldon claimed that, if she had made an error, it would have justified his manner, but as it was, "no lady could stand the manner in which you talk to your stenographers and be a lady!" Mr. Gresham's apology and promise of reform resolved the problem and both boss and stenographer enjoyed a productive and smooth working relationship (and they did *not* marry!).

Success was also measured in the stenographer's ability to serve others, often other women. Even though Lou, the main character in "Women and Their Work," prospered in her stenographic agency, it was not by this that she measured her success. She had trained hundreds of girls in the ways of stenography and typing, making the "untidy . . . neat, the sickly well, the morbid, wholesome, the selfish more warm hearted." The author concluded that Lou had succeeded, "not alone because she ha[d] worked hard, but because she ha[d] taken the world to herself in a wise and friendly way; ha[d] learned to serve and to cajole it.''

There were some important messages in these fifteen stories. First, if a woman conducted herself in a refined, dignified, feminine manner, if she worked diligently and seriously, if she attempted to serve her boss and others less fortunate than she, then she would not only gain acceptance and respect in the world of the office, but also earn more responsibility and money. Second, and less obviously, the relationship between a female clerical worker and her male boss does not have to pose a problem as long as she does not relinquish her "womanliness: ornament and protection." It is, of course, highly significant that most of these stories were written by women for a journal that catered primarily to female clerical workers. These were, then, practical lessons and moral tales that could have both tapped and generated feelings of the enormous promise that clerical work offered women during this period.

Of course, romantic relationships were inevitable between men and female stenographers, and some of the stories playfully explored the new romantic possibilities opened to both men and women when women entered the office. Two stories, "Typewritten," and Robert Barr's "The Typewritten Letter," tell of somewhat older, seasoned, yet shy bosses who fell in love with their stenographers, but were unsure of what to do. In both stories, the bosses resorted to dictating their proposals of marriage to their completely oblivious and business-like stenographers. The stenographers in each story, "sensible" and "modern girls" who belong to good families that had "come down in the world," took an inordinately long time to realize that they were, in fact, receiving marriage proposals. The situation was funny because of the awkward way in which the boss attempted to change a business-like relationship with his stenographer to a personal one. And both stories were resolved when the stenographer, after finally realizing what was going on, continued the pretense by accepting the offer of marriage with a business letter resigning her stenographic position for a "better situation." In other stories, romances occurred between sympathetic men and women in the office simply because of proximity. Again, there was no peril depicted as a result of this mixing of the sexes in the office; rather, in these stories, the office was as suitable a place as church to find an appropriate mate, particularly because, as was the case in almost all of these stories, the parties involved came from the same class and ethnic backgrounds.[45]

The final variation found in these stories was a hybrid between the female Horatio Alger story and the office romance story, and this hybrid appeared toward the end of the period, in the years 1905 and 1906. Four stories in *The Phonographic World* had plots that became commonplace by the 1920s: the finding of a husband as the reward for a female clerical worker's diligence and compliance with feminine qualities. In Edith Azalia Adams's "The One Thing Needful," Miss Brown needed to learn that her boss would not tolerate lateness and sloppy work. After her boss deducted money from her paycheck, Miss Brown resolved to improve her performance and was so successful that she began to cast around for a better-paying position. The possibility of her departure provoked the boss's proposal, which was accepted. In Marion Mitchell Barr's "A Mistake in Identity," it was the stenographer's high moral standards and impeccable business etiquette that qualified her for marriage. Evelyn Harvey became very disturbed when her married boss began to pay her inappropriate attentions. She submitted her resignation, which caused great financial hardship for herself and her dependent mother. The boss called her in to discuss her resignation and revealed that the man who had made advances was his identical twin, who had taken over while the real boss was on vacation. Improper advances from a boss were apparently legitimate overtures from his twin brother, and the stenographer's virtue was rewarded with a proposal of marriage.[46]

The Cinderella story, therefore, which became the standard plot of almost all working girls' stories by the 1920s, evolved in this trade journal as a mixture of two earlier plot configurations: the female Horatio Alger story and the office romance. This evolution of the female clerical work story in this particular trade journal is suggestive. The authors, primarily women, who had a female clerical readership in mind, were apparently most concerned about women's accommodation to the day-to-day routine in the office, not her vulnerability to vice. They depicted, and therefore probably considered, female clerical workers to be serious participants in the world of work. They were also not especially preoc-cupied with the issue of marriage. Perhaps it was assumed between the author and reader that the female clerical worker would marry and therefore it was not necessary to state this explicitly; but the enormous debate surrounding this issue in the nonfiction articles suggest that this was, in fact, very much an issue.

The complete absence of the marriage issue in many of these stories suggests the enormous promise held out to women who engaged in clerical work. It is in these early stories that we see the first glimmer of a real ambivalence about reconciling work and marriage. But other readings of these stories were possible, and some female readers may have focused on their moral lessons: the need to maintain their feminine qualities within the office setting to succeed, however they determined to measure that success. It was precisely because clerical work was in a transitional state regarding its status within the labor force and regarding its gender association that cultural depictions of the clerical work could pose the possibility of at least temporarily ignoring, or at most permanently defying, women's ultimate conventional life choice: marriage.

The image of the female clerical worker also appeared in other places. The contrast between the characters and plots in the trade journal's short stories and those that appeared in the popular novels and movies of the era could not have been greater. There were some obvious differences in these cultural depictions. Novelists and movie makers were usually men, and their art was not specifically designed for an audience of female clerical workers. To many who both made and consumed this art, the world of the office was foreign territory and the female clerical worker was a new, peculiar, and untested creature. Therefore, in popular cultural depictions, female clerical workers were often tantalizing and stereotyped characters. This new character in the world of work put herself in the position to do something most women could (or would) not: she crossed two previously insurmountable barriers, those of class and sex. The office was a setting where women of middle-class or lower-class backgrounds could mingle with businessmen of higher classes. A woman who ventured into the "dangerous" male office could, perhaps, capture a rich husband.

In the earliest depictions, clerical workers appear as unusual, often immodest women who not only placed themselves in a setting where they had to work perilously close to men, but who also sometimes welcomed that proximity. This was true of Cornelia McNabb, a character in Henry Blake Fuller's *The Cliff Dwellers* (1893), a novel that tells of the web of relations among the business men and women who worked in an office building. Set in Chicago during the 1890s, a period of explosive growth and social dislocation, the novel depicts the evils of greed and the false values of the rich and those aspiring to social station. Cornelia McNabb, the building's public stenographer, illustrated this theme. Cornelia left her modest rural home in Wisconsin for the pleasures and opportunities of Chicago. She learned quickly that the only way for a woman to make a decent living and mix with the right sort of people was to become a stenographer. While she worked as a waitress, she studied stenography and typewriting at a private business college, and she studied the ways of the rich and powerful in the society pages of the newspaper. As she told the main character of the novel, "now then, why shouldn't I be wearing heliotrope satin to dinner sometime?—if not under the name of Cornelia McNabb, then under some other as good or better. Anyway, I'm going to keep my hands as nice as I can; a girl never knows what she may have a chance to become. I don't imagine it will disfigure me much to operate a typewriter."[47]

Cornelia McNabb soon became the general public stenographer for many of the businesses in the Clifton office building. She learned the ways of society people through her contact with both the business men and their wives, who frequently visited their husbands. One wife in particular, Mrs. Floyd, quite inadvertently provided Cornelia with pointers on costume, speech, and behavior. From this interaction with Chicago's society, Cornelia learned "what to do and what to avoid." These lessons paid off. In a short time, Cornelia had become a particular favorite with Mr. Brainard, an important banker, and his son. As Mr. Brainard's daughter explained to the hero of the novel, "Cornelia is a pretty smart girl. Father had become quite taken with her." But Cornelia's spirit apparently impressed Mr. Brainard as well. Miss Brainard continued, "she corrects his mistakes. . . . She talks back. That's where she's bright. It kind of irritates him, I think, to have his—his clerks—his employees seem afraid."[48] And ultimately, Cornelia's manipulations, intelligence, spunk, perseverance, and even her refreshing coarseness, were rewarded. With his father's approval, Mr. Brainard's son married Cornelia McNabb just a few months later.

The female stenographer in David Graham Phillips's *The Grain of Dust* (1911) was a more ambiguous character than Cornelia McNabb.[49] Dorothy Hallowell, the "grain of dust" of the title, entered Fred Norman's life as his barely competent stenographer. Dorothy was from a respectable middle-class family that had fallen on hard times, while Fred was the most successful up-and-coming corporation lawyer in New York City. At first, Fred hardly noticed Dorothy, but it was not long before he became obsessed with her. This obsession cost him dearly; Norman neglected his fiancée and his job until he lost both. After a protracted and difficult courtship, Dorothy agreed to marry Fred, not for love, but for the comforts and security he could provide. Only after several years of marriage and a child did Dorothy and Fred realize that they did care about each other.

Dorothy Hallowell, however, was not simply a social climber. In fact, Phillips deliberately made her character mysterious. Throughout the novel, Fred was never sure whether she was setting a good trap or was a good girl facing difficult circumstances. As his obsession began to take hold of him, Fred wondered if this girl was "playing upon him." "In his folly he had let her see how completely he was in her power, and she was using that power to establish relations between them that were the very opposite of what he desired—and must have."[50] Fred could never discover Dorothy's true character. He expressed his confusion in a conversation with his sister. "She [Dorothy] is so—elusive. I can't understand her—I can't touch her. I can't find her. She keeps me going like a man chasing an echo."

"Like a man chasing an echo," repeated Ursula reflectively. "I understand. It is maddening. She must be clever—in her way."

"Or very simple. God knows which; I don't—and sometimes I think she doesn't either."[51]

Fred admitted his confusion to Dorothy herself, claiming, "I don't know what kind of girl you are. I never have known. I've never wanted to know. If you told me you were—what is called good, I'd doubt it. If you told me you weren't, I'd want to kill you and myself."[52] And even though Dorothy never deviated from respectable behavior, her appearance and personality changed throughout the book, making her an elusive character to the reader as well as to Fred Norman.

Dorothy Hallowell not only represented the difficulties that many young, single, self-supporting women encountered as they ventured into the problematic environment of the business office, but also the confusion that accompanied the formulation of an acceptable image of the female clerical worker. Throughout the book, the author provokes the reader to wonder whether Dorothy is a calculating social climber or a young woman in a difficult economic situation who is futilely trying to hold onto her morals. One does not have to take an enormous leap to apply this question to female clerical workers in general. Perhaps, then, this ambivalence about Dorothy Hallowell's place and character bespoke a larger uncertainty about the character, legitimacy, and role of the female clerical worker.

The earliest movies about female clerical workers also depicted them as women, who because of misfortune or, worse, desire, have placed themselves in an immoral environment. These early films were short comedies that were shown in local, small nickelodeons, primarily to audiences with large percentages of working-class wives, mothers, and daughters. Really filmed vaudeville, the plots and characterizations were simple and similar. Nevertheless, these motion pictures did potentially reach enormous numbers of people, providing for those newly arrived immigrants and other working-class viewers a powerful image of American working womanhood and the world of the office.[53]

According to Kathy Peiss, themes about factory employment were less common than those involving office romance.[54] The possibilities of crossing sex and class boundaries in the office were the stuff of laughter.[55] *The Typewriter* (1902) best exemplifies this type of film in its simplest form. It involves a young, pretty typist who first received the attention and then the embraces of her grey-haired boss. They are interrupted by a severe old woman, undoubtedly the boss's wife, who, brandishing an umbrella, drags her husband out by his ear. In the 1905 *Broker's Athletic Typewriter* (the title refers to the operator of the machine, not the machine itself), the boss misinterprets an innocent interaction between a young male employee and his typist and reprimands the young man. After the young man goes, the boss, another gray-haired man, makes advances to the typist, but she resists. She begins, in fact, to throw her boss around the room. While the boss is on the floor, his wife, another severe old woman wearing black, comes in and begins hitting him with yet another umbrella. In *She Meets with His Wife's Approval* (1902), the boss and his secretary conspire to trick the boss's wife. A matronly, tall woman enters the business office to find her husband and his secretary hard at work. She scrutinizes the young woman, but is apparently mollified by the woman's appearance, and she leaves after her husband gives her some money. As soon as she is well gone, the secretary takes off a mask that she had been wearing on her face, and the boss and his secretary begin to kiss.

These cultural representations seem intended both to shock and to elicit laughter. During this early period, a woman engaging in clerical work was a titillating prospect to the general public (see Illustrations 4 and 5). Whether a young female resisted or encouraged the advances of her boss, some interaction between the two seemed inevitable. Whether she was cast as a victim or the vamp in the office setting, she was not a respectable, good girl. And yet there was a mixed message here. As Kathy Peiss states, "visually and thematically, these films constructed a notion of modern American womanhood that reaffirmed the flamboyant cultural style popular among many young American-born working women and . . . created new aspirations among the foreign-born."[56] The young, pretty typist or stenographer stood in sharp contrast to the doughty, unfashionably dressed, bespectacled matron married to the boss. Clearly, the young female office worker represented a new type of woman, not altogether acceptable, but not completely unsympathetic either. The mingling of the older, dignified business man and the young, pretty, sexually aware, streetwise, and socially ambitious female clerical worker was the stock situation that provoked laughter from these nickelodeon audiences. But just like the movies and the nickelodeons that they appeared in, these characters of female clerical workers would probably not have been entirely acceptable to most members of the respectable middle class. Because the clerical worker in these depictions was identifiable as a woman overstepping her "proper" sphere, a woman who put herself in an environment not entirely hospitable to women, she was not the all-American girl next door. Just as the image had the power to provoke a reassessment of Victorian morality, the female clerical worker, battling victim, or brazen vamp was a sensation—not a "true" woman. She had not yet evolved into an acceptable stereotype within the cultural currency available to most Americans.

By the second decade of the twentieth century, the experts and clerical workers whose voices appear in the trade journals increasingly came to believe that women had the skills necessary to work as clerical workers, and that they brought refinement, morality, decorum, and neatness with them into the office. Women not only had work discipline but also a limited commitment to work that made them cheaper workers. Clerical work, no longer a threat to women's traditional roles as wife and mother, was a good training ground for the future wife. None of this was automatic or sinister; both men and women, perhaps for different reasons, sought to legitimize women's presence in the office in the only way and using the only language that was available at the time. It was necessary to legitimize women's entrance into the world of the office by arguing her essential "difference" or "otherness." Because of the pervasiveness of the sexual division of labor and its rules within the workplace, women could only safely and properly engage in clerical work if the occupation itself became feminized, that is, if the nature of the job itself required a female worker. It is this reconstruction that began within the trade journals during these years.

Simply seeing a female clerical worker on the screen, or reading about her as the main character of a book or short story, even in the most simplistic, sensationalized, or stereotypical way, must have had an impact. Women's entrance into the masculine world of the office was necessarily accompanied by and also provoked and was hastened by, a change in the cultural image of the female clerical worker. I find it difficult to envision such an unprecedented shift from male to female work occurring only as a result of economic and structural changes. Regarding issues of gender (or race, ethnicity, religion, age, or geography, for that matter), neither men nor women act as perfectly rational economic beings responding simply to wages, hours, and working conditions or the impersonal forces of supply and demand. The simple appearance of the character of the female clerical worker in various cultural forms may have posed the possibility of this type of employment for those men and women exposed to this image. The changing and diverse image of the female clerical worker provided women who either wanted to or had to work with "cultural currency." If the specie glittered in any individual woman's eye, she could attempt to grab and redeem it. If a woman thought it worthless, she could let it be. That increasing numbers of women grabbed at the coin ultimately changed its value. The image of the female clerical worker and the economic reality of the clerical labor force interacted dialectically throughout the period, affecting women's occupational perceptions and desires as well as the nature of clerical work itself.

CHAPTER 5

Separate but Not Equal in the Changing Office

*T*HE ECONOMIC changes that occurred between 1890 and 1920 in Chicago affected clerical work and clerical workers. Chicago's economy grew at an extraordinary rate, particularly in those sectors that employed a large number of clerical workers. Larger enterprises used the services of greater numbers of white-collar employees to keep records and to coordinate the firms' varied activities. The sheer increase in volume alone of goods, capital, trade, manufacturing, and so on required more record keepers of property.

As the number of clerical workers necessary to a firm increased, the expense of the office staff also grew. Theoretically, this made it in the interest of employers to seek ways to minimize the costs of clerical services and to maximize their efficiency. And, to increase productivity and profitability, owners and managers in these larger firms sought to rationalize, routinize, and mechanize office functions. To accomplish this, some office managers from the largest firms borrowed freely from the scientific management theories of Frederick W. Taylor.[1] Efforts by office design experts to create a smooth and efficient flow of work through an office setting may have predated the widespread dissemination of Taylor's ideas.[2]

Profitability and efficiency were not the only goals motivating capitalists and managers, however. Who fills what position in society and what value that position commands is determined by more than market forces. As Heidi Hartmann tells us, "capitalist development creates the places for a hierarchy of workers, but traditional marxist categories cannot tell us who will fill which places. Gender and racial hierarchies determine who will fill the places."[3] That black women could not enter clerical jobs until the 1960s is certainly proof that employers were not only interested in those workers attainable at the lowest wages.[4] Similarly, that white women were traditionally cheaper workers than white men does not, in and of itself, explain why employers hired more women as office staffs began to grow. Recent scholars have uncovered the capitalists' strategy of segmenting labor forces not only to undermine working-class unity, but also to reduce wages generally by provoking competition among groups for jobs. Workers were divided by underscoring racial, sex, ethnic, and skill differences.[5]

And, just as the sex and skill level of clerical work was changing, so too was the position of clerical sectors in firms and the nature of clerical work changing. It is impossible to understand the rationalization and differentiation that took place within the clerical sectors in some firms, as well as the clerical labor force in general, without understanding the interaction of capitalism and patriarchy at this particular time and place. Obviously, as large-scale organizations sought the most cost-effective way to run their office forces (as smaller firms tried to compete), managers needed to devise new jobs, new organizations of work flow, as well as the position of members of these office forces within an occupational hierarchy. These managers, whether they wanted to or not, were increasingly placing white, native-born, predominately young, single, female workers into some of these jobs, and this reality itself altered the nature of these jobs and their positions within the hierarchy of the firm. Therefore, we can stand the standard structural argument for the feminization of the clerical labor force on its head;[6] not only did the advent of monopoly or industrial capitalism, which altered the size and nature of the office force and routinized some office jobs, facilitate women's entrance into the office, but also, the women who were entering these jobs affected the size, nature, and position of the office forces and the value that society placed on these occupations. Women's presence in the office not only signaled fundamental shifts in the nature of American capitalism, but also altered the direction and expression of these shifts. The sex of the worker had at least as powerful an effect on the definition and position of a job as did market forces.

Chicago's Economy

By 1890, even though Chicago was a diverse industrial city, the city's economic development had certainly not ended. During this period, Chicago became a significant service-oriented, merchandising, retail, and distribution center within the national market.[7] The downtown business district, the Loop, became the center of activities of the city. An observer in 1910 stated that "within an area of less than a square mile, there are found the railroad terminal and business offices, the big retail stores, the wholesale and jobbing businesses, the financial center, the main offices of the chief firms of the city, a considerable portion of the medical and dental professions, the legal profession, the city and county government, the post office, the courts, the leading social and political clubs, the hotels, theaters, Art Institute, principal libraries, the labor headquarters, and great number of lesser factors of city life."[8]

The downtown prospered as office buildings and transportation and communication services completed the look of this urban landscape. Office building construction in the city that first built a skyscraper in the United States boomed during the first decades of the twentieth century.[9] In 1910 alone, 1.5 million square feet of office space was opened for use.[10] In 1906, the electrically powered street railroad system replaced the cable cars that had been in use for over twenty years. By 1910, these elevated trains, the "els," circled or looped around the central business district. This rapid transit system brought large numbers of workers and consumers into the central business district each day.[11] In addition, facilities such as post office service, electric lights, and telephones grew in response and contributed to the enlargement of the business sector. As early as 1871, the post office system in Chicago was the second busiest in the United States, employing 482 clerks.[12] In the 1880s, electric lights and telephones became available, and both of these services were significant businesses in the city in the following decades.[13]

The central business district, with its supporting transportation and communication systems, created precisely the conditions necessary to support the kinds of firms that would employ a large number of clerical workers. Manufacturing firms established downtown business offices where managers and planners conducted their activities. By the middle of the 1890s, Chicago had become the headquarter city for thirty-six of the country's largest industrial combinations. By 1920, Chicago supported the second largest number of headquarter offices in the United States.[14]

In addition, those firms involved in the purchase and resale of commodities, banking, credit, brokerage, investment, and insurance relied heavily on large numbers of clerical workers.[15] Chicago continued to function as a conduit for the foodstuffs and natural resources of the hinterland and these commodities greatly strengthened the financial institutions of the city. The Board of Trade, the Stock Exchange, and local banks matured into strong, independent financial institutions. With the establishment of the Board of Governors of the Federal Reserve System in 1913, Chicago became the capital of the seventh district, serving a 300-mile radius. Between 1909 and 1924, the number of banks in Chicago increased almost fourfold, exceeding Philadelphia in commercial deposits.[16] LaSalle Street in the Loop became the home for many of these financial institutions, as it still is today.[17]

New, innovative distributive industries also employed large numbers of clerical workers. During the late nineteenth century, wholesale dry goods establishments expanded their operations and added retailing to their functions. By 1920, seven of the largest department stores in the United States, the Fair Store, Rothschild and Company, the Boston Store, Hillmans, Marshall Field and Company, Mandel Brothers, and Carson, Pirie, Scott sold their vast array of wares on State Street in the Loop. Some retailing establishments capitalized on Chicago's services and connections to the hinterland. As a result, the mail order house was born in Chicago. In 1872, Montgomery Ward and Company began offering merchandise to rural customers through a catalogue.[18] In the late 1880s, Sears moved his small, mail order business from Minneapolis to Chicago, and within twenty years, Sears, Roebuck, and Company rivaled Ward for this mail order market.[19] By the 1920s, Chicago supported ninety-three mail order firms employing tens of thousands of clerical workers.[20]

Women and the Clerical Labor Force in Chicago

The entrance of women into this expanding clerical sector is really three separate stories. Women entered the three major categories of clerical work (bookkeeper, cashier, accountant; clerk; stenographer and typist) at different times and at different rates. Women's early entrance into and complete capture of stenography-typing was followed by important inroads into the clerk category. Overlaying this was a steady increase of women's participation in the bookkeeper, cashier, and accountant category, although this occupational category was increasingly less important within the female clerical labor force in Chicago.

Between 1890 and 1910, Chicago's working women made the growing occupation of stenography-typing their own. In fact, much of the increase in women's labor force participation in clerical work was a result of women's employment in stenography-typist positions. The rapid increase in the number of stenography-positions between 1900 and 1910 altered the distribution of the clerical labor force. Of the entire clerical labor force, which included bookkeepers and accountants, clerks and copyists, and stenographer-typists, stenography-typing contributed only 13 percent of the total clerical labor force in 1900. By 1910, however, almost 24 percent of the total clerical workforce was employed in stenography-typing positions. In 1890, stenography-typing positions accounted for only 19.3 percent of the female clerical labor force; by 1910, stenography-typing accounted for 50.7 percent of all women in clerical work (see Tables 8, 9, and 10). To be a female clerical worker during the period between 1890 and 1910 increasingly meant being a stenographer-typist. The appearance of a clerical category that was almost exclusively the domain of women, and the increasing importance of this category relative to other clerical jobs, certainly functioned to perpetuate the identification of women and office work. The extension of this association to other clerical categories indicates, perhaps, that during this period, clerical work in general came to be regarded as "women's work."

Between 1910 and 1920, women began to enter another office job, the clerk's. Although women certainly began to enter clerk and copyist positions starting in 1870, women never accounted for more than 20 percent of the clerk labor force in Chicago. By 1920, however, 35 percent of all clerks in Chicago were women (see Table 9). This occurred because women were taking more of the newly opening clerk positions than ever before. Between 1900 and 1910, women took only a little more than a quarter of all the new clerk positions. During the next decade, employers hired equal numbers of men and women for new clerk positions (see Table 13). Although women did not quite constitute a majority of the clerk labor force, women's entrance into the clerk category was significant since clerks were the most numerous clerical position. Throughout the period between 1900 and 1930, the majority of office positions in Chicago were clerk positions (see Table 8).

Table 13. Number and Percentage of Males and Females Taking New Clerk Positions in Chicago, 1910–1930

YEAR	NUMBER OF NEW POSITIONS	NUMBER OF MALES	PERCENT MALES	NUMBER OF FEMALES	PERCENT FEMALES
1910	6,879	4,942	72.3	1,907	27.7
1920	53,285	26,389	49.5	26,896	50.5
1930	31,146	16,307	52.4	14,839	47.6

Source: U.S. Bureau of the Census, *Population—Occupational Statistics, 1910,* vol. 4, pps. 165, and 544–547; U.S. Bureau of the Census, *Population—Occupations, 1920,* vol. 4, pps. 149, and 1076–1080; U.S. Bureau of the Census, *Population—Occupations by States, 1930,* vol. 4, pps. 423–429, 447–450, 456–457, and 463–465.

Women also began to work more frequently in bookkeeping, cashier, and accounting positions after 1900, but the growth of this category and the growth of women's share of these jobs was steady and unspectacular.[21] Although almost one-quarter of all clerical workers were bookkeepers, cashiers, or accountants in 1910, only 17.9 percent of all clerical workers were bookkeepers, cashiers, or accountants by 1930 (see Table 8). Even as this position was losing ground relative to other clerical occupations, women increased their participation and took new positions in this category at a fairly constant rate (see Table 14). Women increased their participation in this category of clerical work at a rate slightly greater than the rate of increase in these positions, so the percentage of female bookkeepers, cashiers, or accountants did increase within

Table 14. Number and Percentage of Males and Females Taking New Bookkeeping, Cashier, and Accounting Positions in Chicago, 1910–1930

YEAR	NUMBER OF NEW POSITIONS	NUMBER OF MALES	PERCENT MALES	NUMBER OF FEMALES	PERCENT FEMALES
1910	8,467	3,602	42.5	4,865	57.5
1920[a]	11,718	4,852	41.4	6,866	58.6
1930[a]	5,515	2,439	44.2	3,076	55.8

Source: U.S. Bureau of the Census, *Population—Occupational Statistics, 1910,* vol. 4, pps. 165, and 544–547; U.S. Bureau of the Census, *Population—Occupations, 1920,* vol. 4, pps. 149, and 1076–1080; U.S. Bureau of the Census, *Population—Occupations by States, 1930,* vol. 4, pps. 423–429, 447–450, 456–457, and 463–465.
[a]Includes auditors.

this relatively small clerical category, from 30.2 percent in 1900 to 45.4 percent in 1920 (see Table 9).

These three stories contributed to the same ending: by 1920 a majority of the clerical workers in Chicago were female. Was the entrance of women into stenography-typing positions between 1890 and 1910, and the entrance of women into clerk positions between 1910 and 1920, provoked or occasioned by "deskilling," rationalization, or mechanization of those jobs? The answer is no and yes.

Women, Skill, Rationalization, and Clerical Work

Recently, scholars have been significantly revising the standard explanation that the deskilling of clerical work, as a result of technological and organizational changes, made some office positions less appealing to men, allowing women to enter them.[22] Shirley Dex, for example, maintains that "the concept of 'skill' which forms the basis for both occupational classifications and occupational ranking" is socially constructed, affected by unionization, prevailing attitudes, the concept of the family wage, women's "natural suitability" for certain types of jobs (nursing, childcare, etc.) and, most powerfully, by the sex possessing the skill. In other words, what women do is simply considered less skilled. Dex mentions specifically that "when women take up new skills which have resulted from technological change, as with the case of typewriters . . . there is a tendency for the jobs to be thought of as less skilled than the earlier form of technology, if women fill the jobs. In the case of typewriter operators, one could argue a case that using a typewriter involved greater skill than that involved in the hand copying of the superseded male clerks."[23] Sam Cohn, in his study of the process of occupational sex-typing among clerical workers in two industries in Great Britain, states forcefully that "the overall feminization of clerical work cannot be attributed to an increase in the percentage of low-status positions."[24] Ava Baron states even more forcefully, "the study of deskilling actually is a study of the demasculization of work. . . . Skill is conceptualized as something men have, and which women lack."[25]

Between 1890 and 1920 in Chicago, only certain clerical positions, primarily in the largest firms, experienced deskilling, mechanization, and routinization. Throughout much of the period, however, a wide diversity of conditions characterized the general category of office work. The one trend that did occur, however, was that the sexual division of labor within the office evolved and became pronounced. In other words, certain spaces and functions within the office were increasingly associated with women while certain jobs and positions within the firm were considered appropriate for men. A more historically specific analysis of the transformation of the clerical labor force reveals that the rationalization and devaluation of a clerical job was not a necessary prerequisite for women's entrance in that particular field.

The stenographer-typist, the most feminized clerical job, for example, had more skills than the worker he or she replaced, the copyist. Women's entrance into stenography-typing positions in the late 1880s, and domination of the field in the period between 1890 and 1910, then, is in no way related to any objective process of deskilling. A comparison of two of Chicago's female clerical workers separated by only five years reveals the differences between the skill levels of copyist and stenographer-typist positions. Isabel Wallace, who worked in a pension office in Chicago in the fall of 1885 to help her mother financially, had some college education but no specific training for her clerical work. And she really did not require any. She was apparently hired to help record and post pension vouchers. On a particularly heavy work day she described her output: "filled out about 150 vouchers yesterday and 190 today. That means write the name 3 times and date once then a very large number amount and your initials. Those numbers have to be very accurate and names spelt [sic] perfectly correctly." Isabel repeatedly complained to her mother that although the work was easy, it was tedious.[26] Effie Jones procured work in Chicago in 1890 only after receiving training in stenography and typing. Effie's work experiences varied, but she always used these two skills. The women who were pouring into stenography-typing possessed more specific skills than their male or female predecessors. Isabel Wallace would not have lasted until lunchtime at any of Effie Jones's jobs.

Since most of the earliest stenographer-typists engaged in both stenographic and typing functions, a great deal of skill, requiring specialized training, was necessary to perform effectively in these jobs. On the most practical level, it would have been impossible for those women seeking copyist positions in the 1870s to have filled positions as stenographer-typists in the 1880s without some additional specialized training in addition to the language and writing skills they already possessed. Therefore, the standard arguments attributing women's entrance into clerical positions to the deskilling of these positions seem inappropriate when examining the stenography-typing positions between 1890 and 1910.

If the women engaging in these more highly skilled stenography-typing positions, however, found themselves in impersonal, highly rationalized and mechanized workplaces, it could be argued that despite the greater skill required, the nature of the labor process made these jobs undesirable to men. In fact, women conquered all varieties of stenography-typing positions during this period, not just those experiencing rationalization, routinization, or mechanization. The work experiences of the female stenographer-typist varied greatly depending upon the type of office in which she worked. She could be found in a small office, in a large mail order house, and in the individually run office of a public stenographer.

In 1890, Effie Jones left her Iowa home for Chicago. She lived in a boarding-house, and upon arriving, took a course in a business college to learn stenography and typewriting. Her first position was in an import agent's office in the Loop. She wrote her father after starting her first position and described her work situation favorably. She began as a substitute stenographer, as the usual male stenographer was on a two-week vacation. She wrote, "I write about twenty-five letters a day, and address the envelopes, and that is all. The office boy folds and seals the letters after they look them over, and they do their own copying, so it is a very easy position. They only pay me $6.00 a week, but say they will pay me more next week if I suit them." She wrote that "they always had a man before, and said they did not know whether a lady would do or not, but I think I will do just as well." The dictation was not difficult and she worried about losing her speed. "They spell almost all of the names out for me, and have me write them in long hand, and it is a very good plan, as no one ought to be expected to spell them correctly who is not acquainted with them." Her hours were from 8:30 A.M. to 5:30 P.M. with an hour for lunch. She reported that the "office is very nice and I have a nice desk right by the window. We are opposite the Post Office and I amuse myself looking at the people who are always around them, when I am not busy."[27]

Two years later, Effie Jones procured a position as a stenographer in a law office across the street from City Hall. Although she does not mention her salary, her position commanded more work and responsibility. She describes one particularly busy period "as positively amusing." "Every desk in this office is connected with electric bells and speaking tubes with every other desk, and I would be in one room, writing away for dear life, and would hear my bell going. Then would come an ominous silence, then a head would be poked into the room where I was, 'Going to keep Miss Jones long?' 'Yes, been waiting all day for her, and now I am going to finish this.' 'Well, Miss Jones, you come in to my room as soon as you are through there' and before I would finish there, I would have a date or two made in some of the other rooms."[28] At this new position, she usually worked from 9:00 A.M. to 5:00 P.M., but during these busy periods, she worked from 8:00 A.M. to 6:00 P.M. She had an assistant who, under her direction, attended to all of the routine correspondence. And in addition to taking dictation, Effie appears to have done some periodic paralegal work as well. Her boss sent her to the Law Institute to look up specific cases and to report back to him.[29]

Two years of working had not made Effie Jones bitter and tired, but worldly, and enthusiastic about life around her. She rapturously described all the festivities surrounding the World's Columbian Exposition and her tramping adventures with friends. She acknowledged the flirtatiousness of the young lawyers in her office, but took it upon herself to protect her young assistant from "the frivolity of mankind in general." And Effie was ambitious. She wrote that she would remain at her present position, "unless I get sick, die, or get married—until I can get into newspaper work." She would ultimately marry, but whether she got into newspaper work before marriage is unknown (see Illustration 6).

Although Effie Jones worked hard, her working conditions were favorable. Had she found her first position as a stenographer for Sears, Roebuck, and Company, her work experience would have been extremely different. When first seeking work at Sears, Effie would have been taken to the stenographic division of the training school. If she performed adequately on a test, she would have been accepted for employment, with her salary determined by the results of her test. During the first weeks of employment, Effie would have had to attend the training school to learn the special business procedures at Sears.[30] In 1902, twelve years after she began at six dollars a week, the average weekly wage for a beginning female employee at Sears was four dollars.[31] Her hours would have been longer at Sears, as well. The day started at 8:00 A.M. and ended at 5:30 P.M., with a forty-five-minute lunch break. And, during the weeks before Christmas, Sears required employees to work an extra hour a day.[32]

Effie's experience on the job would have been less pleasant at Sears. Rather than a pleasant desk by a window, she would have worked in an enormous room filled with between 150 and 200 women, all pounding on typewriter keys. Rather than moving from office to office to take dictation, involving personal contact with her boss, or going to do research at the Law Institute, which bespoke a certain trust and responsibility, Effie would have received work from two possible sources: from a correspondent in the letter-writing department or from a graphaphone cylinder delivered directly to her.[33]

Effie's day would have been rigidly scheduled and her behavior at work strictly disciplined. The company kept records on the punctuality, attendance, productivity, and behavior of its clerical employees. Attendance, deportment, punctuality, and quality of work were computed monthly and the total used as a basis for salary.[34] The company routed the work entering the stenographic department, as in many other departments, on a schedule system. A clerk stamped a time on each piece of work coming in and the various departments were required to act upon it within the stated time. The company kept records of the work coming in and out and computed the productivity of each individual employee. In the Sears company newspaper, *The Skylight,* the column "Banner Records" reported the most productive workers in each department.[35] And discipline was strict. Effie would have had to punch in at 7:55 A.M. and be in her seat by 8:00 A.M. when the time light signal went on. She would have had to give advance notice of absences, and if she failed to do so for three consecutive days, she would have been dismissed. She would have had to refrain from unnecessary talking. She would have been prohibited from entering a saloon within a certain perimeter around the plant.[36] (This latter restriction would probably not have been a problem for Effie.)

The stenographer who worked in the small, personal office, and the stenographer who worked in the large, tightly controlled company have contemporary equivalents.[37] Today Effie Jones might have the title of executive secretary, administrative assistant, office coordinator, or even paralegal secretary. The stenographer-typist at Sears was one worker in what we today call a typing pool or word processing center. But, there was a small group of stenographer-typists who combined elements of the contemporary clerical pool and of temporary services: the public stenographers.[38] As mentioned earlier, some of these stenographers worked as newspaper and court stenographers, but some extended this service to office settings. In firms, in partnerships, or as individuals, they worked in their own rooms in an office building and took in work from the various establishments in the building. They billed their services by the hour and by the volume of work done.

One such stenographer, Astrid Rosing, recalled how her start as a stenographer helped her ultimately to run her own company. She reported that "it was the year after the panic [probably 1893]—I was in my early twenties then—that I rented an office in the Rookery Building, hired a stenographer and myself, went out after business from dealers, contractors, and large manufacturers." Astrid Rosing claimed that when she started, her greatest obstacle, "despite a small amount of initial capital and hard times, was that I was young and a woman." By 1921, however, when this article about her life appeared, much had changed. "Today, that [working as a stenographer] wouldn't seem so unusual, but then, girls were not doing such things."[39]

Between 1890 and 1910, therefore, women filled and increasingly dominated a variety of stenography-typing positions. Depending on her skill, ambitions, contacts, and, unfortunately, personal appearance, a woman could choose among a variety of positions with varying status. Public stenography, which resembled the work of a small businessperson more than that of a wage worker, provided a good employment opportunity for a particular group of female clerical workers. These were older women, many living on their own, who rented their own office space, determined the conditions and pace of their work, and remained stenographers for a significant period of time during their working lives. The female stenographer at Sears, however, did resemble a closely monitored factory worker. Effie Jones, in her small law office, enjoyed the close working relationship with her boss and perhaps, like her male counterparts, wished to use her position as a stepping-stone to a newspaper position. Clearly, these stenographic positions were not equally routinized, rationalized, or mechanized during this period, and yet women entered them all. And, except for some of the routinized clerical jobs at Sears, one cannot find any evidence of deskilling in the type of jobs described here. Both Effie Jones and the women who took jobs as public stenographers were directly replacing men without any significant alteration in the actual day-to-day function of the job itself.

Women's invasion and capture of stenography-typing positions was to have a profound impact on women's work experiences as more offices systematized their work processes and adopted business machines.[40] As large office forces began to drain more of the profits of firms in salaries, managers sought to increase the productivity and profitability of their office employees. The functions of the stenographer-typist were sometimes divided into smaller actions, measured, separated from individual bosses in pools of workers, and paid for by piece rates rather than by straight salaries. Although it is unlikely that even a majority of those firms employing office workers incorporated these principles into their office practices, efficiency in office design and work flow was undoubtedly a popular goal among managers as early as the 1910s.[41]

What is important to remember is that the rigorous application of scientific management principles to the running of the office, and the resultant routinization and rationalization of some stenography and typing positions, began *after* women had already entered this occupation. Many women were not at all pleased by this development. In February 1919, *System* magazine published an exchange between a female stenographer and William H. Leffingwell, the foremost authority of the day on scientific management in the office. The question put to the contributors was, "shall I have a central typing department?"—and the workers replied, "no." This female stenographer complained that she lost interest in her work after the new president instituted new office management techniques. She recounted, "his first step toward reorganizing was segregating the stenographers, who are the only women the firm employs. He had a room fitted up for us way off from the rest of the force, as he claimed the noise of our machines, distracted everyone's attention, and made it impossible to concentrate, and that he had proved to his satisfaction that efficiency was acquired through segregation." The new working procedures, she claimed, discouraged initiative, promotion, privacy, and in the long run, productivity. Each woman stenographer was assigned work from a head operator: "no one has any special person to work for. . . . We are summoned by a buzzer and the one nearest finished with her allotment is sent to answer the call. We are simply human machines, required to turn out a certain amount of work each day and draw our salary each week. No initiative desired; no responsibility—and no progress." Before the reorganization, this stenographer felt that she had a chance for advancement; she had worked her way up from an "extra girl" to a stenographer in the manager's office. She felt that she was a valuable asset to her boss, cared about her work, and hoped to become his private secretary. The reorganization, however, changed all that; the work became a grind and she lost all her interest and enthusiasm. Leffingwell refuted these abuses point by point, claiming that promotional schemes and incentive mechanisms within the typing pool would foster greater productivity and better attitudes towards work.[42]

Although it is difficult to determine how often managers adopted scientific management techniques in their offices during the first two decades of the twentieth century, the ever-increasing numbers of clerical workers certainly provided the occasion for such reorganization, and not just among stenographer-typists. Between 1910 and 1920, the number of clerks in Chicago's clerical labor force increased dramatically, coinciding with an almost equally dramatic increase in women's participation in these clerk positions. In addition, women continued to gradually enter the routinized, lower-level bookkeeping positions.[43] Because of the trend toward routinization, rationalization, and mechanization in the office, these clerk and bookkeeping positions were fundamentally different from their nineteenth century namesakes. When women entered these clerk positions between 1910 and 1920, they were entering into jobs that were significantly different, and probably deskilled and devalued.

If women's entrance into stenography-typing predated significant rationalization of some of these positions within the world of the office, the reverse was true for clerk and bookkeeping positions. Male office workers expecting to advance to a stable white-collar position promising a family wage were experiencing some difficulties as a result of the volatile economy.[44] The positions they expected to use as stepping-stones were undergoing some serious changes. By the beginning of the twentieth century, various business magazines in Chicago began to report that clerk positions were no longer stepping-stones to higher-level positions in a firm. As the business of running a business became more complex, owners sought to hire experts trained in professional, technical, or managerial fields. Private collegiate schools of business started in response to businessmen's requests for men trained to take high-level positions without the usual apprenticeship.[45] In 1911, when North-western University's School of Commerce broadened its course offer-ings, the magazine *Chicago Commerce* reported that "in the past, a young man who secured a position with a firm in the process of formation . . . may have obtained in actual business life, the training best adapted to the needs of the time. The situation at present, however, is essentially different. This is a day of specialization. . . . The dearth of men properly qualified for positions of large responsibility is a situation which con-fronts nearly every large employer."[46]

As firms began to expand and divide work into departments, the clerk became more of a detail man than a bright young man learning the ways of the firm for future advancement. The editors of *System,* a Chicago magazine devoted to modern business practices, even equated the use of clerks to old-fashioned business practices. In 1902, they wrote that "old established industries have a tendency to clerks rather than to system and that in many cases eats a large hole in the profits. The office methods of our grandfathers are continued and as new departments of business are established, each with its staff of clerks, the office expense grows out of all proportion to the volume of business transacted without system."[47] In 1910, a writer in *System* reported that the "demand for men of the clerk class—men who perform a certain number of hours of detail work in the office for a certain number of days in return for a certain number of dollars—is liable to remain fairly steady." The illustration accompany-ing the article pictured a weary, middle-aged man seated on a stool at a high, slanted desk, with a visor on his head, and featured the caption, "he is merely a cog in the machine." "Necessary as clerk-work is, however," the article continued, "and helpful as practical experience in this phase of business may be, the man who sinks into its mechanical routine loses the opportunity for development along the lines that lead to big salaries."[48] Therefore, at around the turn of the century, the position of clerk began its decline. It was no longer assumed that a clerk's position would provide a young man with the promotional and educational oppor-tunities that it once had (see Illustration 7).

It would be simplistic to assume, however, that women were able to take these clerk and lower-level bookkeeping positions in increasing numbers starting around 1910 only because of the decline these positions experienced starting a decade before. There is, of course, some evidence that this did occur in some instances. Cost-conscious managers, after becoming aware of office machinery, replaced expensive male workers with machines and with inexpensive, usually young, female workers. One scientific manager, for example described how computing wages at one firm "required two full days for the six clerks" who often made mistakes. "Today," the manager continued, "all of this work is done by two girls with the aid of an adding and computing machine. Here again is a large saving—the services of two girls cost $8.00 for two days, where the services of the six men cost $24.00" and there were fewer mistakes.[49] Although probably more prevalent in the 1920s than in the 1910s, historians Sharon Strom, Margaret Hedstrom, and Priscilla Murolo all provide evidence of this kind of replacement of expensive male workers by cheaper, younger, female workers and office machines.[50] Despite obvious savings, there was no wholesale replacement of male clerks and lower-level bookkeepers with females. In fact, for the whole period covered in this book, men were the majority of clerks and bookkeepers in Chicago. Women were not simply taking over the lowest level clerk and bookkeeping positions, even though they certainly took these positions in large numbers starting in 1910.

What was occurring during this period was not only the degradation of some clerical positions, but also the continued development of the sexual division of labor within the office setting. During the next ten years, then, women began to take *certain* clerk and bookkeeping positions just as these positions underwent rationalization, routinization, and mechanization. To completely understand how and why women were able to engage in the clerical jobs they did when they did, one must not only understand how the evolution of industrial capitalism affected the office, but also how the sexual division of labor, as an expression of a larger system of patriarchy, followed women into the world of the office.

Women, Clerical Work, and the Sexual Division of Labor

The increasing division of labor in the office and the concomitant devaluation of many office jobs that began around 1910 only extended the sexual division of labor in the office that began with the widespread entrance of female stenographer-typists into that setting. These two developments, related yet distinct, interacted to produce two separate occupational hierarchies within the office, one for women and one for men. This evolution was not always smooth or automatic. Many companies that had traditionally employed large numbers of male clerical workers already had established occupational hierarchies. As women increasingly entered lower-level positions in these hierarchies, managers in these companies were faced with the disturbing prospect of promoting women into the higher ranks in these firms. Within the federal civil service, where promotion was based upon a mixture of political, personal, and objective standards, sex was a crucial determinant of salary. Cindy Sondik Aron reports that there were salary levels beyond which women were not permitted to go.[51]

Some Chicago companies, particularly railroads, attempted to bar women from employment because employers did not want to have to promote women within their ranks. In 1898, the Chicago and Northwestern Railroad announced that it would discharge all female clerks and stenographers that had been employed for less than two years, citing potential promotion as a reason. "Can you imagine a woman as general superintendent or general manager of the affairs of this great Railway system?"[52] By 1903, the Chicago and Northwestern Railroad was apparently still committed to its goal, because "women stenographers are always women stenographers . . . unless they get married. They are not fitted for promotion under civil service rules in force on railroads. They cannot run a handcar, lay rails, build tracks, or operate trains and are therefore limited to the keys of a typewriter."[53] Apparently some commentators believed that "many concerns, railroads, insurance companies, and other corporations are . . . anxious to obtain young men for such positions [stenography positions] that they have fresh material on hand for promotion in case of vacancies in more important positions."[54] As a result, articles appeared throughout the period in various business and trade journals in Chicago concerning the shortage of male stenographers available to meet the demands of the marketplace.[55]

Certain stenography-typing positions, therefore could function as stepping-stones, while others would remain as relatively dead-end positions. During this period, the promotability of stenographer-typists appeared to have more to do with the sex of the worker than with the specific positions of the worker within the hierarchy of the firm. In other words, the job provided different opportunities depending upon whether the employee was male or female. The myth of advancement through the ranks of the company applied as often to young men starting as stenographer-typists as it did to those beginning their careers as office boys, clerks, or bookkeepers. The writers in the *Gregg Writer,* for example, reminded its male readers of the career potentials in stenographic positions. "The young man who today takes his place in the shorthand or typewriting classroom may confidently look forward to the time when his knowledge of the two arts will place him at the stenographer's desk. After that, his progress up through the various stages of correspondent, chief clerk, manager, president, etc. will be swift and sure, if he is made of the right stuff."[56]

On the other hand, the woman who chose stenography-typing was "assuring herself of an opportunity to secure pleasant and profitable employment and to be associated with pleasant people whose interest and influence will prove invaluable to her." If she should ever have to work later in life, she would have a marketable skill.[57] Knowing stenography-typing would teach women lessons in economy, discipline, and independence, and, in case of a family emergency, provide women with a means to provide for herself or a dependent. As Theodore Roosevelt claimed, "every girl should have a thorough business training. . . . It makes her self-reliant, not a clinging vine, and if she marries, she can contribute strength to the partnership."[58] When a woman entered a stenography-typing position, the employer's expectation, as well as that of much of society, was that the job was not a stepping-stone to anything except marriage.

Some room for advancement existed, but the occupational goals for women were separate and more limited. One writer in *The Phonographic World* revealed the upper limits on women's occupational advancement in clerical work. While objecting to the recent restrictions on female employment in certain companies, this writer maintained that many women had worked their way up to responsible, well-paying positions as a successful public stenographer, a private secretary, a court stenographer, or the head of a stenographic department.[59] Two managers of employment departments, F. C. Henderschott, from New York Edison, and F. E. Weakly, employment manager at Montgomery Ward and Company, Chicago, also revealed what occupational advancement meant for female clerical workers. In a manual on their practices and policies, they detailed two occupational hierarchies for female office workers. One hierarchy featured six clusters of three jobs; each cluster progressed from a position that requires almost no training to an "ad-

vanced class of work which is closely related" to the entry-level position.
The clusters progress from left to right.

1. Entry check	Mail reader	Letter checker or correspondent
2. Draft clerk	Biller or typist	Supervisor or ledger clerk
3. Order filler	Merchandise checker	Supervisor or special clerk
4. Addressing machine	Typist	Dictaphone operator or stenographer
5. Sorter	Pricer	Special clerk or stock record keeper
6. Errands	Paster	Addressing machine operator

Presumably, a young girl could begin her work life as an errand girl
(cluster 6), advance to addressing machine operator, then jump to cluster
4, and with extra training, reach the pinnacle of her career as a dic-
taphone operator or stenographer. Henderschott and Weakly also provided a more linear advancement hierarchy, this one based on jobs
clustered around grades on tests of dexterity, arithmetic, and general
intelligence.

Grades	Jobs
90	Correspondent, letter checker, secretary
85	Record clerk
80	Reader, stenographer, dictaphone operator, biller, pricer, rack work
75	Division checker, draft clerk, classifiers, indexers
70	Order filler, typist, entry checker
65	Addressers
60	Paster, errands, sorter, tubes
50	Bagger

Again, according to this occupational hierarchy, the ultimate goal for
a young woman starting her working life as a clerical worker was to
become a correspondent, letter checker, or secretary. The companies

from which these hierarchies came apparently provided no way for women to advance into any higher-level management positions. Those clerical jobs associated with female workers were effectively separated from a larger occupational hierarchy within the firm.[60]

The existence of two separate occupational hierarchies within offices is also evident from the National Industrial Conference Board's findings from the early 1920s on clerical salaries in manufacturing enterprises, railroads, public utilities, mercantile establishments, insurance companies, and banking institutions in eighteen cities throughout the United States.[61] Some 2,699 of the clerical workers examined were from Chicago. The board analyzed twenty separate clerical occupations by salary range and by sex (see Table 15). Not surprisingly, women dominated the

Table 15. Number and Percentage of Male and Female Clerical Workers from Chicago in National Industrial Conference Board Study by Occupation

OCCUPATION	TOTAL NUMBER	NUMBER OF MALES	PERCENT MALE	NUMBER OF FEMALES	PERCENT FEMALE
Chief Clerk	78	69	88.5	9	11.5
Senior Clerk	664	227	34.2	437	65.8
General Clerk	92	48	52.2	44	47.8
Payroll Clerk	59	36	61.0	23	39.0
Order Clerk	68	25	36.8	43	63.2
Mail Clerk	32	15	46.9	17	53.1
Labor-Saving Machine Operator	300	112	37.3	188	62.7
Shipping Clerk	134	131	97.8	3	2.2
Cost Clerk	57	41	71.9	16	28.1
Ledger Clerk	36	26	72.2	10	27.8
Cashier	27	21	77.8	6	22.2
Head Bookkeeper	53	48	90.6	5	9.4
Switchboard Operator	77	4	5.2	73	94.8
File Clerk	94	10	10.6	84	89.4
Inexperienced Typist	114	17	14.9	97	85.1
Experienced Typist	131	4	3.1	127	96.9
Junior Stenographer	106	3	2.8	103	97.2
Senior Stenographer	154	12	7.8	142	92.2
Secretarial Stenographer	71	13	18.3	58	81.7
Junior Clerks	352	90	25.6	262	74.4

Source: National Industrial Conference Board, Inc., *Clerical Salaries in the United States, 1926* (New York: National Industrial Conference Board, 1926), pp. 39–48.

lowest-paid clerical jobs, and even those women in the more important clerical occupations received less pay. Table 16 details male and female clerical workers ranked by the median weekly salary range in each occupation by sex. Women's jobs are clearly clustered at the bottom and men's at the top. The National Industrial Conference Board estimated the average weekly salary for all clerical workers to be approximately $25.00 a week. If we take the $26.00–$24.01 range in Table 16 as a midpoint (payroll clerk, both men and women) we find that 1,527 out of the 1,747 women in this survey, or 87.4 percent, were found below this midpoint, whereas 700 out of 952 men, or 73.5 percent, were found above this midpoint. Female clerical workers, therefore, were found on the bottom of the salary scale.

This type of analysis, however, does not take into account the reality of the sexual division of labor in the office. Office hierarchy was not one continuous linear ladder, with women simply cut off from the opportunities at the top. Rating office jobs by salary in separate men's and women's lists reveals the two hierarchies that were present in the office (see Table 16). Note that for five occupations, head bookkeeper, senior stenographer, payroll clerk, experienced typist, and mail clerk, men and women had the same median salary range. And, for three positions, labor-saving machine operator, switchboard operator, and inexperienced typist, women's median salary range was actually higher than men's. Delineating positions by the percentages of men and women in them reveals more clearly the dual occupational hierarchies embedded in this list. The clerical occupations that appear in Table 17 were either more than two-thirds men or more than two-thirds women. As this table demonstrates, there are clearly two separate occupational categories here. Women's occupational opportunities existed primarily within the occupations they had traditionally held since the 1890s, stenography and typing. Men's opportunities remained predominately in various clerk and bookkeeping positions, particularly those that appear to have a specialized function. Even as the office was rationalized, then, many women remained in those jobs that had traditionally been their domain, stenography-typing; and men continued to dominate their traditional positions, clerking and bookkeeping.

And yet women did begin to enter some clerk and bookkeeping positions in increasing numbers after 1910. Table 18, which ranks occupations more than 50 percent male or female, shows that many of these

Table 16. Occupations in National Industrial Conference Board Survey Ranked by Median Weekly Salary Ranges for Male and Female Clerical Workers in Chicago

OCCUPATIONS/MALE	SALARY (IN DOLLARS)	OCCUPATIONS/FEMALE	SALARY (IN DOLLARS)
Chief Clerk	65.00–55.01		
Head Bookkeeper	50.00–45.01	Head Bookkeeper	50.00–45.01
Cashier	45.00–40.01		
		Chief Clerk	42.00–40.00
Secretarial Stenographer	40.00–35.01		
		Secretarial Stenographer	35.00
Senior Clerk	35.00–30.01		
Cost Clerk	35.00–30.01	Cashier	35.00–30.01
Senior Stenographer	30.00–27.51	Senior Stenographer	30.00–27.51
Shipping Clerk	30.00–26.01		
Order Clerk	30.00–26.01		
General Clerk	30.00–25.01		
Ledger Clerk	27.00–24.51		
Junior Stenographer	26.50–25.01		
Payroll Clerk	26.00–24.01	Payroll Clerk	26.00–24.01
		Machine Operator	26.00–23.51
		Senior Clerk	25.00–20.00
		Junior Stenographer	23.50–22.01
		Switchboard Operator	22.50–21.01
Experienced Typist	22.00–20.51	Experienced Typist	22.00–20.51
Junior Clerk	22.00–20.01	Cost Clerk	22.00–20.01
File Clerk	22.00–19.01		
		Ledger Clerk	21.50–20.01
Machine Operator	21.00–19.01		
		General Clerk	20.00–18.01
		Shipping Clerk	20 and under
		Order Clerk	20 and under
		Inexperienced Typist	19.50–18.01
		File Clerk	19.00
Mail Clerk	19.00–16.01	Mail Clerk	19.00–16.01
		Junior Clerk	18 and under
Switchboard Operator	16.50–15.00		
Inexperienced Typist	13.50 and under		

Source: National Industrial Conference Board, Inc., *Clerical Salaries in the United States, 1926* (New York: National Industrial Conference Board, 1926), p. 39–48.

Table 17. Occupations More Than Two-Thirds Male and More Than Two-Thirds Female Ranked by Median Weekly Salary Range

OVER TWO-THIRDS MALE	(SALARY, IN DOLLARS)	OVER TWO-THIRDS FEMALE	(SALARY, IN DOLLARS)
Chief Clerk	65.00–55.01		
Head Bookkeeper	50.00–45.01		
Cashier	45.00–40.01		
Cost Clerk	35.00–30.01	Secretarial Stenographer	35.00
Shipping Clerk	30.00–26.01	Senior Stenographer	30.00–27.51
Ledger Clerk	27.00–24.51		
		Junior Stenographer	23.50–22.01
		Switchboard Operator	22.50–21.01
		Experienced Typist	22.00–20.51
		Inexperienced Typist	19.50–18.01
		File Clerk	19.00
		Junior Clerk	18 and under

Source: National Industrial Conference Board, Inc., *Clerical Salaries in the United States, 1926* (New York: National Industrial Conference Board, 1926), pp. 39–48.

women took a variety of low-level clerk positions, which probably were entry-level office positions for women. But women were not simply entering those clerk positions at the low end of the occupational hierarchy. Table 19 lists all clerk positions, ranked according to men's median salary. The columns on the right indicate the percentage of women in these occupations and the median weekly salary range they received for performing the same work. Eight of the fifteen positions listed contain close to or more than 50 percent women. Five of the eight positions are found at the low end of the male clerk hierarchy; therefore, most women did work at the most routinized and devalued clerk positions.

Three of the clerk positions dominated by women, senior clerks, order clerks, and general clerks were not at the bottom of the salary ranking, however. As Table 19 demonstrates, when women performed these positions, they ranked low on the hierarchy relative to men. Of course, it is impossible to determine with these data if men and women with the same job title performed exactly the same work. Nevertheless, the severe devaluation of these three positions when women performed

Table 18. Clerk and Bookkeeping Positions More Than 50 Percent Male and More Than 50 Percent Female Ranked by Median Weekly Salary Range

MORE THAN 50 PERCENT MALE	(SALARY, IN DOLLARS)	MORE THAN 50 PERCENT FEMALE	(SALARY, IN DOLLARS)
Chief Clerk	65.00–55.01		
Head Bookkeeper	50.00–45.01		
Cashier	45.00–40.01		
Cost Clerk	35.00–30.01		
Shipping Clerk	30.00–26.01		
General Clerk[a]	30.00–25.01		
Ledger Clerk	27.00–24.51		
Payroll Clerk	25.01–24.01		
		Machine Operator	26.00–23.51
		Senior Clerk	25.00–20.00
		Switchboard Op.	22.50–21.01
		General Clerk[a]	20.00–18.01
		Order Clerk	20.00 and under
		File Clerk	19.00
Mail Clerk[a]	19.00–16.01	Mail Clerk[a]	19.00–16.01
		Junior Clerk	18.00 and under

Source: National Industrial Conference Board, Inc., *Clerical Salaries in the United States, 1926* (New York: National Industrial Conference Board, 1926), pp. 39–48.
[a]General and mail clerk included in both lists since percentages were so close to 50 percent.

them suggests that the sex of the worker contributed significantly to the (lack of) value of the job.

Looking at the three jobs at the bottom of the male clerk/bookkeeping hierarchy is also revealing. When women worked as labor-saving machine operators, mail clerks, or switchboard operators, their median weekly salary range was the same or higher than men's. These three jobs were also dominated by women with 62.7 percent, 53.1 percent, and 94.8 percent, respectively. Although women were able to make more money than men doing the same work, their presence in large numbers devalued the job within the male occupational hierarchy. These three positions were relatively new on the scene, products of the rationalization and mechanization of the office of the 1910s and early 1920s, and may have been dominated by women early on. The sexual division of labor, therefore, had two separate effects on women's work in bookkeeping and clerk positions: women who did high-status jobs that were

Table 19. Clerk and Bookkeeping Positions Ranked by Male Weekly Median Salary Range with Percentage of Women in Job Category and Women's Median Weekly Salary Range

MEN'S JOB AND SALARY	(SALARY, IN DOLLARS)	WOMEN'S PERCENTAGE AND SALARY	(SALARY, IN DOLLARS)
Chief Clerk	65.00–55.01	11.4	42.00–40.00
Head Bookkeeper	50.00–45.01	9.4	50.00–45.01
Cashier	45.00–40.01	22.2	35.00–30.01
Senior Clerk	35.00–30.01	*65.8*	25.00–20.00
Cost Clerk	35.00–30.01	28.1	22.00–20.01
Shipping Clerk	30.00–26.01	2.2	20 and under
Order Clerk	30.00–26.01	*63.2*	20 and under
General Clerk	30.00–25.01	*47.8*	20.00–18.01
Ledger Clerk	27.00–24.51	27.8	21.50–20.01
Payroll Clerk	26.00–24.01	39.0	26.00–24.01
Junior Clerk	22.00–20.01	*74.4*	18 and under
File Clerk	22.00–19.01	89.4	19.00
Machine Operator	21.00–19.01	62.7	26.00–23.51
Mail Clerk	19.00–16.01	*53.1*	19.00–16.01
Switchboard Op.	16.50–15.00	*94.8*	22.50–21.01

Source: National Industrial Conference Board, Inc., *Clerical Salaries in the United States, 1926* (New York: National Industrial Conference Board, 1926), pp. 39–48.

considered highly skilled and were highly paid within a male occupational hierarchy, often received less pay; and, women's domination of some low-level bookkeeping and clerk positions occurred while these jobs were severely devalued in the male occupational hierarchy, rendering them more viable occupational opportunities for women than men.

The existence of the sexual division of labor within the office and its extension within the clerk and bookkeeping categories throughout the 1910s and 1920s begs the question: why did women occupy some clerk and bookkeeping positions and not others? A variety of explanations is possible. In some cases, most notably that of the shipping clerk, the work involved physical labor and was therefore deemed inappropriate for women. Men also seem to have occupied what the National Industrial Conference Board referred to as the more specialized clerical occupations. For example, the board claimed that general and ledger clerks occupied positions of similar grade and importance, yet "the work of the ledger clerk . . . is somewhat more specialized, consisting chiefly of the posting of items from various sources to the proper ledger accounts."[62] Three of these positions, mail clerk, order clerk, and machine operator, were entry-level jobs for young men. Women may have found it easier to enter a clerk position when their competition was a younger man. And it is possible that many of these clerk positions were actually rationalized versions of functions women had traditionally performed as stenographer-typists. With help from an office boy, stenographer-typists in small offices (like Effie Jones, mentioned earlier) often performed many duties such as opening, distributing, and dispatching the mail, filing correspondence, and composing and typing bills and orders. In larger offices, when these functions became segregated, rationalized, and mechanized, it is possible that their gender association did not vanish. Women may have dominated certain clerk occupations (and not others) because these functions had already become "women's work."

Conclusion

The transformation of the clerical labor force was not a simple phenomenon involving the direct replacement of men by women as the jobs they engaged in experienced degradation caused by the evolution of industrial capitalism and scientific management. The story of the change in clerical work and the clerical labor force was much more complicated and involved the interplay between capitalism and patriarchy against an historical backdrop. The growth of Chicago's economy precipitated an alteration in the configuration of the clerical labor force starting around 1890. While the male clerical labor force remained relatively stagnant, the female clerical labor force grew and also took on distinctive characteristics of its own. The most important characteristic of women's clerical experience between 1890 and 1910 was women's entrance into, capture of, and continued domination of a wide variety of stenography-typing positions.

In some of the larger firms, clerk and bookkeeping positions traditionally dominated by men, as well as some of some stenography-typing positions, were divided into several separate positions and rationalized, rendering them completely different from their nineteenth century namesakes. Women did not enter into all of these positions en masse or simply because they were becoming devalued and routinized. Just as functions were divided into specific job categories for the sake of efficiency in the office, so too the sexes in the offices were increasingly divided into two organizational hierarchies because of the proscription against promoting women into managerial ranks. There was (and is) nothing natural about this evolving sexual division of labor within the office; it was the construction of those in the positions of power to construct it and was entirely consistent with the general sexual division of labor in the larger society. The sexual division of labor in the world of the office was the result of the interaction between a set of evolving contemporaneous social/cultural assumptions held by male employers and managers about women's position in the world of office work, and the actions of women themselves. The transformation of office jobs and the clerical sector in any individual firm was affected as much, therefore, by the sex of the people taking these jobs as it was by economic and structural trends.

But it was not simply the world of business that adapted to this intrusion of women and changed in special ways because of them. The institutions and organizations of the city of Chicago, both public and private, that were increasingly concerned about the dislocations and difficulties endemic to burgeoning American cities, slowly, and in some cases reluctantly, focused their attention on this new group of women workers.

Illus. 1: The masculine office. Circuit Supply Company, Chicago, 1910. Photo courtesy of the Chicago Historical Society, 890-B.

Illus. 2: The correspondence between the piano and the typewriter. Advertisement for Royal Typewriter Co., Inc., from *System* (March 1920). Photo courtesy of Triumph-Adler—Royal, Inc.

Illus. 3: The gender ambiguity of the stenographer position. Advertisement for Smith Premier Typewriter Co., from *Gregg Writer* (Sept. 15, 1904).

Illus. 4: "How would you like my job?" The female clerical worker as vamp. Color postcard with 1909 postmark. Courtesy of the author.

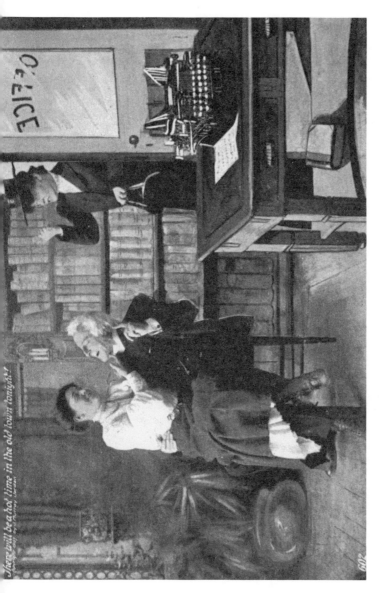

Illus. 5: "There will be a hot time in the old town tonight!" The female clerical worker as vamp. Color postcard, copyright 1907, J. Murray Jordon Publishers, Phila. Courtesy of the author.

Illus. 6: Female stenographer in a moderately-sized, predominately male office. Auditor's office, Bowman Dairy Co., Chicago, 1912. Photo courtesy of the Chicago Historical Society, 86:49 B2F4.

Illus. 7: Large, segregated, male office space. Pulman Co., Chicago, 1916. Photo courtesy of the Chicago Historical Society, P. 18774.

Illus. 8: Eleanor Association Residence, Club 6, the living room. Publicity photograph from late 1910s or early 1920s. Photo courtesy of the Parkway Eleanor Association.

Illus. 9: Eleanor Association Residence, Club 5, the dining room. 1918 publicity series. Photo courtesy of the Parkway Eleanor Association.

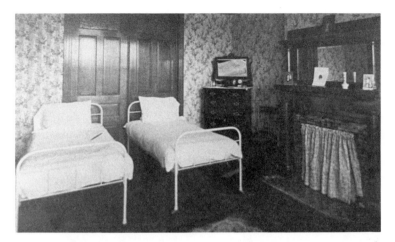

Illus. 10: Eleanor Association Residence, bedroom. Publicity photograph probably taken before 1915. Photo courtesy of the Parkway Eleanor Association.

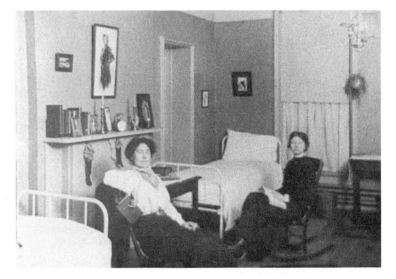

Illus. 11: Roommates at an Eleanor Association Residence. Photograph from Eleanor Association photograph album, no date. Photo courtesy of the Parkway Eleanor Association.

Illus. 12: Three "kid party" frolickers, October 1925, from Eleanor Association photograph album. Photo courtesy of the Parkway Eleanor Association.

Illus. 13: Large, segregated, female office space. Pulman Co., Chicago, 1916. Photo courtesy of the Chicago Historical Society. P 19553.

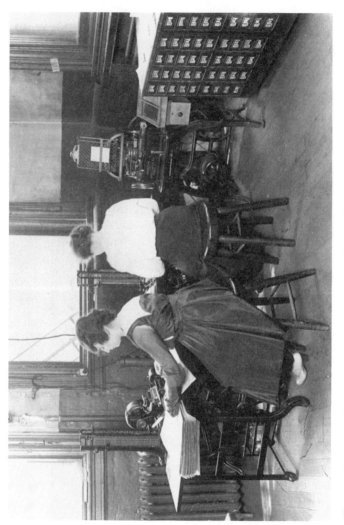

Illus. 14: Women working at addressograph machines. Pulman Co., Chicago, 1917. Photo courtesy of the Chicago Historical Society, 1982. 157 B1 F12.

CHAPTER 6

From Home to School to Office in the Progressive City

*T*HE WOMEN training for clerical positions in schools, working in offices, and availing themselves of public and private accommodations throughout the city certainly did not go unnoticed. The wave of women into clerical jobs between 1890 and World War I attracted the attention of educators as well as that of members of philanthropic, business, labor, religious, and women's groups in the city. Early twentieth century reformers, however, whether they were interested in social efficiency, economic equity, or humanitarian or cultural uplift, did not put female clerical workers high on their list of priorities, particularly early in the century. Since educators considered men the primary breadwinners in their future families, matching the student with the best job training was more important for male students than for female. The relatively better wages, hours, and working conditions as well as the ethnic background of female clerical workers rendered them less compelling recipients of charity, aid, and cultural uplift than their foreign sisters and brothers working in factories and sweatshops. Philanthropic, business, women's, religious, and public organizations and institutions slowly, and in some instances, reluctantly, turned their attentions to the specific situations and problems of the female office worker by the second decade of the twentieth century, and only because it was impossible to avoid these new female workers on the urban scene.

Even if most urban reformers did not pay attention to female clerical workers specifically, they were greatly concerned by the increasing number of women who had to work in the city. Members of various reform, civic, and women's organizations believed that a working girl faced perils at almost every corner. The rapidly growing city contained large populations of strange immigrants, fortune-seeking drifters, saloons, dance halls, houses of ill repute, all within tantalizing proximity to more reputable neighborhoods. A "home girl," who did not venture into the city without a chaperone or companion, would never have to come into contact with the vices of the city. The life of the working woman exposed her to a variety of compromising situations, particularly if she lived on her own. If she had recently arrived from a small town or rural area, she quickly needed to find a safe place to live and some sort of employment. Rooming-houses and boarding-houses were not always safe and respectable places to live. Some employment agencies took advantage of the naiveté of newly arrived girls. On the streets, in the trains or buses, and in her workplace, she would come into contact with men of all sorts. Also, she was responsible for seeking out her own leisure and companionship when not at work. Because she had no family to guide, protect, and comfort her, contemporary observers argued, the young girl recently arrived in Chicago was most vulnerable to the dreaded white slave trade and prostitution.[1]

Even women who lived with their families did not escape danger or temptation. During the day, the working girl was beyond the watchful eyes of relatives. The close proximity of all classes of men at work often tempted women to stray from the path of purity. Clerical workers were particularly susceptible to this kind of evil influence. As Jane Addams noted, the female office worker, "so recent an outcome of modern business methods . . . has not yet been conventionalized. The girl is without the wholesome social restraint afforded by the companionship of other working women and her isolation in itself constitutes a danger."[2]

In response to this situation, many of Chicago's organizations began to shift the focus of their activities in an attempt to "conventionalize" the experience of Chicago's growing female clerical labor force. These organizations were not responsible for women's entrance into clerical jobs; rather, the reformers' actions responded to and hastened this dramatic change in the female labor force. Although these groups acted upon their own specific concerns and agendas of activity, by the late teens the activities of these groups on behalf of female office workers helped to legitimize this form of employment, created the opportunity for more women to choose clerical work, and, in some cases, helped to define what it meant to be a clerical worker. The actions of these organizations, therefore, contributed to making clerical work "women's work." Nevertheless, the slow reaction of these groups to the female clerical worker and her needs underscores that it was women themselves, in their relentless pursuit of good employment, who began the process of redefining clerical work as a woman's job.

Commercial Education in the Chicago Public Schools

Just as the opportunities offered by private business colleges in Chicago facilitated women's entrance into clerical fields, the introduction of commercial education courses in the public schools helped to facilitate the association of women with clerical work. Although private business colleges certainly opened opportunities for women to receive the training necessary to engage in clerical jobs, the fees kept many away. After 1900, the Chicago public schools began to offer their first commercial education courses and women took these courses in increasing numbers between 1900 and 1930.

Recent scholars of the public school system during the Progressive era claim that school, civic, and industrial leaders hoped to alter schools to train good workers and citizens. The increasing numbers of immigrants and children of immigrants in the schools, as well as the increasing complexity of the American economy, prompted school officials to differentiate students according to their vocational potentials and the needs of the marketplace.[3] Training in vocational subjects and citizenship were products of the attempts by school, civic, and industrial leaders to provide an education to suit their diverse needs and the needs of the student body. These courses helped to perpetuate class divisions and the values of the dominant culture, rather than providing meaningful choices or the opportunity for growth and advancement for students.[4]

School curricula and policies may have also perpetuated gender divisions in society.[5] Presumably, school leaders were persuaded by the reasonableness and efficiency of training students in vocations adapted to their future jobs and stations. Since these leaders, as well as most members of American society, assumed that women and men would perform different functions after school, one could expect to see these educators advocating different vocational tracks for boys and girls. For vocational training in industrial pursuits, the differentiation by sex was clear and mirrored the sexual division of labor in industry. Boys, for example, could learn the rudiments of carpentry or mechanics, whereas girls could learn sewing, hatmaking, or embroidery.

Since the Chicago schools were influenced by the larger community and particularly the business community, one would also expect to find business, civic, educational, and women's rights leaders debating the merits of commercial education for women in Chicago's public school system.[6] Business leaders had a stake in procuring cheap office help and it seems reasonable to expect that they might encourage school officials to provide girls with the opportunity to train in these skills. If school officials in Chicago believed, or were persuaded by Chicago's business community, that clerical work was "women's work," one would expect to find these officials directing women into clerical education courses.

This, however, is not what happened in Chicago. Gender distinctions within commercial education were not immediately evident and only evolved slowly throughout the period.[7] Chicago's school board officials did not promote commercial education as a particularly female endeavor until women began to dominate clerical courses and clerical jobs. Throughout this period, it seems, women's attendance in commercial courses altered educational policy, not the reverse. As they had done in private business colleges in the late nineteenth century, women chose to train themselves for clerical occupations.[8]

The Board of Education of the City of Chicago first considered commercial education long before women entered office work in any significant numbers. As early as 1877, the public school's evening school program included both bookkeeping and stenography, along with algebra, geometry, mathematical drawing, and natural philosophy. Enrollment in these commercial subjects accounted for 60.7 percent of the approximately 128 students who attended evening classes weekly.[9] By 1892, the evening school program consisted of four courses, mechanical drawing, bookkeeping, shorthand, and typing, with typing compulsory for those studying shorthand.[10] These commercial courses contributed greatly to the popularity of the evening school program. The report on evening schools in 1895 stated that "the introduction of type-writing machines has been very beneficial. The classes in stenography have been increased in numbers and in interest and many of those studying last year are now employed."[11]

The tremendous success and apparent popularity of the evening program as well as of private business colleges prompted school officials to offer commercial courses in public schools. As in many other cities in the Midwest, Chicago's board of education first considered commercial education in the public, day, high schools in the 1890s.[12] In 1890, the English High and Manual Training School, originally started in 1883 under the auspices of the Commercial Club of Chicago and called the Chicago Manual Training School, opened its doors to Chicago's boys desiring training for life's work. In 1893, the English High and Manual Training School began offering commercial courses. The superintendent reported the year after stenography and typing courses appeared that, "it would in every way be desirable to extend the work of the English High and Manual Training School to include broader work in bookkeeping, stenography, and typewriting, and the study of commercial law. In other words, there is a demand for what may be denominated a business course in connection with an English High and Manual Training School in each division of the city."[13] This school and its curriculum were for boys. In addition to commercial courses, the school offered courses in mechanical drawing and carpentry, forge and foundry work, and machine shop, as well as standard high school courses in English, history, mathematics, and natural sciences. The commercial course involved substituting book-keeping and stenography for mathematics courses such as algebra, geometry, and trigonometry.[14] Thirty-five of the 476 male students in the English High and Manual Training High School enrolled in business courses during the 1897–1898 academic year.[15] Opportunities for boys to obtain commercial training grew as administrators extended manual training to each division of the city.[16]

Expanding manual training courses was only one way school officials attempted to accommodate the demands of the student body and Chicago's business community. The educational leaders of Chicago wanted to do more to prepare young men for the commercial world. In the late 1890s, these leaders began to voice their desire for a separate commercial high school in the city of Chicago. Nationally, some educators believed that there was a greater demand among boys for commercial training because of the lack of apprenticeship training in business establishments, and the development of collegiate and denominational schools of business.[17] A public high school of commerce would supply the kind of training that Chicago's businessmen desired. The president of Chicago's school board, E. G. Halle, expressed this in his annual report of 1898. After stating that the continued health and progress of the United States depended upon opening foreign markets, Halle claimed that "the building of the Nicaragua canal, the development of trade with

South American peoples will offer an opportunity to Chicago which it will certainly be to its interest to seize and utilize. It is one of the standing complaints of our large business houses that they find difficulty in filling their most important positions with men. . . . Here in Chicago we need to provide facilities for such education as liberally and fully as we have provided facilities for other branches of secondary training."[18] President Graham H. Harris reported a year later that this proposed four-year commercial high school "should not be a school where simply book-keeping, stenography, telegraphy, and typewriting may be taught to prepare boys for clerkships, but a school where opportunities should be offered for science, math, commercial geography, commercial law, banking, political economy, civics, and modern languages."[19]

Educators had their own professional reasons for advocating a separate commercial school for boys. During this time, they repeatedly expressed concern over the 70 percent to 30 percent ratio of girls to boys in the high schools. This commercial high school would provide just the incentive needed to keep boys in school. In his annual report for 1899, Superintendent Lane wrote, "we are educating our girls better than our boys because we do not give our boys the opportunity to be trained for the occupations they must follow. Americans are rightly generous to women, but such partiality in this instance will produce an ill-balanced relationship."[20] These educators believed that commercial training would attract and keep boys in school because, to these officials, commercial work was men's work.

Interest in a separate four-year commercial high school for boys heightened during Edwin Cooley's superintendency between 1900 and 1909. Cooley was an active advocate of all types of vocational training in the public high schools, and even after his tenure as superintendent lobbied for bills to establish a dual system of schools, based on the German vocational school model, which allowed for the tracking of students into vocational and academic courses. Although Chicago's business community continued to lobby the board of education to provide the training necessary to transform Chicago's boys into "men of affairs," principals' and teachers' organizations, women's organizations, and the Chicago Federation of Labor were all opposed to this dual system and Cooley's efforts failed.[21]

Commercial courses weathered the controversy. Although the separate four-year commercial high school for boys never materialized, commercial courses did appear in the general high schools during this time.[22] High school students could elect to take courses in commercial geography, commercial law, accounting, stenography, and typewriting as early as 1900. To ensure that commercial students received a well-rounded education, these electives were only offered in certain years in a student's four years of high school study.[23] First-year electives included commercial studies and accounting; second-year electives included stenography and typing; third-year electives included commercial geography and advanced stenography and typing; and fourth-year electives included commercial law. The design of this curriculum reflected the board's desire not only to provide skills offered by private business colleges, but also to train young men for higher posts in the commercial world.

Cooley believed that these courses did achieve one of the goals of Chicago's educators. He reported as early as 1910 that "the percentage of boys was gradually increasing," and he attributed this to "the greater elasticity in the program of study and to the introduction of commercial or business subjects."[24] The commercial courses in both the day and evening schools were apparently popular. Enrollment in commercial courses in the day school increased from 300 in 1901 to 4,490 in 1913, when those enrolled in commercial courses accounted for almost one-fifth of those in high school.[25] Enrollment in commercial subjects accounted for more than one-half of those taking evening school classes in the high school in the 1909–1910 academic year. Men and women took advantage of these courses in equal numbers. Slightly more than half of those enrolled in stenography and typing evening courses in 1909 were men.[26]

When Cooley left the school board in 1909, then, commercial education had become a legitimate and established part of the school elective course offerings. The most significant aspect of Cooley's commercial education program was his response to the refusal of the board to establish a separate four-year commercial high school for boys. By making elective commercial courses available in the general high schools, Cooley placed these courses designed to train young men for business in schools dominated by female students. Instead of keeping boys in school, Cooley had inadvertently created the opportunity for more women to take commercial courses.

Chicago's next superintendent of schools, Ella Flagg Young (Chicago's first female superintendent) further solidified commercial training in the high schools. In her first year as superintendent, she instituted two-year vocational courses in the high schools, claiming that "the day has passed in America when two years in the life of a boy or girl who is going out without a college education can be treated as of little value in the High School."[27] In the years to follow, the commercial course became a permanent fixture in the academic high schools, not the technical high schools. Young reported in 1912 that, "because of the need for emphasis on composition in English, classes in stenography and typewriting are not admitted to the technical school. They are trained in the academic High School. On the other hand, all classes in two-year vocational courses excepting those in stenography and typewriting are admitted to the technical High School only."[28]

The comprehensive high school offered several courses of study to the student including the general course, science course, normal college preparation course, commercial course, office preparation course, technical course, general trades course, household arts course, arts course, architecture course, and a preparation for pharmacy course. The commercial course lasted two years, while the office preparatory course lasted four years. The four-year course offered comprehensive business training with relevant general high school courses such as mathematics, modern languages, and history. The student in the two-year commercial course could concentrate on bookkeeping or stenographic practice, with additional courses offered in business English, arithmetic, rudimentary science, business forms, and penmanship.[29] Enrollments in these commercial courses increased dramatically in the teens. Between 1913 and 1918, the number of students in commercial courses in the high schools increased 115 percent, while overall high school enrollment increased 53 percent.[30]

Although enrollment figures for commercial courses suggest that these courses were popular among students, Chicago's business community was still not satisfied with commercial education in the high schools. In 1912, the City Club of Chicago conducted a study of vocational training in Chicago and other cities. The general opinion of the employers polled was that commercial training was inadequate in scope and substance. Employers expressed a general dissatisfaction with the theoretical and practical training in the high schools. They objected to the burden of excessive academic work, and suggested that the division of labor in offices had come about "as much from the lack of well-educated office employees, as from advanced business organization."[31] They recommended a more practical business-oriented two-year commercial course, and again, the establishment of a separate four-year commercial high school to train young men for opportunities in the business world.[32]

Chicago's board of education made several attempts to meet the needs of the business community. In 1913, Ella Flagg Young started a department of commercial education, which included two members of the Chicago Association of Commerce to act as advisors.[33] The board also established a vocational supervision department to help match students to available jobs, and, in 1917, opened a junior college of commerce and administration.[34] Because of the demand created by the war effort in this same year, the board offered five-month intensive courses in stenography and typing for high school graduates.[35] And, in 1919, in response to state legislation, the board started a continuation program, which provided instruction, often in commercial subjects, to all employed minors between the ages of fourteen and eighteen years.[36] The continuation program institutionalized an already existing cooperative relationship between certain businesses and the board of education regarding commercial education. Two years before the legislature required these schools, the board of education and the office manager at Swift and Company had already arranged for the board to furnish instructors for and supervision over the commercial course taught at the company, while Swift paid attending employees for hours missed from work, and furnished classrooms, textbooks, supplies, and equipment.[37]

Although none of these programs and activities were specifically designed for women, starting in the 1910s, some administrators and educators began to acknowledge the business community's demands for women trained in commercial skills. In 1911, the president of the school board, J. B. McFatrich, wrote that "the increase in demand for the services of women in commercial and industrial life has broadened the scope of our conception of the field for technical schools and is directing the attention of school authorities to the necessity for special training for girls who desire to qualify for a business career."[38] Ella Flagg Young believed that "it [was] impossible to limit all girls in the industries to dressmaking, millinery, and cooking." She insisted that women were well suited for other types of work, as evidenced by the great number working in the factories and commercial houses.[39]

In response to businessmen's demand for workers, students' demand for courses, and educators' desires to train students for their lives after school, the board of education opened the Lucy Flower Technical High School for Girls in 1912. Although the stated objective of this school was to prepare young women for efficient careers in the business world or in the home, the school did not offer a commercial course until 1917.[40] Although the reason for this delay was never stated outright, a number of explanations are possible. Many administrators, educators, and employers still may not have thought of commercial education as a type of women's vocational training. Since commercial courses were available in the comprehensive high schools, their inclusion in this school may have seemed redundant, particularly if resources were limited. The quality of the English and language training in the Lucy Flower school may have been considered below the level necessary for adequate commercial training. Finally, educators and administrators may have felt that other types of vocational education, such as homemaking, cooking, sewing, and childcare, were more important for women. It is significant that commercial education was not included in the only vocational school for girls in Chicago until 1917 and equally significant that commercial education was never explicitly or overtly oriented to female students during this period.

Women, apparently, did not need any encouragement from educators to take commercial courses. Despite the board's efforts to supply a clerical labor force suited to the many needs of the business community, most commercial students continued to attend the two-year commercial courses in the general, local, high schools. In 1913, almost ten times as many students enrolled in the two-year course as had in the four-year commercial course; in 1915, only 35 students graduated from the four-year course, while 712 graduated from the two-year course.[41] The majority of the students in the two-year courses were women. In 1913, 70 percent of students in the two-year courses were women, as opposed to 44 percent women in the four-year business course, and this trend would continue until 1930.[42]

By 1920, most women had access to the basic training required to procure office jobs in Chicago through the public schools. What had started as a policy designed to provide the business community with young men trained in four years of courses in a variety of commercial topics had turned into a bifurcated commercial education program with a two-year vocationally oriented course attracting large number of female students, and a less popular four-year course that had a majority of male students. There is little evidence to suggest that any individual or group orchestrated this outcome. Rather, the evolution of commercial education in the Chicago public schools was haphazard, affected by a variety of interest groups, economic considerations, and educational policy, as well as the demands of the students and their parents. As John Rury succinctly states, commercial education in public schools "bore a unique relationship to the labor market. It developed in response to a growing demand from educational consumers, from students and to a lesser extent from businessmen" and "offered what was probably the period's clearest example of the schools responding directly to the demands of the labor market."[43]

Vocational Guidance and Placement

In the late teens, vocational guidance and placement bureaus and other employment agencies began to report an oversupply of poorly trained young women seeking office positions. As early as 1916, Charles Boyd, the superintendent of the Illinois Free Employment Bureau, complained that his office was "besieged by applicants for clerical and office positions." He added that women no longer wanted domestic work, which was plentiful, and that the schools ought to train more women in domestic science.[44] Like public school officials, individuals involved in vocational guidance and placement could not ignore female clerical workers. As one might expect, business organizations such as the Chicago Association of Commerce endorsed vocational guidance and placement services in Chicago's public schools to minimize training and turnover costs for Chicago's employers. Vocational placement and guidance in the public schools was just one program designed to involve and educate students in business ethics and life. Women's, philanthropic, and religious organizations also offered humanitarian reasons, such as the safety and protection of female workers, for vocational guidance and placement activity. By establishing services for young working girls, older women, college women, and daughters of poor, immigrant families, these groups facilitated the entrance of many different types of women into popular commercial courses and into clerical positions.

The first and most important effort for vocational guidance and placement services in the Chicago public schools began in 1911 in response to a variety of economic and social problems. During this year, "the state of Illinois allowed a child to leave school the day he was fourteen years old and go to work. Worse than that, they allowed him to leave school to hunt work."[45] Three social workers at the Chicago School of Civics and Philanthropy, George H. Mead, Sophonisba Breckinridge, and Edith Abbott, believed that vocational guidance and placement in the public high schools would encourage children to stay in school longer. In addition, the service would steer students away from dead-end jobs and preempt the need for young, inexperienced workers to visit exploitative private employment agencies or answer possibly deceptive advertisements in the newspapers. The need for a vocational bureau became apparent after Breckinridge and Abbott finished a report of the employment opportunities for children who left grade school to go to work. This report was directed to the Chicago's Women's Club, the Chicago Association of Collegiate Alumnae (the predecessor of the American Association of University Women), and the Women's City Club, and these three organizations quickly became involved in the work of the new organization, the Joint Committee for Vocational Training for Girls.[46] A recent graduate of the School of Civics and Philanthropy, Anne S. Davis, functioned as the placement director, vocational advisor, and employment investigator for those fourteen-year-olds to sixteen-year-olds seeking counsel.

Within just five years, this fledgling organization became incorporated within the educational system of the city. One year after its start, it expanded its focus to include boys as well as girls. In 1914, other organizations in the city began to participate in the work; representatives from thirty-one clubs, including the Chicago City Club, the Chicago Association of Commerce, and the Chicago Women's Aid, and various representatives from industry, contributed money, support, and staff.[47] And, in 1916, the Board of Education of the City of Chicago took over financing and administering the work of the Vocational Bureau. The Vocational Supervision League continued, however, "to encourage legislation to raise the minimum school age, to provide protective legislation for children already in industry, and to encourage a system of vocational training in the schools which [would] equip children to become skilled workers in some definite field." The League's scholarship committee enabled poor students to take advantage of the vocational training in the high schools.[48] A large part of the scholarship work was conducted by the Committee on Scholarship for Jewish Children, organized in December 1915.[49]

Although the business and philanthropic groups involved in the vocational guidance and placement movement clearly endorsed clerical courses and work as a positive vocational choice for high school students, these organizations never explicitly advocated clerical training and work as a particularly female vocational choice. For example, during the early part of the twentieth century, women's groups in the city were concerned that the board of education was not offering female students technical and industrial education equal to that offered to male students.[50] When the Albert Lane Manual and Industrial Training School opened in 1908, the women in the Association of Collegiate Alumnae were dismayed that there were no classes for girls in the new school.[51] Two years later, the association sent a resolution to the board of education requesting the establishment of a coeducational technical high school. Despite this apparent call for equality between male and female students, these women's groups did not envision women in woodworking or machine or shop classes, but in cooking, sewing, and domestic science courses.[52] The Lucy Flower Technical High School for Girls, which opened in 1912, reflected the notions these club women held regarding what vocational education meant for women; the school did not offer a course in commercial subjects until 1917.

The business groups involved in vocational guidance and placement activities were less explicit about differentiating vocational education for the sexes, and their activities indirectly contributed to women's entrance into clerical training and work. Between 1912 and 1916, the Chicago Association of Commerce actively participated in the work of the league. Raymond Booth, employed by the association, worked with Anne Davis to keep children in school and enrolled in vocational education courses. He described the vocational subject as "purely economic," "a connecting link between the schools and the industries."[53] While working in the schools, when Booth discovered that a child between the ages of fourteen and sixteen was contemplating dropping out, he would send his or her parents a letter. "Your _____ tells me that _____ does not expect to go back to school this fall. This letter is written to let you know that there is not much chance for boys and girls to get good work until they are sixteen, because the best employers will not hire them. The trades never employ children under sixteen, and there are only a few offices that will hire them while they are so young. . . . *It is best for him or her to take studies that will prepare him or her to start in a good trade or in office and commercial work, including shorthand, typewriting, and bookkeeping.* This extra time spent in school will mean more wages all the rest of his or her life because he or she will be able to take and hold a better job"[54] (emphasis added). Other than the Lucy Flower school, there were limited vocational opportunities available for female students except commercial studies. Because of the lack of comparable vocational training options for female students, advocating vocational training for female students probably came to mean advocating commercial education for female students.

Other organizations inadvertently aided women's placement into clerical positions during the period before World War I. In 1912, the Association of Collegiate Alumnae also became involved in another sort of employment service, the Collegiate Bureau of Occupations.[55] The purpose of this downtown bureau was twofold: to encourage women to attend college and to place the college woman who did not want to teach. A position in a business office was just one of many options available. Helen Bennett, the manager of the bureau, reported on her success in placing women in high-level office positions. For example, in 1916, she reported that a call for a bookkeeper in a real estate firm came into her office. One of the two brothers who owned the firm "strongly preferred a man for the positions. We were able," she continued, "to suggest just the right kind of young woman who won over the anti-feminist brother."[56] College women were able to take the most interesting and potentially promotable clerical positions. In 1917, Bennett reported to have placed secretaries with "the Red Cross, with various associations working on behalf of war relief, with all political parties, with the Little Theater, the Engineering Experiment Station of the one of our large universities, heads of departments in other universities, literary men, a well-known social authority who is making a technical survey, the magazine of Poetry, a daily newspaper which wanted a girl to do some secretarial work and to work into reporting, and with all kinds of publishing and business houses."[57] The placement officers of the bureau enthusiastically encouraged college-educated women to pursue a wide variety of fields, from chemists, to housekeepers in settlements; office positions of all types clearly fit into this roster of alternative occupations for the college woman.[58]

The Chicago branch of the Young Women's Christian Association (YWCA) also provided an employment service that aided women's entrance into clerical occupations, without acknowledging women's special relationship to these jobs. During its earliest years, the leaders of the YWCA were not convinced of the benefits to women of clerical employment. Even though the leaders recognized in the 1870s that the typewriter could supply remunerative employment for women, "the Young Women's Christian Association organized with trepidation classes in this new skill. There was hesitation in doing this because the women felt the work of a typist might be too great a strain, both mentally and physically, on a young girl."[59]

The way the YWCA administration viewed clerical work as an occupational option for women reflected the goals and purpose of the organization itself. In its early years, the leaders of the YWCA viewed the woman who worked outside the home as in need of charity and safety. The YWCA was "a place where young persons forced to engage in gainful occupations and depend on their own exertions for a living could retire for protection from the world."[60] Until 1917, the services of the employment bureau reflected this stated purpose by placing women into positions that women had traditionally dominated as nurses, domestic servants, governesses, companions, maids, and seamstresses.[61] These positions extended women's roles in the home into the work place and provided "appropriate" employment until a woman married.

In 1907, the reporter from the employment bureau was dismayed, however, because those using the service were no longer requesting these traditional jobs. "Never has good help been so scarce as in the past year," she claimed. "Girls prefer to go into offices or stores or factories rather than into private families."[62] The statistics from the employment service bear out this reporter's observations. Table 20 demonstrates an erratic increase in the percentage of women placed in clerical positions through the association's employment service.

Because of their own concerns, reformers, educators, administrators, religious leaders, and businessmen provided a variety of services from which future or newly trained female clerical workers benefited. During the years before World War I, female clerical workers increasingly availed themselves of a variety of educational, vocational, and

Table 20. Percentage of Clerical Placements in the Chicago YWCA Employment Bureau, 1896–1917

YEAR	TOTAL PLACEMENTS	CLERICAL PLACEMENTS[a]	
		NUMBER	PERCENT
1896	283	000	0.0
1898	270[b]	25	9.3
1899	297	26	8.8
1900	316	23	7.3
1901	350	19	5.4
1902	391	30	7.7
1904	413	50	12.1
1905	424	57	13.4
1906	537	79	14.7
1908	414[b]	78	18.8
1909	465	94	20.2
1910	484	38	7.9
1911	533	81[c]	15.2
1912	648	147[c]	22.7
1913	560[b]	173[d]	30.9
1914	444[b]	130	29.3
1915	360	70	19.4
1916	450[b]	68	15.1
1917	480	66[c]	13.8

Source: Chicago Young Women's Christian Association, *Annual Reports.* YWCA of Chicago Collection, *19th Annual Report* (1895), p. 30; *22nd Annual Report* (1898), p. 35; *23rd Annual Report* (1899), p. 36; *24th Annual Report* (1900), p. 33; *25th Annual Report* (1901), p. 43; *26th Annual Report* (1902), p. 30; *28th Annual Report* (1904), p. 22; *29th Annual Report* (1905), p. 23; *30th Annual Report* (1906), p. 28; *32nd Annual Report* (1908), pp. 24–25; *33rd Annual Report* (1909), p. 24; *34th Annual Report* (1910), p. 26; *35th Annual Report* (1911), p. 22; *36th Annual Report* (1912), p. 23; *37th Annual Report* (1913), p. 23; *38th Annual Report* (1914), p. 18; *39th Annual Report* (1915), p. 21; *40th Annual Report* (1916), p. 23; *41st Annual Report* (1917), p. 21.

[a]Includes stenographers, cashiers, office clerks, reception room clerks, bookkeepers, secretaries, and addressers.

[b]There were slight discrepancies between the number of total placements provided and the sum of the listed occupations placed. In every case I used the larger number.

[c]May include retail clerks. Listing only mentions "clerks."

[d]Includes retail clerks.

placement services that were not specifically intended for them. By the end of the period, many of those involved in these organizations began to recognize the special needs of the female clerical worker and the necessity for orienting services to her. Just as women's presence in the office contributed to the altering of the gender association of some clerical jobs, so too did women's presence in places that trained and placed workers provoke new attention to the nature of those employment services.

At the Office: Female Clerical Workers' Unions

Women's entrance into the office in significant numbers coincided with the first efforts to organize female workers into trade unions. Organizing was probably not a completely foreign idea to some female clerical workers. General stenographers joined in unions and professional associations throughout the period and qualified women participated in these short-lived efforts. Kittie Van Bodengraven, the president of the Stenographers' and Typists' Association of Chicago, pointed to the success she perceived the National Shorthand Reporters' Association had had in securing high wages and favorable legislation, and claimed that "there is no reason in the world why an organization of commercial stenographers should not be able to do the same thing."[63] The rapid expansion of women into commercial stenography, low-level clerk positions, and business machine operation all created the possibility for more wide-spread and, perhaps, more successful organizing. The National Women's Trade Union League recognized the needs of female clerical workers and attempted to remedy their lack of power in the workplace and to increase wages, improve hours and working conditions, and control entry into the field.

Organizing Chicago's stenographer-typists was on the agenda of Chicago's branch of the Women's Trade Union League from its inception. In 1905, just one year after the Chicago branch was founded, the Stenographers' and Typewriters' Union #11691 appeared in a directory of unions affiliated with the Chicago Federation of Labor.[64] This organization did not last and late in 1908, league members held meetings to form a new Stenographers' and Typists' Association. In 1909, Chicago became one of the five cities in the United States with a stenographers' and typists' union affiliated with the American Federation of Labor

(AFL).[65] The organization met the second and fourth Friday of every month at the Central Eleanor Club, the service and social club of the Eleanor Residences. At the club's rooms downtown, stenographers and typists could listen to talks of professional interest. In addition, members also apparently had the "advantages of the sick benefit fund, the use of the library, and membership in the chorus," courtesy of the Women's Trade Union League.[66] This union was small, with between 100 and 200 members by 1911.[67] Perhaps in response to this low membership, the Stenographers' and Typists' Association asked the organizing committee of the league for help building up the union and the league arranged for an organizer "to canvass as many offices as possible," and for an employment agency to begin the work of the union in earnest.[68]

This union shared many of the goals of the professional associations of the specialized shorthand reporters. League officials believed that the major problem facing stenographer-typists was the decreasing wages caused by "the younger element . . . more and more crowding in, who because of inexperience and inefficiency, and mostly because of financial pressure, accept the most paltry wages."[69] Organizers believed that training, controlling, and grading entrants into the field in a central employment agency would combat this depression of wages. The agency would grade its own workers by having stenographers work as public stenographers in their own employment agency. "In this office, the workers, during their employment would be trained or tested, graded and placed in outside positions as applications for workers were received."[70] In addition, the union would provide free advice to beginners, free medical advice to women, classes in dictation, punctuation, English, and Spanish, free library and reading room privileges at the league, and lectures and social occasions.[71]

Chicago's stenographer-typists did not respond to the 1912 organizing drive. A league report in 1913 stated that "a good many applications were taken care of and some requests from employers for stenographers filled. In December, 1912, the office was given up, as the expense was too great. However, the organization had gained both in members and in publicity so it was felt that although the results were not as great as had been hoped, the work was not wasted."[72] In fact, the union vanished from the list of unions affiliated with the Women's Trade Union League after this date.[73]

The Office Employees Association, formed in 1912, was a more successful union, particularly in the period following World War I.[74] Starting as a union of employees in union offices, the union grew dramatically in 1917, when it began to include workers in the civil service, and by the end of the 1920s, clerks in the civil service constituted the largest percentage of the membership.[75] This union engaged in a number of successful strikes during the late teens and early 1920s, when its membership approached a thousand members.[76] Women, however, never formed a large percentage of the most numerous workers employed in clerical work at city hall—clerks. In 1926, only 18.1 percent of the clerks in the civil service were female. And even though women filled 78.9 percent of the stenographic positions, these positions made up only 26.2 percent of the total clerical workforce in the civil service.[77]

These activities did more for the civil service workers, mostly male, than for the mass of female clerical workers in the business world. During the first decades of the twentieth century, efforts to organize Chicago's female office workers failed. There is a variety of possible explanations. Most importantly, most female clerical workers, particularly stenographer-typists, did not appear interested in a union. Organizers commented on the indifference and even hostility many clerical workers felt towards unions. Kittie Van Bodengraven, the president of the Chicago's Stenographers' and Typists' Association, claimed that "many stenographers—women especially—will scorn the idea of such an organization."[78] Alice Bean, who successfully organized clerical workers in New York City, claimed that "average American office workers do not feel that they are 'wage earners' but have a notion that they are professionals and, therefore, it would be degrading to join a union. They leave unions to factory workers."[79] In addition, the focus of this early union was ill suited to the mass of less-skilled clerical workers. Like the quasi-professional shorthand reporters' associations, these organizers attempted to control, limit, and grade new entrants into the field to keep wages high. They envisioned a strictly regulated craft union. Because of the influx of women into the field and the increased mechanization and rationalization in many newer clerical fields, however, this style of union organizing was inappropriate. The dispersal of small numbers of clerical workers in a larger number of offices may have made union organizing logistically difficult and expensive. It is also possible that the Women's Trade Union League did not commit enough resources to get the organizing drive going. The league abandoned the 1912 drive in Chicago after just one year. Poor, immigrant women who worked in unsanitary, unsafe, low-paid, factory jobs probably merited more immediate attention from the league. There were certainly some limited successes in organizing clerical workers during this period in other cities, most notably New York City, but most were short-lived and did not receive the support from the male-dominated trade union movement necessary to achieve success.[80]

Those women who joined together to promote union organization among women could no sooner ignore the increasing numbers of female clerical workers in their purview than could public school officials and educators, or reformers and businessmen concerned with vocational training and placement. Female clerical workers commanded attention precisely because they were entering positions in the office, the business district, and the world of work where they had not been found previously. Individuals in these disparate arenas reacted to the presence of these women based upon their own professional needs and programmatic visions. The actions of these educators, reformers, and businessmen were often not directly geared to accommodate the female clerical worker, but she often benefited from their actions. Even if most female clerical workers in Chicago remained unorganized, many did seek out commercial education courses and vocational and placement services to help them with their personal journeys from home to school to office. This special, institutional attention solidified, legitimized, and endorsed women's claim to clerical positions.

PART III

Clerical Work as Women's Work, World War I–1930

CHAPTER 7

The Promise of Clerical Work: Image and Reality

*I*N *1919*, a resident in a women's boarding house in Chicago wrote that "no matter how independent the woman, a home is the thing to which she looks forward. But the office experience of many of these girls will create a taste for a daily going out into the world. . . . There is satisfaction and contentment in the triumphs and trials of earning one's bread that is not to be gained in the dependency on human affection; and numberless women are now enjoying making the wheels turn noiselessly in some office who in other decades got their satisfaction from a kitchen or apartment."[1] Clerical work, and the possibility of relatively good wages and independent living, certainly had the potential of altering some women's perceptions of the world of work. The remarkable ambivalence of this young woman's statement suggests that women's concern with reconciling fulfilling work and home life is not an entirely contemporary phenomenon. The continued entrance of women, many of them young, into the ranks of the white-collar labor force during the first decades of the twentieth century coincided with, and was encouraged by, the loosening of many of the social, economic, and political restraints experienced by the nineteenth century woman.[2] Even though the "flapper," vamp, and rich heiress are commonly associated with the new image of womanhood emerging in the 1920s, the working woman was also an important symbol of women's increasing activity within society.[3] The young, single, white-collar woman of the period after World War I was an important transitional figure, both personally and historically, and at least some of these women recognized their unique position.

Clerical work held promise for women. Clerical work was still a relatively new job for women and it was one of the best jobs available to them. Just as Horatio Alger's tales encouraged young boys to set out in the world of work with right values and hard work to achieve success, so too did the popular media of the period after World War I dangle a number of promising possibilities for women. The possibilities were varied and the promise not always the same. Obviously marriage was the one universally, so it seemed, desired prospect for young women engaging in clerical work. But to claim that the image of the female clerical worker in the 1920s was a young woman simply bent on marrying above her station would be far too simplistic. A clerical position could be a way to achieve a number of goals besides domestic bliss.

Image

The coincidence of the continuing sexual division of labor and "scientific management" in offices and the regularizing of women's positions within offices and the city helped to produce the stereotypical female office worker that would become an enduring image throughout the twentieth century. During the 1920s, as the loosening morality of the youth, particularly female youth, received the attention of the nation, clerical work came to represent a form of employment specifically identified with that period in a woman's life cycle between childhood and marriage. In novels, short stories, and films, the female clerical worker of the 1920s could find an easily recognizable and sympathetic character with which to identify.

After World War I, the female clerical worker did become more of an acceptable and identifiable character in various types of cultural depictions. In movies, short stories, and novels, the female clerical worker was no longer simply the innocent victim of lecherous men, or the fallen woman distracting and ruining men; she also appeared in more diverse and appealing roles. Although much of the concern and sensationalism that was characteristic of early cultural depictions of women engaging in office work abated by the 1920s, the mingling of the sexes and different classes still provided the basis for most of the plots of popular fiction and movies. The office provided the perfect setting for what would become one of the most common themes in depictions of female clerical workers throughout the period, the Cinderella story. Although some women did work in these films, they were "still victims of the Cinderella syndrome," realizing their fates "through Prince Charming rather than assume the onerous burden of becoming an entity in [their] own right."[4]

The vast majority of plots of novels, short stories, and movies ended with the female office worker marrying the man of her choice, but analyzing these films only on the basis of their endings obscures the importance of the action of the plot. In these movies, female clerical workers are rarely victims or vamps, but are everyday women who act as office or day-time wives. These female clerical workers, because of their loyalty, virtue, and initiative, are able to help some man, either the boss, a fellow employee, or a sweetheart, because of the contacts, money, and independence she has by engaging in clerical work. The movies and short stories that appeared after World War I still dwelled on the complications that ensued when the classes and sexes mingled in the office, but also demonstrated that certain kinds of behavior that had previously been considered improper for women were now accepted and even desired. In fact, these cultural images of female clerical workers may have provided an important alternative to the "true woman" of the nineteenth century, and to the sexually liberated and, perhaps, threatening flapper of the 1920s. The female clerical worker of the 1920s appeared as a fun-loving, attractive, resourceful, and good girl.

This was exactly the image of the stenographer in one of the earliest feature films about a female office worker. Filmmaker James Montgomery Flagg made *The Stenog* in 1918 as part of a series of films called "Girls You Know."[5] The movie opens with pretty Miss Pitman (Pitman is a form of shorthand writing) daydreaming behind her typewriter. A friend of the boss suggests that he send her on a one-week vacation. He says, "she would probably choose Coney Island—don't let her. Send her to the mountains where it's quiet and restful." The stenographer has a dreadfully boring time in the mountains and escapes with one day left to spend a fun-filled day with her beau at Coney Island, where she receives a proposal of marriage from her young man. Miss Pitman rejects the respectable rest home in favor of the modern amusement park and finds a husband.

In many of these films and stories, the female clerical worker was a woman of respectable, middle-class background who found love by becoming a more sexual, "natural," or "modern" woman. Just as Cinderella had done, she changes from a moth to a butterfly, but unlike Cinderella, she does this on her own initiative. A short story, "The Bite of the Lotus," which appeared in a Chicago woman's magazine, told of the adventures of a stenographer and her boss on a desert island. The boss, an editor, had taken his proper, respectable, thirty-five-year-old stenographer and her mother (as chaperone) to test whether spending time on a desert island does provide the setting for a romantic novel. Miss Simpson gasped as she asked if her boss wanted to fall in love with her. And even though he protests that she is not very promising material, within a few days on the island, Miss Simpson's appearance and demeanor changed and the two fell in love.[6]

In the films of the 1920s, this theme of transformation emphasized the juxtaposition of the old and new types of womanhood.[7] In the popular film *His Secretary* (1925), a "plain and severe stenographer" overhears her two bosses making fun of her appearance. In revenge, the office worker visits a dressmaker and a beautician and transforms herself into a beautiful woman. She arranges for a male friend to play her enraged husband and burst in during a kiss between her and her newly attentive boss. Later on, she reveals her deception and the two marry. Likewise, in the musical *The Golden Calf* (1930), the "plain and old-fashioned girl" stenographer transforms herself into a hosiery model with perfect measurements (hence the title of the film) and presents herself to her boss, a commercial illustrator, for a modeling position. She gets the position and a husband. The opening song in this musical, "You Gotta Be Modernistic," sums up the theme of this genre of film.

The female clerical worker in the films of the twenties, however, usually had to do more than merely transform herself to get her man. In the majority of the films, the female clerical worker, who often starts out as an attractive and modern woman, involves herself in some family or business intrigue, contributes to its resolution, and then wins the affection of her chosen man. She does this by using her feminine wiles, her business acumen, or a combination of the two. For example, in *Smile, Brother, Smile* (1927), Mildred Marvin, a secretary of the Bonfillia Cosmetic Company, helps her fiancé rise in the same company. She intercepts messages from a rival company, allowing her fiancé to prove himself. And, in addition, she transforms herself into a ravishing creature in a modeling demonstration of the product, thereby assuring her fiancé's success. The comedy *From Ladies Only* (1927) began with the boss, Clifford Coleman, discharging all of his female office workers because of their "excessive concern with perfume and hosiery." His secretary, Ruth Barton, warns him that she will exact a price for any information he needs from her after she is gone. Before long, Coleman concedes that Barton is indispensable to the firm and offers to reinstate her. She does not return, however, until he agrees to rehire all of the other women. And of course, after all of this, Ruth and Clifford discover that they love each other.[8]

The image of the female clerical worker was that of a woman who was not only modern, pretty, resourceful, and unafraid to use her feminine charms, but also fundamentally good. Her character in films and short stories often stands alone for virtue and right values amidst a corrupt or decadent society. For example, in the short story, "The Little Petticoat Patriot," Elsie Dean, a stenographer to the managers of a clothing manufacturing establishment, is shocked to discover that her firm is profiting at the expense of soldiers in World War I. When the young, handsome, absentee owner of the firm returns, she resists his advances because she assumes that he is also involved in the profiteering. Before long, however, she learns that he had returned to alter the evil ways of his company. Her high ideals had made her the obvious recipient of her boss's affections.[9] In *Sin Takes a Holiday* (1930), a lawyer marries his stenographer to make his high-society girl friend jealous. Grace, the stenographer, then goes on a trip to Paris to allow her boss to take advantage of the ploy. During her stay she meets a wealthy man who takes her to shops and helps to transform her into a beauty. He proposes marriage, but she remains true to her legal husband and returns to the United States to discover that he loves her too.[10]

The film *The Office Wife* (1930) combines many of the elements of films mentioned above and capitalizes upon this image of the office wife.[11] Pretty, young Ann Murdoch gets a chance to become the boss's private secretary because Andrews, the older, spinsterish-looking private secretary, had fainted after hearing of the boss's imminent marriage to a stylish society woman. Ann is thrilled with the increase in pay and status and later, while discussing all of this with her roommate-sister, she reveals her true intentions. "Let me tell you something," she protests, "I'm not going to give the best years of my life to getting stung like Andrews. Don't you suppose I know what this business game is for a girl?" she continues, "about as fair as a marriage game." After a few difficult months on the job, Ann makes herself completely indispensable to her boss and they get more personal. Over time, she reveals two important messages to both the boss and the audience. First, that she is a good, old-fashioned girl at heart. As she and the boss are walking in a park one afternoon, a child playing comes near and the boss asks her if she likes children and she says yes, she does. He queries, "I suppose they're a little out of fashion," to which Ann replies, "I guess I'm just old fashioned." But, even if she is an old-fashioned girl, she does not embrace nineteenth-century Victorian morality. Her complicated personal life (Ann does have a beau throughout this entire flirtation), her alluring attire, and her flirtatious ways, and even her efficiency in organizing the boss's private and professional affairs, tempts the boss until he succumbs and kisses her. The final obstacle in the way of the two lovers uniting is the boss's society wife. Ann's goodness is underscored as the boss discovers that his glamorous society wife is tiring of him and having an affair with someone else not long after their marriage. Presumably, Ann, the good, efficient, all-American girl, would appreciate her wealthy husband and perform as well as a wife at home as she had at the office.

Sometimes the virtuous and good female clerical worker had to suffer through a period of martyrdom before the quality of her character was rewarded. She often encountered resistance as she attempted to marry into a higher status or enter high society. In *The Trespasser* (1929), a popular film starring Gloria Swanson, a stenographer, Marion, elopes with Jack, a boy from a wealthy family. The boy's father induces him to annul the marriage and arranges a more appropriate match. Marion has Jack's baby in poverty, returns to her former position, and suffers a breakdown from financial pressures. Her employer helps her and ultimately bequeaths Marion a large fortune. After she has proved her virtue and crossed the class boundary on her own, she is rewarded. Jack's society wife dies and she is reunited with him. In similar movies, the female clerical worker perseveres against the prejudice and decadence of the upper classes and is ultimately rewarded by a favorable marriage.[12]

By the 1920s, the image of the female clerical worker had changed from a passive victim or active vamp, to an honest, resourceful, hardworking, fun-loving, good girl.[13] She was not always as completely passive, pure, and chaste as the nineteenth century true woman; but, she was not a frivolous and promiscuous society girl or flapper. She was a girl trying to be good in a changing world, and she almost always got the right man in the end. This image of the female clerical worker undoubtedly had appeal. These films and stories not only provided characters with whom real clerical workers could easily identify, but also depicted a powerful fantasy—the promise of a good marriage if one worked hard, kept up to date, and remained good.

These popular images never really provoked any questioning of women's ultimate fate of abandoning work for marriage and children. One film, *Summer Bachelors* (1926), safely and comically posed the possibility that a female clerical worker might actually choose to shun marriage. The main character of this film, Derry Thomas, decides that she will never marry after witnessing her sisters' unfortunate experiences with men. She organizes a club where men whose wives are away for the summer can meet single girls. She herself meets and falls in love with Tony, whom she believes to be married. After learning that he is single, she rejects his advances. During a party, she is placed under a hypnotic trance by a psychology professor. Only then can she admit her love. Tony arranges for them to be married before she awakens from her trance. When she does, she is at first displeased, but then becomes reconciled to her fate.

These movies rarely included a serious depiction of the work experience of the female clerical worker or the difficulties female clerical workers encountered in reconciling their work and personal lives. In a number of novels about female clerical workers written during the same period, however, authors examined the female clerical worker and her relationship to American life more critically. C. Wright Mills observed that "in serious literature white-collar images are often subjects for lamentation; in popular writing they are often targets for aspiration."[14] Mills was certainly correct when noting that these novels focus on how a female clerical worker attempted to chart a course between two seemingly mutually exclusive goals: success at business and a fulfilling personal life. After his analysis of some of these novels, Mills observed that "career has been substituted for marriage," and concluded that, "the conflict of the white-collar girl is resolved . . . she is in the nunnery."[15]

Actually, this assessment is too simplistic. These novels do not depict the life of the white-collar woman negatively, just realistically. If she has trouble reconciling work life and a personal life, it is not her fault; rather, it is the fault of the "capitalist system," the "class system," or of unsympathetic or ignorant men, or other uncontrollable, outside forces. The female clerical worker in these novels is not always a white-collar nun. Like the female clerical workers in the popular media, the white-collar woman in these novels are ordinary and undistinguishable women.

Her work experiences, however, permit her to grow into a woman who is not at all commonplace.

Booth Tarkington's *Alice Adams* (1921), Sinclair Lewis's *The Job* (1917), Nathan Asch's *The Office* (1925), John Dos Passos's *U.S.A.* (1937), Christopher Morley's novels, *Kitty Foyle* (1937) and *Human Being* (1935), and Ruth Suckow's *Cora* (1929) all seriously consider the life of the female clerical worker between the turn of the century and 1930.[16] The female clerical worker in these novels came from similar backgrounds, shared certain personality characteristics, traveled similar paths from home to school to work, and held similar views regarding work, marriage, and their futures. These similarities reveal the issues that critical observers of the day felt were important when depicting the lives and work experiences of the female white-collar worker.

All of the female clerical worker characters came from modest middle-class or working-class families living in small towns or urban backwaters. In all of these novels except for *Human Being,* the young girl's decision to train for clerical work was precipitated by illness or death of a father, or some other economic calamity in the family. Minnie Hutzler in *Human Being* seemed motivated to train for and engage in clerical work by a simple desire to make something of herself. In all of the novels except *Alice Adams* and *Cora,* the young woman ultimately leaves her home town environment for exciting and well-paid work. Tarkington ends his novel with Alice deciding to attend a business college. Cora Schwietert began working in an office to help lift her family from its day-to-day struggle for survival. Cora's father was a lovable German immigrant who had spent most of his life traveling, with his family in tow, from town to town, trying to make his tailoring business work. His repeated failures provoked Cora to single-handedly take over the coordination of the family's budget. In most instances, these characters received their business training in high schools and private business colleges. In Lewis's *The Job,* Una Golden, on the death of her father, decides that her small town in Pennsylvania holds nothing but low-paying jobs and unappealing widowers. She decides to take her mother with her to New York City, and enroll in a private business college.

Even though these women do encounter challenges in their pursuit of employment, they are by no means exceptional women. The authors present these characters as conventional, well-intentioned, warm-hearted girls. Lewis describes his main character, Una, as "important, not because she is an Amazon or a Ramona, but because she is representative of some millions of women in business, and because in a vague but undiscouraged way, she keeps on inquiring what women in business can do to make human their existence of loveless routine."[17]

The female clerical workers in three of these novels were unable to reconcile fulfilling work and marriage. In *U.S.A.*, Janey Williams becomes emotionally attached to her boss, J. Ward Moorehouse, and foregoes any personal life of her own to remain his faithful stenographer. After her father's financial ruin and loss of a rich suitor, the main character in *Alice Adams* decides to "enter the wooden stairway leading up to Frincke's Business College—the very doorway she had always looked up to as the end of youth and the end of hope."[18] In *The Office*, an interesting novel about the effects of a business failure on the workers in an office, the stenographer, Gertrude Donavan, consents to marry a lowly bookkeeper when her fantasy was to run away with the boss.

Yet even in *U.S.A.* and *Alice Adams* the fates of the two female characters were not that grim. In all of these novels, clerical work itself provided the potential for fulfillment and advancement. Although Janey Williams never married, she found her work in various legal and public relations firms engaging and remunerative. Although Alice Adams feared the entrance to the business college, once up the stairs she caught a hint of new independence. "Half way up the shadows were the heaviest, but after the place seemed brighter. There was an open window overhead somewhere, she found, and the steps at the top were gay with sunshine."[19] In fact, Una Golden, Minnie Hutzler, and Kitty Foyle all enjoyed office work and achieved a remarkable degree of success in their business lives. Lewis wrote in *The Job*, "it must not be supposed that Una or her million sisters in business were constantly and actively bored by office routine. . . . She [Una] had real satisfaction in the game of work—in winning points and tricks, in doing her work briskly and well, in helping Mr. Wilkins to capture clients. . . . She was rather more interested in her day's work than are the average of meaningless humanity who sell gingham and teach algebra and cure boils and repair lawnmowers, because she was daily more able to approximate perfection, to look forward to something better—to some splendid position at twenty or even twenty-five dollars a week. She was certainly in no worse plight than perhaps 95 million of her free and notoriously red-blooded fellow citizens."[20]

Engaging in clerical work gave these fictional women an independence that was altogether new. And with this independence came two new problems. First, many of these female characters had to forge a new sort of morality for themselves. In the company of men at work, and alone in a large city, the values of their home towns and mothers no longer seemed relevant or helpful. After a short time in business schools or offices, these female characters often became accustomed to male company and manners. Una Golden, Minnie Hutzler, and Kitty Foyle all sought physical, emotional, and intellectual companionship with men, and had unsuccessful love affairs. They did not despair their transgressions, just that their affairs did not succeed. In his novel, *Human Being,* Morley described Minnie Hutzler as a woman whose "personal scruples were delicate and clear. Her virtue was more consistent, perhaps, more certain, than that of many circumspect sisters who would have buzzed her frailty. The gift of her favors was a prerogative, not a perquisite. It was truly a gift; to be granted at her own pleasure, not by rule or rote; she was willing to assume the consequences."[21] These were women who had forged a new morality out of their personal needs and the necessities of their lives as working women.

Because of their new morality and independent work lives, these female characters often had trouble finding fulfilling relationships with men. They valued the independence afforded by office work and were reluctant to enter any relationship that would threaten that freedom. In fact, after their failed affairs, Una Golden, Minnie Hutzler, and Kitty Foyle shied away from any further serious relationships with men. It is interesting that these three novels end with the possibility of the heroines' imminent marriage. But these new marriages would have to be altogether different. All three women had achieved success in their careers and had no intention of giving up work for marriage. In addition, even though they still acknowledged a need for a personal relationship, none was willing to relive earlier mistakes. At the end of *The Job,* Una Golden had worked her way to a responsible position as a partner in a hotel chain. As she was introduced to her staff, she recognized that one of her employees was Walter, a man that she had been in love with over a decade before when she was still a lowly stenographer. She had succeeded while he had remained at the same level job. Despite this difference in position, they acknowledged their persistent feelings for each other. Yet Una had no intention of relinquishing her job, security, and responsibilities for marriage as she had done in a disastrous prior marriage. Walter implored her to marry him, claiming that she need not give up anything and that they could both continue to work. She considered the prospect. "Maybe . . . the business woman will bring about a new kind of marriage in which men will *have* to keep up respect and courtesy."[22]

Ruth Suckow's *Cora* merits special analysis not only because it is even more ambiguous than the other novels discussed, but also because it was written by a woman and may be based on some of the author's own experiences.[23] This novel is not simply about the meaning of the experience of clerical work, but more generally about gender roles in American society. Throughout the book, Cora faces responsibilities and desires that come into conflict, and expectations that are not fulfilled. To help her family, Cora takes a clerical position, and because she is intelligent, hard-working, and possessed of a cool and attractive demeanor, she works her way up in her company until she is indispensable. In fact, Cora herself acknowledges that were she a man, her job title, salary, and promotability would have been better. Nevertheless, this position allows her to take care of her family financially, until all that remain in her household are her mother and an unmarried aunt.

Years of self-sacrifice take their emotional toll, however. Just as Cora was about to be promoted to the coveted position of manager, she, and friends and family alike, decide that she needed "a change." Cora decides to go on a vacation to Yellowstone where she meets a man whom, a week later, she marries. At first, Cora enjoys the love, attention, inactivity, and adventure of her married life, but things begin to sour quickly. In just a few months, her husband vanishes, leaving Cora with a child. After several months of recuperation, Cora returns home with her daughter. Finding inactivity intolerable, Cora reenters the world of work, and once again, finds herself in a high-level office job. Before too long, she joins a rich society lady in a business venture in children's clothing that makes her quite comfortable. The story ends with Cora, not a particularly "maternal" parent, fussing over her daughter's dress while waiting for her evening's date with a rich married man.

This is certainly not a standard Cinderella story and Cora is not a typical female character. She spends, in fact, most of the novel shunning what society considered to be natural gender roles for women. Cora was the financial and emotional strength of her family; she arranged for the jobs and even spouses of her siblings; she rebuffed any serious advances from suitors. When she finally "submitted" to a week of pleasure, the results were disastrous. It was Cora's ability, in fact, to work, to command respect in an office, and to do something productive, that saved her in the short term and that gave her life meaning throughout the book, even as she grew weary and tired of its routine and unequitable rewards.

Cora can certainly be read as a cautionary tale; perhaps, if Cora had not been forced to deviate from behavior acceptable for women, her life would have followed a more "normal" path. Certainly, Cora was continually faced with having to make a choice between taking charge of her family's future or submitting to the winds of fate (as her sisters did). But I do not think that this is the overriding message here. Cora did not perceive a choice, but only one logical course of action. And, more importantly, the book reminds the reader over and over again of the importance and the strength of women's friendships. The book, in fact, opens with the teenaged Cora frolicking with her best life-long friend. It was Cora's friendship with Evelyn, who came from an upper-middle-class family, that instilled in Cora the desire to do better for herself and her family. In addition to Cora's close familial relationships with women, she also belonged to women's clubs, befriended two professional women, who by all appearances were engaged in a "companionate" marriage, and named her daughter after the hospital nun who provided her with strength after her husband deserted her. Suckow emphasized the importance of sisterhood at the end of the book. Cora's affair with a married man certainly attracted notice by the women of the neighborhood and even Cora tried to scrutinize her own reasons for engaging in this behavior. Nevertheless, it was what she wanted to do and she walked out of the door to meet her companion, leaving her daughter with her mother and aunt. Tongues wagged in the neighborhood, but not Mrs. Rawlins's. A gossip and busybody, "Mrs. Rawlins, although quite unnoted for tolerance, was the one who stuck up for Cora . . . and admired in Cora things that she would never have forgiven in another woman," because she, "was one woman who did as she pleased." Mrs. Rawlins defended Cora because, "she's got *some*-where, anyway!" (emphasis in original).[24] Cora's work permitted her to do what she wanted and to make a success of herself. Certainly, this is a different portrayal of women's relationship to the world of work than most "traditional" depictions.

By 1930, the image of the female clerical worker had evolved from the victim or the vamp to an appealing, new woman. In the films of the 1920s, the female clerical worker was usually a good girl. She was not, however, an "old-fashioned girl" or a "flapper." She embodied the freer morality of the 1920s, yet clung on to the hard-working virtue and goodness of an earlier time. In the short stories and in the movies, she almost always married her Prince Charming, yet the ways she went about attracting her husband were altogether new.

In the novels written after World War I, the character of the female clerical worker was more complex. The women in these novels sought to redefine their relationships to the world of work and to the world of men and marriage. As it surely would have been for any male character, the key to success for these female characters was both a fulfilling personal and work life. And, at least in some of these novels, the authors presented the possibility of this outcome for their readers. Those women who did not achieve this ideal were subject to forces beyond their control. The female clerical workers in these novels were not stereotypes or nuns; they were very human characters facing real challenges and conflicts.

Reality

Did these images of clerical workers in the popular media reflect or affect real clerical workers during the 1920s? Because of the social services and relatively good wages provided clerical workers in the 1920s, many office workers could lead secure and independent work lives. This circumstance, so unusual for working women, provoked some female clerical workers in Chicago, at least, to overtly question traditional assumptions about women's relationship to the world of work.

Between 1898 and 1930, thousands of Chicago's single, independent, young, middle-class, white-collar women, who called themselves business women, lived in Eleanor Association residential clubs. Eleanor residences provided safe, respectable, home-like low-cost housing, and a vast array of social services that allowed white-collar women to lead relatively independent lives. At its peak, the Eleanor Association boasted of six residences located throughout the city, a downtown lunch-room and social center, a junior club, a lodge, and a summer camp for inexpensive vacations, all for business women.[25] The voices that appear in records of the Eleanor Association provide us with a unique and rare insight into the feelings, thoughts, desires, preoccupations, and hopes of the clerical worker between World War I and the stock market crash of 1929.

The leaders of the Eleanor Association started the residential clubs and other services to ease the transition between home and work for the women of this new occupational group. An editorial that appeared after the death of Ina Law Robertson, the founder of the Eleanor Association, stated, "Miss Robertson was not a reformer in the popular sense. . . . Her business was to make the transition of women from home to life in business easier and less dangerous. She was really a home-maker on a grand scale."[26] In the midst of unsettling changes, the leaders of the Eleanor Association created a home-like refuge for these women and perhaps functioned as surrogate mother figures. Miss Robertson de-scribed the first residence as an appealing alternative to rooming houses. "Its rooms are kept clean and as neat as possible. Single beds are the rule, from one to three in each room. There are double parlors, a good reading room with a modest library, and a commodious office. Two good pianos, a sewing machine, and a Remington typewriter are for the pleasure and profit of the guests. The dining room is large and has good heat, light, and ventilation. Each table seats eight persons. The table is selected with care, meals are well cooked and daintily served."[27] The Eleanor clubs stood as a haven or way station between the security of family, home, traditional values, and a changing new world. After recalling her disheartening search for housing in Chicago, one resident wrote in the *Eleanor Record,* "I looked around at the quiet restfulness of the parlor, the cleanliness of the rooms, and almost wept at the luck that brought me to such a lovely home."[28] (See Illustrations 8, 9, and 10.)

In some ways, the Eleanor residences were more appealing than the homes that many women left behind. Each residence had its own club council, which democratically decided house rules and activities. In addition, although many residents had the responsibility of supporting themselves, they were also freed from some of the domestic chores they would undoubtedly have been required to do if they lived at home, such as cooking and shopping for food. Time-consuming and boring activities such as sewing, laundry, darning, and spring cleaning were often organized collective activities in the residences. The parlors in each of the residences were available to each woman for entertaining whomever she wished, usually women from her office or a particular beau. There was a 10:30 curfew for residents, but exceptions could be made if a woman desired to stay out until 11:30 to attend entertainment in the city. And important to some residents, the Eleanor clubs sponsored socials with men's organizations, particularly with the Young Men's Christian Association's residences or colleges.

The leaders of the association envisioned that these residences would not only provide safe and home-like housing for the business woman, but also teach her lessons in sorority, civic duty, and service. The leaders promoted these ideals through various institutional structures as well as by the establishment of customs and organized rituals. Women were encouraged to spend their leisure hours together, either in organized cultural activities, such as lectures, hikes, and exercise classes, or in cleaning and house activities. In addition, the association opened the Eleanor Camp in Lake Geneva, Wisconsin in 1909, where, for a small expense, business women could spend their two-week vacations in the fresh air. Every month, one day was set aside to celebrate the birthdays of residents born in that month. The large cake was baked with a penny, a thimble, and a ring inside to indicate which woman had riches, spinsterhood, or marriage in her future. In addition to pledges and songs, the members and officials engaged in a candle-lighting ceremony on special occasions. This ritual involved each woman lighting her own candle from a central flame symbolizing the passing of the Eleanor "light" to each member, and to demonstrate the connection among the Eleanor women. The leaders of the Association chose the name Eleanor because it meant "light" in Greek. The symbol of the association was the betty lamp, a small hand lamp from colonial days. It was chosen because it would "represent not only the ideal of the greater light, but also the little light which each would carry with her as she goes through life."[29]

Residents of the Eleanor clubs, however, needed little organized prodding to form strong bonds among themselves. The Eleanor residences were environments where women could maintain their friendships and family ties. One official of the club remembered that many women were accompanied to the residences by at least one parent. "When they applied for a room in one of our clubs," she stated, "parents seemed more reconciled to leaving them because they thought they would be in good hands."[30] In other cases, women came together in groups from their home towns. For example, in September 1920, the Club Five reporter stated, groups of girls from Pennsylvania, Texas, and Minnesota had come to take an expert course at the Gregg School to improve their clerical skills, and five girls from Mississippi Women's College had moved in so that they could study music at the Columbia School of Music. "Occasionally," the Club Five reporter exclaimed, "the better part of a whole town moves in."[31] In 1915, an *Eleanor Record* reporter commented that five sets of sister were occupying rooms in her club and exclaimed, "Come on girls and bring your sisters with you!"[32]

The residences also provided the opportunity for new female friendships to develop. These female friendships apparently were quite strong and fully accepted throughout the 1920s. Often, the *Eleanor Record* reporters revealed these bonds by proclaiming the joy of certain women when their married chums returned to the club for a visit. Sometimes, women left the club to follow another woman. In October 1927, for example, the Club Five reporter wrote that "Annette Kesphol couldn't get along without Edna Naystrom and so she has gone to join her in Philadelphia."[33] In February 1923, the Club Three reporter claimed that her club was suffering from a "friendship complex," and proceeded to list the various couples inhabiting the club.[34] The strength and acceptability of these friendships comes through in this account of an incident in Club Six: "Time—After 10:30 P.M. Place—Miss Laura Holmes' room. Miss Gunn is peacefully sleeping. Miss Holmes loves her 'roomie' and so she tiptoes over to her and lightly touches her lips. True to her name, Miss Gunn gives out the most unearthly shriek. The entire second floor is aroused; they all have visions. Then they learn the truth. Miss Holmes had merely bestowed a kiss!"[35] (see Illustration 11).

The leadership of the Eleanor Association also encouraged women to participate in civic issues. One pet project of the association's officials was the Eleanor League. Founded in 1915, this organization housed young women between the ages of fourteen and eighteen who were not able to continue school. The association provided the building and volunteers from its membership for this self-supporting organization.

Eleanor women could also participate in the Eleanor Women's Model City. In conjunction with the Women's City Club of Chicago, the Eleanor Club organized interested members into a model city in which women took a specific task to learn how city government works. Monthly talks by Chicago's city officials supplemented this educative process. And in 1916, the U.S. presidential election caused a great surge of activity and discussion in the clubs. The *Eleanor Record* printed statements by Eleanor Association officials endorsing their favorite of the three candidates, and women were encouraged to register and vote.[36] A Club Two correspondent wrote, "the final assurance of victory of the President came as a relief to everybody, for we had almost talked ourselves out of breath!" In Club Four, "it's almost over and our pulses are back to normal. My, what a thrill we had!" And finally, the Club Five reporter was glad for the peace in her house now that the election was over. "We were a house divided against itself for Wilson and Hughes and the library was the scene of many a hot pre-election debate."[37]

Eleanor Association leadership and residents could agree on the importance of sorority and civic duty, but the issue of work and service revealed the generational differences between the two groups of women. Both the association's leaders and the residents believed that work was a positive experience for a young woman, but for different reasons. The motto of the Eleanor Association, "Love and Service," not only spoke to the civic and political activities of women, but also prescribed the attitude that the leadership believed was appropriate for women to have toward their work. As one sponsor of the association expressed it, "The [Eleanor] ideal is to give young women the opportunity to develop the best that is in them. The highest impulse in human life is love, and life dominated by love reaches its highest development. But love demands expression and must be kept alive and flowing by activity. The ideal of Eleanor work, therefore, is love expressing itself in service."[38] The leaders expected women to bring the ideals of "love and service" to all of their endeavors, personal, political, or pecuniary. Women's special qualities would enhance her desirability and uplift the workplace. Work, the leadership believed, was a form of service, an activity which would provide not merely a livelihood for the person engaged in it, but also a valuable service to society.

As time went on, however, the residents of the Eleanor clubs began to delineate between service and profit. Although these women seemed anxious to take up civic and service activities throughout the teens, this interest did not persist into the twenties. Female residents no longer wanted to work to express the ideals of "love and service," but to get ahead. They did not seem to need any further justification for working than the hope that if one works hard, "one gets just what she goes after."[39] In an article describing the efforts of two sisters who took over their father's business after his death, the author rejoiced that these women succeeded, "never once compromising their womanhood by their work, but rather enobling the work by their doing it." But the reporter also stated that the qualities that brought about their business success were common sense, activity, diligence, and self-dependence, not particularly feminine qualities.[40]

In fact, the women who wrote about their work in the *Eleanor Record* saw the business woman of their generation as someone "who has ideals in her work, who is not merely tiding over until she marries, but is paying herself into her profession in order to get back an increase in her own value."[41] This vanguard role required that these women pay special attention to their behavior so that they would "not bring down condemnation upon the whole class of working women." Apparently, they felt that their appearance was as important as were the ideals they brought to their work. One Club Six reporter stated that "we musn't dress too much or 'they' will say we spend all our money on clothes; we musn't dress too little or 'when women go into business they lose all their femininity'; we musn't be too independent; there was never a time when women found it so hard to know what to do and when and how to do it."[42] When this statement was made in 1915, the role of the business woman was still fairly new upon the commercial scene, but these young, independent and trained women clearly desired to advance beyond the gains they had recently made. Many women of the Eleanor Association were constantly trying to better their positions by taking courses in business colleges and night schools.

Even if the business women of these clubs did not embrace all of the values that the leaders attempted to foster among its residents, the price, comfort, safety, and company in the clubs may have outweighed this intrusion to many business women. During the early, crucial years of women's entrance into clerical occupations in Chicago, residential clubs like the Eleanor clubs undoubtedly helped many young, single, out-of-town women adjust more easily to living and working in the city. Even if these business women ultimately left these residences to take up house-keeping on their own or with friends, or married, the residential club provided a safe haven or way station that endorsed values familiar to these women.

Within this comfortable, safe, and familiar institution, these women were able to create and express their own culture. In the Eleanor Association's monthly journal, the *Eleanor Record,* residents of the clubs reported on their perceptions of themselves and their relationship to their world. These women perceived that they were personally and historically at a transition point. Personally, Eleanor women regarded their stay in the boarding-house and in the world of work as transitory. For these years, they existed between their role as a child in a family and their role as a wife and mother in a family. Historically, Eleanor women saw themselves standing between two worlds. They pictured the past as a traditional, Victorian world, a world of true womanhood, and the world of their grandmothers and mothers. Eleanor women saw a different world around them, however. They saw a new world where women bobbed their hair, wore short skirts, worked for personal satisfaction, and embraced a freer morality.

Club residents revealed their perceptions of their personal and historical positions in their play life. They engaged in performances and parties called "man parties," "kid parties," "old maid or spinster parties," and mock weddings and funerals. These events are best understood as a form of ritualistic behavior for the following reasons. First, these performances were entirely the creation of the young women in the clubs, with no prompting from the leadership or any other group or individual outside the residences. Second, many of the activities occurred on such ritualistic occasions as Halloween, wedding showers, St. Patrick's Day, and birthdays, although Eleanor women altered the traditional behavior that one associated with these events. Third, Eleanor women repeatedly evoked certain images and metaphors in their performances and parties, suggesting that these images and metaphors were easily and generally understood by the participants.

Anthropologists have recently begun to examine the appropriateness of defining and analyzing rituals in modern, western society. Barbara Myerhoff claims that rituals "deal with paradox and conflict," providing a new meaning to life changes, and the relationships of the individual to his or her society. Individuals in modern society have, perhaps, greater need for this process, but "are left to devise for [them]selves the myths, rituals, and symbols needed to endow life with clarity and significance."[43] Examining these rituals along with what the residents said about their lives, as well as in light of their historical positions in the transformation of clerical work, will provide the most complete picture of how Eleanor women saw themselves and their world.

Between 1916 and 1924, the writers in the *Eleanor Record* reported on twelve "kid parties." Kid parties involved the women residents exchanging their everyday clothes for the garments of male and female infants and small children. Kid parties could occur spontaneously in a corridor of a residence, but, most often, they occurred on Halloween celebrations, birthdays, St. Valentine's Day, and wedding showers. In July 1916, a reporter from Club One described how new residents were "naturalized" into the Eleanor residence through a "Juvenile Party." During one Halloween party, "dressed as children, the guests passed down the receiving line of ghosts, followed the old witch to her den to receive a fortune dipped out of her caldron, and then betook themselves to old-fashioned games." The reporter continued that "the years fell away from us and we leaped back into childhood with leapfrog."[44] During one wedding shower, "all sorts of kid games were played, after which the frolickers assembled in the parlor. Here the bride-to-be was enthroned on a cushion in the center of the room, while the girls formed a circle about her on the floor" (to give her gifts).[45] During a birthday party, "many of the girls were dressed as boys and were remarkably like boys with their shingle hair cuts, and they had a delightful time playing 'make me a child again, just for tonight.' There was nothing dignified about that party and everyone had an exceedingly good time."[46] Women often commented on the contrast between their childhood play and their demeanor at work. "One could scarcely believe," wrote one reporter, "that the host of children . . . would the next day be sedate and efficient business women."[47] And similarly, after a weekend hike, one woman reported, "one would never guess that Monday morning would find this same group of 'happy kids' sitting behind a desk with all the dignity that goes to make up a stenographer, secretary, and other positions the girls hold."[48] (See Illustration 12.)

Women in the residences also dressed up as Victorian spinsters for "spinster conventions" and "Old Maid Clubs." Between 1916 and 1924, four of these events were reported, two occurring for no apparent reason, one for a birthday party, and one on Easter Sunday. During these rituals, club members dressed in the fashions of 1882, in leg-of-mutton sleeves, miniature waistlines, and befeathered hats, and spoke of or acted out the outdated expectations placed on women's behavior in those days. In 1916, girls with birthdays in February staged a suffrage meeting, "in which different types of women were represented. After a choice song on leap year, 'the Hope of All' had been sung, Susan B. Anthony cut the cake with a huge carving knife."[49] In May 1924, a spinsters' convention at Club Six debated the subjects of "women's spear" [sic], and modern dressing. After religious speeches in Club One on Easter Sunday, 1922, a performance began that consisted of a farce and musical sketch called the "Old Maids Association." The secretary of the association called the roll, and the "members" answered with quotations such as "of all the saddest words that ever was writ, the saddest is these—I'm single yit!" After this, the "Watch and Wait Committee for Incoming Widowers and Bachelors" suggested the possible availability of two widowers and two bachelors. "As the meeting was about to adjourn, the maids desperately resolved to live up to the aim of the Club, 'Women's highest duty is to adorn a home.' At this crucial moment, Professor Makerneux [make her new] stepped in. After the ladies recovered from such a shock as seeing a man—an attractive Frenchman at that—he proceeded to make each maid anew with his magical machine." The maids were then transformed into a flapper, golf champion, artist, co-ed, nurse, bride, and so on, allowing them to "fulfill the motive of the club as quickly as they chose."[50]

Professor Makerneux was not the only man who appeared in these rituals. Men appeared in "man parties," a mock prom, a mock wedding, and a mock funeral. At the mock prom, couples promenaded through the first-floor rooms. Those women who dressed as men represented stereo-typical images of manhood. One women "presented a very striking male, the type that one usually encounters on the links or on the tennis courts," and the reporter warned the girls to beware because " 'he' casts a wicked eye." A "regular beau brummel, and an engineer on the Santa Fe Railroad" also appeared as dates for the Club residents.[51] In 1916, when two Club Four women announced their intentions to marry, the residents enacted a funeral with a woman dressed as a lawyer overseeing the procession. This procession "entered to the strains of Chopin's Funeral March, led by a tiny Cupid and made up of a lawyer, and four mourners bearing a small box. This was found to contain various and sundry articles dear to the hearts of the girls, but which now must be willed to friends left in single blessedness. Among these articles were two large packages of love-letters, bequeathed to the library of Club Four for the benefit of those who have not the privilege of perusing such choice bits of literature." One resident dressed as the lawyer, "read the will with great dignity, while the mourners wailed . . . over the loss of the two from our midst."[52]

On St. Patrick's Day, 1923, the women who lived in Club Three staged one performance for their male guests and one for themselves. In the parlor, a symphony orchestra "rendered everything but symphony. Jazz was its main feature." In addition, the reporter stated that two women were dressed like their grandmothers, "or better still, the old-fashioned girl . . . and sang, 'Crinoline Days'." While all of this was going on upstairs, downstairs in the recreation room of the club, other club women were enacting another ritual . . . a mock wedding. Several women dressed up as the groom and other male members of the wedding party. One woman played the role of a recently escaped inmate of an insane asylum and attempted to stop the ceremony, but another woman, dressed as a guard, took her away, and the wedding continued.[53]

These activities were not simply expressions of play and frolic. Because of where these enactments took place and because of the historical circumstances of those who devised and participated in them, this leisure activity suggests deeper meaning. The Eleanor residences not only provided these white-collar women with the social space in which to enact these rituals, but also may have actually provoked this activity. The clubs allowed women to live relatively fulfilling, independent lives. Future decisions, therefore, could be a matter of choice, not necessity. These rituals reveal how these women perceived their transitional positions both personally and historically and how they assessed their choices for the future.

On a personal level, the evocation of childhood was, obviously, a striking theme. In the clubs, residents could maintain their childhood friendships and family ties. Groups of women from the same family or home town often lived together in the residences and residents who came alone had a houseful of "sisters" available for companionship and play. The friendships that developed at the Eleanor Association were apparently strong. Even though the Eleanor residents were independent, twentieth-century women, they still clung to strong emotional ties with other women to ease the transition from home to the world of work.[54] Kid parties helped these women to maintain or recreate the close relationships of their youths.

Kid parties often occurred at turning points in a woman's life, and involved the juxtapositions of the carefree play of childhood and the reality of the residents' lives. Women chose to dress up like children to celebrate when one in their midst aged a year or had decided to marry. The presence of the carefree child at a birthday celebration or a wedding shower posed an opposition to the purpose of the celebration itself, between a forward movement in an individual's life cycle and the childish images of their pasts, suggesting that these women perceived that their present life was a sharp departure from their pasts.

Kid parties may have also expressed how these women felt about their work and independent lives. Clerical work was a relatively new occupation for women, and employers required that their stenographers possess a respectable and responsible manner, in addition to the requisite skills. Club women claimed that they took their work seriously and saw the business woman of their generation as someone, "who has ideals in her work, who is not merely tiding over until she marries, but is paying herself into her profession in order to get back an increase in her own value."[55] The pages of the *Eleanor Record* are filled with accounts and advice from women, many of them residents in the club, who had struggled, but achieved success in their careers.[56] Nevertheless, at kid parties a responsible, serious business woman could delight in undignified and raucous behavior. Descriptions of these parties often included how, the next day, these "kids" turned into dignified business women.[57] The activities of the kid parties, therefore, served as an opposition to the rigorous, new demands on the business woman of the early twentieth century.

These rituals also suggested how these women envisioned their future lives. They appeared to act out two options in their rituals: spinsterhood and marriage. In all of the "old maid club meetings" spinsters appear as ridiculous, desperate old maids with outdated beliefs. This was particularly true during the "Old Maids Association Meeting" on Easter Sunday, 1922, when Professor Makerneux transformed the old maids into modern women. While the Eleanor women mocked the stereotypical image of the Victorian spinster, they may have also been rejecting spinsterhood as an option for their futures.

Marriage fared better than spinsterhood as an option for the future, yet some of the language residents of the Eleanor clubs used to describe marriage suggests that these women were ambivalent about this happy state. In most cases, these women described marriage and success in a career as mutually exclusive. For example, when four women in Club Five announced their intentions to marry, the reporter claimed that these women, with "bright prospects before them in the business world," had "chosen to invest in happiness rather than individual success."[58] The metaphors some writers chose to describe marriage suggest some ambivalence regarding leaving their independent life for marriage. Although the tone was jocular, residents frequently equated marriage to committing a crime, or submitting to an overwhelming force. For example, in 1921, Miss Ona Hill was reported to have left for her Iowa home, "with the avowed intention of committing matrimony." The reporter continued, "[w]e would have like[d] to have had her with us until the close of the school term at least, but Dan Cupid proved too much for her and she finally succumbed."[59] One reporter described the future husband of one of the residents as a "bold brigand" who "might be proud of his plunder."[60] Cupid was often described as a kidnapper, showing up "when we least expect it and taking one of our girls."[61]

Like the reports on the betrothal of certain residents, rituals concerned with or prompted by an imminent marriage revealed ambivalence. On the one hand, marriage brought love, companionship, greater financial security, and familial and societal acceptance. But, the rituals suggested that these women also saw marriage as a sharp break from their independent lives in the Eleanor residences. When one in their midst declared her intention to leave, residents enacted the future separation. During the wedding shower, the bride-to-be was "enthroned on a cushion in the center of the room, while the girls formed a circle about her on the floor." In this ritual, the woman leaving is physically separated from the other members of the club. The equation of marriage with death in the mock funeral also functions to dramatically separate the soon-to-be bride from the residents remaining in "single blessedness" at the club. In the mock wedding, the separation of the bride from the residents is threatened by the insane person, but this disturbance soon ends and the marriage ceremony continues.

These rituals may also reveal how these women felt about the separation brought on by marriage. The wedding shower was different from traditional showers because little children, not mature women, celebrated the bride-to-be's separation from the club. The mock funeral was not a typical funeral either. The presence of the tiny cupid and the love letters in the funeral procession suggested that love, not disease or old age, caused the figurative death of the two women. Therefore, marriage represented two opposing qualities—love and death/separation. In the mock wedding, the traditional ceremony was interrupted by the appearance of the asylum inmate. One can certainly interpret this scene as a form of vaudeville, designed by the women to ridicule insane people. One can also interpret the action of the inmate as embodying the alternative to marriage, spinsterhood, or an opposition to the separation that resulted from marriage, sisterhood. But, as the guard takes the inmate away, the threat of spinsterhood and sisterhood is removed and the opposition is resolved, so the marriage continues. In all of these rituals, some alteration of the traditional ceremony can be interpreted as representing an opposition to marriage. If these women had any doubts about leaving their single, independent lives in the Eleanor clubs, these rituals would have helped them to act out and resolve these doubts.[62]

These rituals also suggest how Eleanor women saw themselves historically as women. Residents played "old-fashioned games" and dressed as "old-fashioned girls." Old-fashioned meant Victorian, or, as they described it, "like our grandmothers." These old-fashioned women were usually spinsters who only wanted to devote their entire life to marriage and a home. Residents seemed to mock both the "true woman" and the spinster in their humorous rituals. At the "Old Maids Association Meeting," the suffrage birthday party, and the St. Patrick's Day Party, modern women stood in sharp contrast to these old-fashioned women. At the "Old Maids Association Meeting," Professor Makerneux transformed the spinsters into a variety of contemporary women. During the 1923 St. Patrick's Day party celebration, the women juxtaposed the images of the old-fashioned girl and the new woman in their entertainment for their male guests. Two women dressed as old-fashioned girls and sang and spoke of what they referred to as "Crinoline Days," while the "symphony orchestra" played jazz and the other women entertained their guests in the costume of the day.[63]

These juxtapositions of old and new images of womanhood suggest that Eleanor women were aware that the image of womanhood was changing. And, there is some evidence that these women, slowly and perhaps tentatively, adopted the new image of womanhood as their own. Throughout the 1920s, reporters often noted how many women in their clubs had bobbed their hair. For example, in April 1924, one reporter claimed that two women (one of whom was the house council president) had bobbed their hair, and, "now must be classed with the flappers, and can no longer be thought of as dignified."[64] One can, of course, interpret this statement literally. More likely, however, this reporter was mocking the image of the flapper as undignified, and also providing evidence of the abandonment of the old-fashioned look by certain residents. If these rituals do, in fact, reveal that these women perceived an opposition between the old and the new images of womanhood, then these perceptions waned by the late 1920s. After 1928, cabarets, with "bohemian atmosphere," began to dominate the play life of the residents of the Eleanor clubs.

The writings, activities, and rituals of the women in the Eleanor clubs provide a unique insight into the life of the independent, single, white-collar woman of the early twentieth century. These women workers valued their female friendships and social space provided in the Eleanor clubs; they took their work seriously, sought to improve their positions; they enjoyed their independent lives. They had fun. Their fun, interpreted as ritual, reflects their view of the world. Eleanor women's rituals drew upon images of the residents' personal and historical pasts, and also depicted the residents' perceived life choices. The rituals helped them to negotiate between the world of work and marriage, and to make sense of the changing role of women in society. Even if these women ultimately abandoned work and an independent life for marriage, we now know they did not do so unthinkingly.

In 1923, a writer in the *Eleanor Record* reported to her sisters in the residences about recent articles on women's achievements in the world of work and ended the article by stating that she believed that, "the next generation will see the business woman more nearly at the top of the list."[65] This was but a fleeting moment in the history of an occupation in transition. Even though characters in novels and certain privileged workers, like those women who lived in the Eleanor clubs, might reflect or even act upon the independence clerical work promised, most office workers from the 1920s on could not ignore the effects of the ongoing interplay of capitalism and patriarchy. Because clerical work had become women's work, it had become devalued work, a reality that many of the daughters and granddaughters of our Eleanor residents probably took as the natural course of events.

CHAPTER 8

The "Conventionalized" Female Office Worker: The Promise Unfulfilled

*L*ESS THAN a decade after Jane Addams warned young women of the dangers and difficulties of clerical work, female clerical workers became a commonplace feature of the business office and institutional accommodations suited to the needs of the female clerical worker began to appear throughout the city. In 1923, the journal of Chicago's business community, *Chicago Commerce,* ran a story that highlighted the fifty-year history of the typewriter. The anonymous writer believed not only that the typewriter had improved business methods, but also that it had contributed greatly to the "economic emancipation" of women. "The typist," the article continued, "blazed the path by which other women entered every department of business." The writer claimed that the entrance of the "girl stenographer and typists" into the business world felled "ancient barriers."[1]

Great changes had occurred; clerical work had become one of the women's occupations, and was considered a proper and legitimate endeavor for white, native-born women. Throughout the 1920s, the female clerical worker became a "conventional" feature of both Chicago and the national scene. Between 1920 and 1930, women assumed a majority of Chicago's office jobs.

Aside from this milestone, however, the demographic characteristics of Chicago's labor force did not change dramatically. The clerical workforce, as a whole, only increased 25 percent and the number of women in clerical work increased 31 percent, the smallest increase since 1870. The share of the total labor force engaged in clerical work remained constant. Likewise, the percentage of male and female labor force participation remained stable. The three categories of clerical work maintained their shares of the clerical work force. And the percentages of men and women in these three categories varied only slightly during the 1920s. By the 1920s, the number of women in office work and the positions they held had reached a temporary equilibrium.

Clerical work became women's work, not only because a majority of those engaging in it were female, but also because clerical work became intimately associated with so-called feminine qualities and was not considered a threat to women's domestic roles. The inclusion of office jobs in the roster of female occupations and the subsequent expansion of women's occupational opportunities was a Pyrrhic victory, however. Although the nature and conditions of work within the office or the configuration of the clerical labor force did not undergo dramatic changes, the transformation of clerical work to a female occupation had a powerful symbolic and material effect. By the 1920s, women were no longer imposing themselves on a male space and occupation and could no longer harbor the mistaken expectation of self-sufficiency and promotion. As "women's work," office jobs could no longer offer the promise of escape from the sexual division of labor and the consequences of ghettoized female employment.

At Work

By the 1920s, the "business girl" or "business woman" was a ubiquitous feature of the business office, but the experiences of clerical workers as a whole were by no means uniform. Office workers as a group probably shared in the general prosperity of the 1920s, but not all clerical workers were prosperous throughout the decade. Still, the wages, hours, and working conditions of most clerical workers were favorable enough to characterize most office positions as good jobs for women. Ruth Shonle Cavan, in a study done in 1929 for the Religious Education Association, using figures compiled from the Chicago Young Women's Christian Association Employment Bureau, the Chicago Collegiate Bureau of Occupations, and the National Industrial Conference Board Study, discovered median salaries ranging from twenty-four dollars to twenty-five dollars per week to eighteen dollars to nineteen dollars per week. Bookkeepers and stenographers earned the highest salaries, those engaging in general office and clerical work, "mechanical operations," and typing earned the moderate salaries, and file clerks earned the lowest salaries.[2] An extensive Women's Bureau study of 9,575 female clerical workers in eighty-one establishments in Chicago in 1931 showed some improvement, even as the Great Depression was deepening. Median monthly salaries ranged from $159 ($39.75 per week) for secretaries to $80 ($20 per week) for file clerks. The Women's Bureau investigator, Ethel Erickson, also examined wage differentials by industry. The lowest median salary for female clerical workers was in mail order houses ($75), with insurance companies ($93), public utilities ($100), publishers ($106), banks ($114), and advertising companies ($117) all following. The best place for women to procure clerical jobs was in investment houses, where the median monthly salary was $127.[3]

Ruth Shonle Cavan examined the budgets of thirty business "girls," most of them from Chicago, to ascertain where they spent their money when their salaries rose. She discovered, as the investigator for the Illinois Bureau of Labor Statistics did in 1892, that female clerical workers who lived at home did not necessarily fare better financially. Table 21 contains an exact replication of the table from Cavan's study; even when making a modest salary, female clerical workers earned enough to take care of most of the necessities of life, with a little remaining for savings.

For most female clerical workers, hours and conditions of work were probably at least acceptable given the prevailing conditions of the day. The most common daily hours of the 9,575 women in the Women's Bureau study were seven and one-half with four and one-half on Saturday, or forty-two hours per week. All but one of the eighty-one offices examined in this study gave vacation with pay to the clerical force, most allowing two weeks. A majority of the offices had definite plans for sick allowance. One half of the offices made group insurance plans available to their employees, most paid jointly by employees and employers. And, a few banks, in particular, provided free lunch and pension and retirement plans to their employees.[4]

The type and size of the firm also affected the nature of the labor process and work experience of the female clerical worker. In general, during the 1920s, it was the largest firms that were most susceptible to scientific management and the mechanization of some of the more overtaxed and expensive clerical functions.[5] Eighty-one large companies in Chicago that undertook to rationalize and mechanize their offices cited

Table 21. "How Business Girls Spend Their Money (Chiefly from Chicago, but Including a Few from Other Midwest Cities), Average Expenditures per Year of Thirty Women"

AVERAGE SALARY	$918[a]		$1,289[b]		$1,650[c]	
	DOLLARS	PERCENT	DOLLARS	PERCENT	DOLLARS	PERCENT
Room, Board	232	25.3	475	36.8	705	42.7
Clothing	248	27.0	296	22.9	232	14.1
Helping Parents	30	3.3	22	1.7	54	3.3
Education	30	3.3	47	3.6	26	1.6
Church, Charity	28	3.0	35	2.7	21	1.3
Recreation	61	6.6	71	5.5	74	4.6
Health	34	3.7	60	4.7	24	1.5
Vacation	30	3.3	50	3.9	96	5.8
Savings	89	9.7	96	7.5	229	13.9
Incidental and Unaccounted for	136	14.8	137	10.6	189	11.4

Source: Ruth Shonle Cavan, *Business Girls: A Study of Their Interests and Problems,* Religious Education Monograph #3 (Chicago: The Religious Education Association, 1929), p. 72.
[a]Nine girls with salaries from $660 to $1,096 per year.
[b]Fifteen girls with salaries from $1,135 to $1,490 per year.
[c]Six girls with salaries from $1,500 to $1,800 per year.

labor saving, convenience, better records, and an easier time during rush periods as the reasons for the changes. One company, for example, that began using an addressing machine in 1920 was able to eliminate the use of a temporary force necessary during the busy season. Another company began using bookkeeping machines in 1929. The female clerk who had formerly kept hand ledgers was trained on the machine, resulting in better work in less time.[6]

As the two case studies above demonstrate, these innovations in rationalization and mechanization did not always result in layoffs. While dictating machines often reduced stenographic forces, bookkeeping machines "have perhaps opened as many fields of employment as they have restricted. Men have been more adversely affected." Similarly, addressing machines did not bring about a "reduction in the number of employees but a reduced printing bill."[7] Nevertheless, in many of these large firms adopting various business machines the story of mechanization sounded the same: cheaper female workers who worked on machines replaced expensive male workers. In one company, for example, a young girl working on a bookkeeping machine replaced three men. "The girl was first paid $30.00 a week, and later cut to $25.00, while each of the three men had received $25.00. One man was retained and shifted to other work and the other two were dismissed."[8] (See Illustrations 13 and 14.)

It is important not to overstate this trend for the 1920s. Only the largest companies had the need and the resources to adopt these rationalized methods of white-collar work. In some instances, the adoption of machines helped overburdened companies keep up with increasing volume of paper work without significantly altering the number of workers or replacing male workers with female workers. In other instances, particularly in the late 1920s, mechanization reduced the force or precipitated the shift to female workers.

The effect of this spotty adoption of scientific management and office machines was to create greater variety within the clerical sector and a more precisely articulated hierarchy among clerical jobs. Ranking the median monthly salaries of Chicago's male and female clerical workers examined in the Women's Bureau survey reveals the two occupational hierarchies for men and women in clerical work (see Table 22). Even though both men and women performed eight of these jobs, men made the same or more money in all but one occupation. Erickson stated that men's higher salaries "indicate(d) a totally different plane of salary values, into the higher classes of which women apparently have not made their way," and she doubted "whether the differences in duties (were) so great as the difference in salary."[9]

Women's occupational hierarchy within clerical work was different from men's and separated from the larger promotional structure of the firm. Women had only the remotest possibility of jumping from a clerical job ladder to an administrative, managerial promotional ladder. Few company records consulted directly stated this, but the effect on women's place in the occupational hierarchy of a firm employing white-collar workers was clear and remains clear to this day.

Two of Chicago's largest mail order houses that employed thousands of female clerical workers clearly targeted young men for promotion through the ranks of the company's occupational hierarchy. A public relations pamphlet issued by Montgomery Ward and Company never explicitly stated that women were not promoted into executive positions, but it is clear that the manager of this company viewed the men and

Table 22. Occupational Hierarchies by Median Monthly Salary of Male and Female Clerical Workers in Chicago, 1931

MALE'S JOB[a]	SALARY	FEMALE'S JOB[a]	SALARY
Security Clerk	$251		
Supervisor	$241		
Semiprofessional	$224		
Accounting and			
Statistical Clerk	$219		
Teller	$177		
Correspondent	$174		
Head Bookkeeper	$162		
		Secretary	$159
		Supervisor	$153
		Cashier; Teller	$138
		Head Bookkeeper	$122
		Correspondent	$120
General Clerk	$115		
		Stenographer	$112
		Telephone Operator	$110
		Machine Operator	$100
Machine Operator	$98		
		Typist	$91
		General Clerk	$90
File Clerk	$80	File Clerk	$80
Messenger	$65		
		Messenger	$56

Source: Ethel Erickson, *The Employment of Women in Offices,* Bulletin of the Women's Bureau #120, U.S. Department of Labor (Washington, D.C.: U.S. Government Printing Office, 1934), pp. 73, 75.
[a]Those jobs done by both men and women are underlined.

women workers in the company as completely different kinds of workers. Montgomery Ward treated male and female workers differently the minute they entered the employ of the mail order house. "[A]ll newly employed men and women" went to the Welfare Department "for instruction before going to their prospective work." Most of the women, who were heading for clerical jobs, "were advised . . . regarding attire, conduct, personal hygiene, and business ethics." "Men," presumably taking entry-level jobs, were "instructed in the nature of the business, the firm's ideals of service to its customers, and employees' responsibility to the house and to each other."[10] The pamphlet detailed the training plan, claiming that, "whenever possible, promotions to positions of responsibility are made from the ranks. The mail order business is essentially unique," the pamphlet continued, "and in order to instruct *young men* of executive ability in the system and policies of the plant, we have instituted our Training Plan under the direction of the Educational Division"[11] (emphasis added). Similarly, a pamphlet issued by the management at Sears, Roebuck, and Company, *Sears Jobs for Sears Men,* detailed procedures for promotion within the company and made it clear that potential executive material would come from the large group of salesmen, not female clerical employees.[12]

The female clerical occupational hierarchy also became longer and more divided in the 1920s. Rationalization, routinization, and mechanization stretched the job ladder downward, adding jobs to the lower end of the hierarchy, particularly in the clerk and bookkeeping categories. In many of these new jobs the "office workers tending machines in the performance of their duties [were] not unlike the factory workers tending a machine in the factory."[13] As the Women's Bureau investigator observed, "promotions become less as the number of routine jobs increased and the opportunities to rise above the clerical field seem uncertain."[14]

At the same time, the upper end of the hierarchy became more exclusive. During the 1920s, the title "executive secretary" or "private secretary" came into general use to describe a highly paid and sought-after clerical position. Immune from scientific management, this exclusive corps of office workers functioned as an executive's office wife, exercising the necessary autonomous activity while acting as his auxiliary in all professional matters. As an adjunct to her boss, the private secretary shared similar roles and qualities with that of her boss's wife. In addition to the many skills necessary to perform the job adequately, the private secretary also needed to project a respectable, yet appealing appearance, maintain a dignified, yet accommodating demeanor, and demonstrate initiative, but not independence, in her work. The private secretary was to remain loyal and faithful to her boss, maintaining all business confidences.[15] During the 1920s, because of this association of secretarial duties and feminine traits, the very word "secretary," as well as "stenographer," "typist," and "office worker," invoked images of female workers.

Divisions within the clerical labor force were not simply based upon levels of skill and experience; the female clerical labor force was also divided by age, marital status, ethnicity, and race. Black women were effectively excluded from clerical work for most of the period examined, but as more and more blacks, many of them young women, migrated from the south to Chicago after World War I, a few black women began working at clerical jobs (see Table 4). These jobs were almost always in black-owned firms. The Women's Bureau survey included data from six black-owned firms (five insurance companies and one publisher) that employed 101 black women as clerical workers. These women tended to be older, more frequently married, and better educated than their white counterparts, yet their salaries, even in black-owned firms, were lower.[16] Despite these opportunities within the black community, clerical work was clearly a white woman's job.

Employers also appeared to want their office workers young and unmarried. Despite the increasing demographic diversity of the white women employed as clerical workers throughout the first three decades of the twentieth century, most clerical workers remained under twenty-five and single. Of the eighty offices that reported on the preferred age of their office staff in the Women's Bureau study, only thirty-one stated that age was not a recognized factor in their hiring policies. Eighteen firms had definite age bars that ranged from thirty to forty-five years of age. Similarly, one-third of the offices did not hire married women for new positions. These bars may have certainly tightened as a result of the Depression under way when the survey was conducted, but they also probably reflected prevailing sentiments that were accentuated as a result of the crisis.[17]

Daughters or members of certain ethnic groups may have had difficulty finding jobs as office workers because of discrimination. The data for this kind of discrimination are sketchy and difficult to document, although it seems clear that Jewish women, in particular, experienced difficulties procuring office jobs. Ruth Shonle Cavan, in her study of Chicago's business women, hinted at this problem when she told of a young Jewish stenographer who had confided in an older worker that she had "great difficulty in finding a position because of her race."[18] A 1934 master's thesis conducted by a sociology student at the University of Chicago documented the existence of anti-Semitism in certain offices in Chicago.[19] Newspaper advertisements routinely specified the desired religion of their prospective job candidate, and employment bureau job application forms sometimes required information about a candidate's marital status, nationality, and religion, as well as housing arrangement.[20]

A woman's age, marital status, race, religion, and ethnicity, therefore, determined whether she could procure work in an office and, once in the clerical labor force, what kind of job she got and her potential for advancement. Clerical work had a different meaning for different types of women and Chicago's educational establishment, with prodding from the business community, became increasingly aware of this throughout the 1920s.

At School

After World War I, educators and educational administrators could no longer ignore the many young women who believed that a clerical position was a good position and they began to focus on the specific problems caused by the enrollment of young women in the two-year commercial courses in Chicago's high schools. Although educators were pleased that two-year courses and continuation programs often kept children in school, they were dismayed because many of these students did not get jobs. Businessmen complained that many of these students lacked adequate language training and business deportment because they were often from poor and immigrant backgrounds. In the 1920s, therefore, educators began to emphasize matching the student with the proper type of clerical training, and also the importance of the "cultural side" of business education. Just as English classes could teach immigrants important lessons in the work ethic, commercial courses could train immigrant daughters in the proper American demeanor in a business office.

In 1921, a vocational advisor made a study of the plans of 596 children leaving the eighth grade in one of the poorest school districts of Chicago. Seventy-one percent of the girls expressed a desire to go to high school, and the largest percentage of these girls, 45 percent, wanted to take the two-year commercial course. The advisor was dismayed by these findings. While 300 students had graduated from this course the year before, only 119 calls for stenographers and typists had come in from employers.[21] Apparently, employers were not interested in young, inexperienced stenographers of this economic background. "The two year stenographic course," the advisor claimed, "is the High School path of least resistance. The girls are falling into it without much thought. Stenography is considered a 'lady-like' occupation, taking minimum preparation and the field of work seems limitless."[22] Poorer, often immigrant girls or daughters, with relatively less training and much less experience than their middle-class predecessors, had more limited and less promising job opportunities.

A 1924 study conducted by the Vocational Guidance Bureau on beginning office positions for young women in Chicago yielded similar results. The director, Anne Davis, reported that girls had been so intent upon securing stenography that they have refused to consider other types of office positions, which were more numerous, and in many cases, Davis believed, more suitable. A study of employers' requirements for different office jobs revealed that the majority of employers demanded four years of training for their stenographers. On the other hand, employers preferred "a younger girl, teachable, cheaper," for the more routinized positions of office clerk, typist, and office machine operator. Davis recommended that, while stenography was certainly superior office work, the girl who could not qualify in personality, language ability, and general knowledge for stenography should be directed to general office work.[23]

Training all young women for stenographic positions was no longer sensible educational policy. By the middle of the 1920s, school officials realized that the two-year stenographic course was not training young women for the positions available in the workforce and also that the women flocking to these courses were not always "appropriate" stenographic material. In 1924, the Board of Education introduced a new clerical course, a two-year office practice course. The course included four semesters of English, three semesters of typewriting, two semesters of bookkeeping or office machines, and no stenography. The board also offered this course in modified form in the newly opened junior high schools.[24]

Cultural training was an important component of the new clerical training of the 1920s. In general, cultural training referred to instruction in citizenship, habits, attitudes, appearance, and character. Chicago's business community enthusiastically supported this type of training as a supplement to commercial training.[25]

This type of instruction was perhaps most important in the commercial training in the continuation schools. In 1920, these continuation schools had an enrollment of 5,161 boys and girls, most of whom were under sixteen years of age and employed in some sort of commercial work in the Loop.[26] The head teacher of the all-girls Winchell Continuation School claimed that even though training in commercial skills was certainly important, courses in hygiene and civics have "given the students the knowledge and opportunities [they] needed to make [them] more efficient business girl[s]."[27] Instruction in diet, sleep, manicuring, skin care, shampoo, clothing maintenance, shoe care, sitting, standing, poise, and dancing was necessary because "a large percentage of these girls [were] of foreign parentage and reared in the most limited environments possible."[28] Jennie Potash, a student at the Winchell School, wrote, "among all other things I have learned, the most important things are manners, and how to act in an office; also always to respect people older than myself; in fact, never to say anything that is not just lady-like and courteous; I have learned to control my temper. I have learned business deportment which had never been taught to me anywhere else."[29]

By the late teens and early 1920s, all groups involved in the efforts for vocational training and placement came to acknowledge commercial training as vocational training for women. The efforts of the scholarship committee of the Vocational Supervision League demonstrated this recognition clearly. The accounts of the children helped by the scholarship committee frequently tell of how the two-year commercial course provided the opportunity the student needed to break the cycle of poverty. Even when a student took the four-year general course in preparation for college, the committee often suggested that the student also take commercial courses to provide the student with the ability to work his or her way through college.

Completing a commercial course was an important goal for poor female students. Clara, who in 1916 was enrolled in Marshall High School, was unable to complete the two-year commercial course because her father, a peddler, could no longer support the eleven children in the family. With the help of a scholarship, Clara was able to finish her two-year course and the Vocational Bureau found her a position as a stenographer for eight dollars a week. By 1923, Clara had advanced to a position of stenographer and office assistant and was earning twenty-seven dollars a week. The League investigator described her as a "very well poised, refined young woman of twenty-three, who has assumed her home responsibilities seriously, and at the same time tried to develop herself. She is very happy in her work, and feels that the family situation is rapidly improving. She is helping make a high school education possible for her younger brother and sisters, as she felt the opportunity given her thru [sic] the Scholarship Association had been invaluable to her."[30] Sadie was another girl who was able to complete the two-year commercial course because of a scholarship. In 1920, the committee reported that "she has been at work a few months and is already earning twenty-five dollars a week. As a mark of her appreciation for the educational opportunity given to her, she has offered her services to teach typewriting at Hull House."[31] Another girl, who had become a stenographer in a lawyer's office through the aid of the Scholarship Association for Jewish Children, wrote a thank-you note to her sponsors claiming, "it is a medium through which the children of the less fortunate, such as I was, who are desirous of getting ahead and not being confined to factory work, can get the proper education."[32]

By the 1920s, the public educational establishment concerned with the training and placement of female clerical workers not only acknowledged women's special relationship to office work, but also the new challenges posed by the new types of office jobs available and the new entrants into these jobs. The rationalization and mechanization occurring in the larger firms created an underclass of clerical workers just as the daughters of southern and eastern European immigrants came of working age. The educational administrators' desires to match the potential clerical worker with an appropriate job and to provide cultural training reveal their assumptions that class and ethnic background determined suitability for certain types of clerical jobs.

Certainly, the ability to train for clerical jobs did provide a path to upward mobility, as the stories cited above attest. Undoubtedly, some daughters of immigrants and immigrant women saw clerical work as a way to escape the danger and degradation of factory work and the slum or ghetto. They also saw clerical work, as well as other white-collar occupations such as retailing and teaching, as a way to "Americanize" themselves. Even though the better wages and working conditions could allow these women to live better lives and help their families, the exposure to American values and customs often caused difficulties within families.

Some daughters of immigrants, and most female clerical workers in Chicago were daughters of immigrants, may have experienced problems similar to May's. May had to battle with her traditional German family to continue her education beyond the eighth grade to train for a clerical job and then, after three years working, for control over her own salary. She won both battles, paying her mother $9.00 a week for room and board and helping around the house. "Now that May had bobbed her hair and had begun to dress as the other girls did, her mother found new matters for criticism. May had joined a Young Women's Christian Association club and began to go to the movies with her new girlfriends. There were too many late hours. . . . The climax came when May wished to spend her vacation away from home." Before her vacation, May left home, but returned when it was over. The conflict between May and her parents was never entirely resolved, however, because it was a conflict between an old-fashioned, thoroughly German mother and her thoroughly American daughter. With bobbed hair, rouge-brightened cheeks, and silk dresses exposing "silk clad knees undaunted to the world," May was not only "hard headed and capable about [her] work and business relations," she was also "capable of spending [her] own money and planning vacations away from home." This caused continual irritation to a mother who believed that a girl "should be fitted for wifehood and motherhood . . . be submissive to her family until such time as she becomes married."[33]

In the City

May was not alone in finding assistance through organizations such as the Young Women's Christian Association. The rapid increase in the number of women engaging in clerical occupations before 1920 prompted many of those organizations concerned with the physical and moral health of working women to redefine the nature of their services. By the late teens and early 1920s, young women were no longer considered in need of charity, but of guidance.[34] It is probably no coincidence that many organizations altered the nature of their services for working women as the nature of the work women engaged in changed. The services provided by these organizations not only helped to "conventionalize" the lives of Chicago's clerical workers, but also revealed how the leaders of these organizations defined the needs of this new occupational group.

The services provided by the reform, civic, business, and religious organizations of Chicago illustrate how these philanthropists and reformers envisioned the female clerical workers' relationship to the world of work. Most activities of Chicago's reform and business organizations did not address the wages, hours, and working conditions of female clerical workers. They believed that the problems of the female clerical worker resulted not from the type of work in which she engaged, but from her sex. These organizations saw their mission as easing the female clerical workers' transitions from small-town and rural life to city life and from school to work and supplied social services for the female clerical worker designed to touch all aspects of her life. In many cases, a job as a clerical worker was actually a solution to the social problems of the working woman, not the problem itself.

Chicago organizations concerned with the city's working women provided safety, promoted sorority, and stressed the importance of service for business women. One of the earliest ways used to achieve these three goals was by providing women living away from their families with cheap, safe, respectable places to live. Between 1870 and 1930, the number of working women living on their own in Chicago increased, particularly during the World's Columbian Exposition and World War I. Generally, three options were available to working women: boarding with a family, renting a room in a lodging-house, or living in a residential club. Although most independent working women lived in lodging-houses and rooming-houses, residential clubs of all sorts did become popular among working women throughout the period.[35]

Business and philanthropic organizations were happy with this development. In the early 1920s, the Chicago Community Trust, with help from the University of Chicago, the Young Women's Christian Association, the Eleanor Association, Illinois Bell Telephone Company, and Marshall Fields and Company, conducted a study to determine the best housing options for young women coming to Chicago for work. Anne Trotter, the director of the survey, examined the three existing options and concluded that the most promising option for young single women was the residential club. She dismissed lodging houses as expensive, ill-equipped, dirty, unwholesome, lonely, and unsafe. "[T]he young woman must eat at restaurants or have light lunches in her room, the character of people with whom she comes in contact is often questionable, but more often the girl or young woman finds herself isolated and alone, without the opportunity for friendly and helpful social contact."[36] Her examination of room registries for lodgings in private homes revealed difficulties in administration and variable results. Residential clubs, she concluded, provided a safe residential choice where a young woman away from home could make friends and have the opportunity for a social life. In addition, participation in the activities of the residence would be a wholesome influence, "pointing to an ideal and exercising a control which is quite unconscious and subtle, but effective."[37]

Although most residential clubs still retained some elements of control over the personal lives of their residents, this negative quality was improving. Trotter reported that many of the earliest homes were "semi-charitable shelters for 'poor, worthy, working girls'." By 1920, however, this conception of the residence was changing in response to the working women served by the residences. "With the . . . advancing status of the business woman, and other modern developments," Trotter maintained, "purposes, names, terms, etc., have changed. Now many such 'homes' have grown to be 'clubs' for self-supporting young women and students preparing for self-support . . . others are clubs for business and professional women. 'Inmates' have become 'residents.' Matrons have been succeeded by superintendents, house secretaries, and directors."[38] Residential clubs provided an important service to all independent working women during the first three decades of the twentieth century and, despite the sometimes strict and condescending supervision, remained popular.[39] By the 1920s, many residential clubs, such as the Eleanor Association, were oriented toward and dominated by white-collar women.[40]

Residential clubs were just one social service designed for the business woman. Many groups concerned with the life of the working woman began to provide a wide variety of other social services to the business woman who worked in the Loop. Reformers believed that these women needed safe, respectable, inexpensive eateries, rest rooms where they could meet friends during and after the work day, organized recreational, cultural, and educational activities, and an outlet enabling business women to serve each other and the community in general.

The Eleanor Association, for example, offered various services to business women who did not live in their residential clubs. The association's leaders met the immediate needs of business women away from home by providing refuge during the working day at the Central Eleanor Club located in the downtown Loop district. In 1918, after moving to larger quarters, the club's membership increased to 2,000 "self supporting business girls," who could eat lunch or dinner at the club, take courses in business English, commercial law, rhetoric, literature, gymnastic dancing, dramatics, chorus, or French, attend lectures on political or cultural topics, or participate in the Eleanor organization through the fellowship, vocational guidance, finance and membership, or civics committees. The leaders of the association designed these committees not only to provide a way for women to receive services, but also to provide an opportunity for successful business women to serve their less fortunate sisters. In addition, the club served as a center of a business women's network in the same way that business men's clubs did. One writer in the Eleanor Association's journal, the *Eleanor Record,* remarked, "A girl who must choose an occupation for herself is interested in what successful women have achieved, and so we are glad to know also those who come to us with more experience. . . . No matter how much we may know of our own work, it is well to know something of other spheres of activity or we are in danger of becoming too narrow."[41]

The Chicago Women's City Club, a club of upper- and middle-class women involved in a variety of civic activities, also supplied services for the business woman who worked in the Loop. Starting in 1917, the club opened its rooms, with a chaperone on hand, between 5:00 P.M. and 9:00 P.M. for any young people who wished to keep appointments or rest until time for their evening appointments. In addition, the board of directors of the club decided to hold a meeting one evening a week each month, "for the benefit of business and professional women who . . . are unable to attend the noon meetings."[42] In 1922, the club oriented its services even more directly to the needs of business women. The rooms of the club were opened all day and business women were encouraged to take advantage of the magazines and books available in the "civic library." The club offered rest rooms where business women could "wash-up" after leaving the office, and an inexpensive cafeteria, "to which she can feel proud to invite her friends." And the club offered talks and lectures on civic and political issues during the noon hour and after 5:00 P.M. so that the business women could take advantage of them.[43]

The Chicago Women's City Club also encouraged business women to become involved in civic issues through its Young Woman's Auxiliary. Founded in 1921, these groups, located throughout the city and suburbs, consisted of 500 business girls whom the leaders of the club described as "potential citizens of this city," who "have not had the advantage of a complete education, nor have they ever been reached before by any organization of civic interest." The three-fold objective of the organization was "Service, Education, and Recreation." Recreation, the club leaders decided, was the easiest way to reach these girls. Not only would wholesome recreation relieve the stress and strain of their labor, but also "teach them how to find the right kind of recreation, instead of leaving them to be the prey of commercialized amusements."[44]

Perhaps the organization that changed the most in response to the transformation of clerical work from men's work to women's work was the Young Women's Christian Association. Starting in 1917, the National Board of the Young Women's Christian Association (YWCA) began acknowledging the need to direct attention and services to the business woman. A writer in the association's journal rhetorically asked her readers, "Have we given enough consideration to the part the women down-town have in creating the atmosphere of the town?" and answered that "the signs of the times indicate that the hosts of earnest, efficient business women are about to come into their own. Their entrance into civic life in other than its commercial phases is going to mean a very wholesome stimulus."[45] At the National Convention of the YWCA in 1922, one hundred business women of the association met for what they referred to as their "Continental Congress," designed to "put the business girls on the map." These women discussed the special needs and desires of the business women of the association, and more importantly, sparked the formation of business and professional women's organizations throughout the country.[46]

The leaders of the YWCA certainly began to notice that business women were beginning to dominate the memberships of their clubs, and given this development, sought to influence this potentially "wholesome stimulus."[47] Through business and professional women's organizations, and girl reserve clubs, the YWCA attempted to incorporate the young business girl into the life of the association and to foster values of sorority and Christian service. The report of the national board of the YWCA to its tenth annual convention in 1928 outlined the problems of the business girls. "There has been, generally speaking, little stimulus to a sense of social responsibility in the work lives of business girls, who are more isolated in their occupations than industrial workers, who show a wide variety in age, educational background and employment conditions, and who lack the sense of group solidarity which comes with a compelling cause arising out of one's economic condition."[48] The Young Business Women's Club of Chicago called this development the "increasing individualism on the part of girls and women in business," and sought to counteract this trend.[49] The Chicago YWCA instituted programs and courses to promote sorority, good citizenship, and service. Members of the Young Business Women's Club were supposed to extend Christian ideals when they went to the ballot box, when they went to work, into every realm of life.[50] One subject taken up by a commission of business women in preparation for a national convention was, "Am I helping create an attitude of business for service rather than business for unfair profit?"[51]

The association officials were well aware, however, that large numbers of business women would not be attracted to these clubs by the thrill of serving others. The clubs also realized that they would have to supply services oriented to the economic and personal needs of the business woman. In 1923, the Chicago YWCA moved its employment bureau from the central YWCA residence, just south of the Loop, to the central branch, in the middle of the Loop. Annie Trotter, the director of the employment bureau, apparently orchestrated this move as a way to better serve the needs of business women.[52] Trotter reported that at its former location, "the major work had been supplying families with governesses and children's nurses." When the bureau moved, however, "great numbers of applicants for business positions crowded the waiting room daily," and, "it soon became apparent that a reorganization of the Bureau was imperative to meet the needs of the new clientele."[53] The employment bureau stopped its placement service for domestic positions and focused on office positions, institutional positions for middle-aged women, and disseminating vocational information.[54] Trotter was actually implementing new directives from the organization's national employment secretary. Now the employment service was "to be for the occupational advancement of young girls and not for the woman who can have no occupational future, as the latter is work for charity organizations."[55] By the early 1920s, the young girl who worked in an office was not a charity case, but a worker who needed special help to advance in her career. Chicago's young business women agreed. In 1924, 92 percent of the placements from the YWCA employment bureau were in business firms.[56]

In 1921, the Chicago YWCA began to notice that business women were also making their presence obvious in other arenas; most women taking courses at the central branch were business women who worked in the Loop.[57] The central club's program was a mix of what the club leaders wished to teach its new constituency and what business women themselves desired. It included social and recreational activities such as "charm school," courses in personality, dramatics, ukulele, courses in citizenship, vocational education, world fellowship, and "talks on suitable dress, business etiquette, and other topics of practical appeal to business girls."[58]

This focus on the personal life of the business woman culminated in 1929. In this year, the journal of the national YWCA reported on a course offered by the Chicago YWCA called "Marriage." With stenographers and bookkeepers in attendance, the ten-week course explored various aspects of courtship, marriage, motherhood, and sex education, in addition to how to reconcile marriage and work if the women desired to do so.[59] This same year, the Religious Education Association, with substantial help from the Chicago and national branches of the YWCA, conducted an extensive study of business girls in Chicago and the Midwest. The director of the study, Ruth Shonle Cavan, stated that "the business girl is, on the whole, a young person of promise. She has possibilities of further development. Because of her own inexperience, because she has often advanced beyond her family educationally and culturally, she needs the assistance of organized agencies." Cavan called on the schools, the YWCA, and the church to provide social services for vocational and personal guidance, and placement information. In addition, she stressed the need for more organized social activities with young men and the use of psychiatrists, psychologists, and sociologists to help maladjusted or troubled girls.[60]

By the late 1920s and during the 1930s, leaders in the YWCA began to take note of the increasing mechanization of clerical work, the possible depression of salaries, and the monotony at the job.[61] Such attention to the work life of the business girl, however, was something altogether new. After the initial failure of the Women's Trade Union League to organize female clerical workers in Chicago, there were no other attempts to scrutinize the conditions of work of the female office worker. Business, women's, religious, and other philanthropic groups focused on the problems of female clerical workers as women's problems. Many, in fact, sponsored programs to facilitate women's entrance into the right clerical jobs because of the widespread belief during the 1920s that clerical work was a good job for women. These organizations oriented their activities, instead, to easing the clerical workers transition from rural to urban life, from school to office, and from work to marriage. And, in recognition of the diversity of backgrounds from which office workers came, they attempted to provide this new occupational group with a code of middle-class morality. The social services that appeared during the 1920s functioned to "conventionalize" the experience of the female clerical workers and thereby incorporate them as participants in the working life of the city. As clerical work became "women's work," both social service agencies and clerical workers themselves identified the problems of the female office worker and consequently, what it meant to be a part of the new female clerical labor force.

As office work transformed into an occupation associated with women and female characteristics, the female office workers' place within the life of the city was ensured. Educational, vocational, residential, and recreational services appeared to meet the special needs these workers had because they were women. And, just as transformation of clerical work from a male to female occupation was approaching its final stage and women could choose office work with greater social and physical comfort, office work's secondary status crystallized. The coincidence, in the 1920s, of the completion of the shift in gender association and the beginning of deskilling and mechanization of some office work jobs ensured clerical work's devaluation for the rest of the twentieth century.

The Promise Unfulfilled

The story of women and clerical work certainly did not end in 1930, but the events of the 1920s did set the stage for the rest of the twentieth century. Once clerical work became acceptable and a good job for a woman, it became easier for many more women to take advantage of this relatively good job opportunity. It also lost its promise. As "women's work," clerical work could not and does not afford women any increased equality in the labor market. In fact, women's domination of certain clerical jobs probably militated against any equality. Women's presence, sometimes alone, sometimes in large numbers, provoked employers to provide for a separate female occupational hierarchy within many firms. It was and is a commonplace that the promotional ladder of most clerical forces culminates with the executive secretary or the supervisor of other clerical staff; certainly, female clerical workers did not become managers or executives even though the myth of upward mobility provided for the lowly male shipping clerk to rise through the ranks to vice president or even president. Female clerical workers made less than men for doing the same work and their jobs had different meanings within the occupational hierarchy of the firm. The use of scientific management and business machines meant that certain clerical jobs, primarily in the largest firms, came to resemble factory labor. Any dignity and satisfaction possible was wrung out of these jobs. Women helped to make clerical work "women's work" and in the process, clerical work lost its promise of remunerative employment and advancement.

The image of the female clerical worker forged during the 1920s has been an enduring cultural stereotype during the twentieth century. Many stories about working women conform to the formula of the Cinderella tale. When the story ends less happily, it is usually because the woman has deviated from some norm or standard of acceptable female behavior. Marriage or death are the standard endings of popular movies, films, and short stories about working women. During the 1920s, as is the case today, a good clerical worker is not only a good worker but also a good woman, and the reward, marriage, validates that womanliness. The most recent film on a female clerical worker, *Working Girl* (1988), is, as was the case in the 1920s, both a Horatio Alger and a Cinderella tale, with the hard-working heroine breaking out of the clerical ghetto and winning the affections of her former boss's lover. She is attractive to this man, not only because she is honest, lively, and intelligent, but also because she is more vulnerable than her upper-class boss and wears feminine clothes rather than a drab, generic business suit.

But there have been some important changes since the 1920s. The demographic characteristics of the female clerical labor force has continued to reflect a wider diversity of ages, marital status, and racial and ethnic backgrounds, even though individual firms or industries may have, until quite recently, discriminated on the basis of age, marital status, or race. Women from all backgrounds have used clerical jobs to provide vital income to their family's budget. A diversity of positions still exists within the clerical sector, but many jobs have become rationalized, routinized, and mechanized, as some firms, during the post-World War II era, began to use computer technology in their offices. The concentration of large numbers of women in typing pools or word processing centers created the conditions that potentially brought the greatest change of all, collective action.

Starting in the 1930s, women did begin to band together more successfully for improved wages, hours, and working conditions. The Great Depression and the organizing efforts of the Congress of Industrial Organizations contributed to some moderate successes in the 1930s, while the increased application of technology and consciousness about comparable worth, child care, and safety at the workplace in part sparked by the women's movement provoked organization of female clerical workers in the 1970s. Many of these efforts have endured through the 1980s and will make a fascinating study for historians in the years to come.

The transformation of clerical work from a male to a female occupation holds important lessons for men and women today. The issues, conflicts, fears, and hopes of the women who were pioneers in the offices of the last decades of the nineteenth century are similar to many recent path-blazers in other male-dominated occupations. Women today have the same basic choice that the first female clerical workers had: a choice between two unsatisfactory options; they can "conquer" a job and make it "women's work"; or, they can work as "equals" within a "male" occupation. Both options are clearly unsatisfactory, the former ensuring second-class status in the workplace, the latter provoking an untenable conflict between commitment to work and commitment to family. The difficulty of the second-class status of many "female" jobs has recently become a desperate situation as many more women each year attempt to raise a family on their own on the depressed wages of women's work within the labor market.

And, the ambivalences and complaisance that many women in the 1920s experienced is similar to that known to many young women today. Just like those young clerical workers coming of work age in the 1920s, many women entering the labor market today did not participate in, or even remember, the recent fights for women's equality. They and other members of American society take much for granted in these times of supposed equality. But, as was true in the 1920s, the struggle has really just begun as we continue to understand how much needs to be changed.

Appendixes

Public Stenographer Data Base

Listed below are the fifty-four public stenographers used for analysis in Chapter 3. These stenographers were first located in the business advertising section of the Chicago City Directory of 1900. Only names of 118 individual women were considered. As these listings had the women's business addresses, home addresses needed to be found in the regular section of the city directory. In some instances, the popularity of the name made positive linkage impossible. In other instances, women did not have a home address listed. Next, women with home addresses were looked up in the Federal Manuscript Census for 1900 to uncover characteristics of their households. Anyone who has used the manuscript census knows the hazards of the terrain. Sometimes addresses did not exist; sometimes stenographers were not at the correct addresses. Fifty-four of these stenographers were located, but this did not eradicate all uncertainty. These census reports were handwritten and are frequently difficult to read or illegible. Sometimes they simply did not make sense. For example, there was one listing that claimed that a stenographer was native-born, and yet this was clearly impossible given her age and the date of her parents' arrival in the United States. In these instances, I went with the majority of the evidence and listed her as foreign-born.

NAME	AGE	MARITAL STATUS[a]	RELATION TO HEAD	NATIVITY[b]
Annie Adams	38	S	daughter to widow	NBNP
Jessie Arensberg	23	S	boarder in hotel	NBNP
Mary Beattie	33	S	roomer with sister	NBNP
Florence Betts-Chumasero	39	D	boarder	NBNP
Mary Brand	35	S	boarder	NBNP
Laura Collins	40	S	boarder	NBNP

NAME	AGE	MARITAL STATUS[a]	RELATION TO HEAD	NATIVITY[b]
Anne H. Cooper	37	M	boards with husband (traveling man)	NBFP–English
Lillian Cox	33	S	roomer with family	NBNP
Josephine Davis	27	S	daughter to married mother (no father present)	NBNP
Mary Davison	45	S	daughter to widow	NBNP
Edna Dickerson	29	S	daughter to widow	NBNP
Althea Dickson	32	S	roomer	NBNP
Marion Drake	35	S	daughter to retired father	NBNP
Susie Garret	29	S	lodger	NBNP
Sophy Green	23	S	head of unrelated household	NBNP
Lenore Henkes	23	S	boarder	NBFP–German and French
Louise B. Herpich	29	S	roomer	NBFP–German
Jessie Holmes	30	W	boarder (two living children not listed)	NBNP
Ella Howe	42	S	daughter to widow	NBNP
Rebecca Hufmeyer	33	S	daughter to widow	NBNP
Emma Jacobson	41	S	daughter to widow	NBFP–German
Lydia Johnson	20	S	granddaughter to widow	NBFP–Swedish
S. E. Kellog	45	D	roomer	NBNP
Genevieve Kingsburg	20	S	daughter to father (manufacturer)	NBNP
Minnie Koehler	38	S	daughter to widow	NBFP–Irish and German
R. E. Lindstrom	27	S	daughter to married mother (no husband in household)	NBFP–Swedish
Emily Louny	16	S	daughter to father (furniture)	NBFP–Swedish
Evelyn Marquardt	17	S	daughter to father (barn foreman)	NBFP–German
Mary McWilliams	38	S	daughter-in-law [suspicious]	NBNP
Minnie Meyer	23	S	boarder	NBNP
Mary Paddock	38	S	head (lived with older sister)	NBNP
Minnie Patterson	34	M	wife to husband (school teacher)	FB–Scots

NAME	AGE	MARITAL STATUS[a]	RELATION TO HEAD	NATIVITY[b]
Cora Powell	23	S	daughter to widowed father (no occupation)	NBNP
Marie M. Price	30	S	daughter to retired father	NBNP
Amelia Ross	30	S	daughter to retired father	FB–Norwegian
Mary Scannel	37	S	head (lived with sister)	NBFP–Irish
Jenette Shaw	30	S	head (lives with sisters)	NBNP
Mabel Shaw	23	S	sister to head	NBNP
Mary Shields	37	S	boarder	NBNP
Hattie Shinn	32	S	daughter to widow	NBNP
Mabel E. Snell	22	S	daughter to lawyer	NBNP
Eliz. Starrett	16	S	granddaughter to lumber dealer	NBNP
Evangeline Steward	24	S	boarder	NBNP
Mary Stocker	38	S	boarder	NBNP
Anna Sullivan	30	S	boarder	NBFP–Irish
Ada Taylor	24	S	daughter to retired father	NBNP
Ida Todd	30	S	roomer	NBNP
Anna Wagner	16	S	daughter to carpenter	NBFP–German
Annie C. Walsh	32	S	sister to widow	FB–French-Canadian
Nellie White	41	S	daughter to widow	NBNP
Ella Willis	25	S	daughter to widow (teacher)	NBNP
Lena R. Wilson	32	S	older sister to head (druggist dealer)	NBFP–Irish
Iva Wooden	38	D	lodger with family	NBNP
Lottie B. Wooley	27	W	boarder (one child living not listed in household)	NBFP–German

[a]S=single, M=married, W=widowed, D=divorced.
[b]NBNP=native-born, with native-born parents; NBFP=native-born with one or both parents foreign-born, nativity indicated; FB=foreign-born, nativity indicated.

Eleanor Association Residences

Data Base—1910

Below are listed the 60 clerical workers who boarded at the four Eleanor residences in Chicago in 1910. I have listed them by the residence in which they lived. An (s) after a woman's name indicates the strong possibility that a sister lived with her in the residence. The sister is listed only if she was a clerical worker as well.

NAME	AGE	MARITAL STATUS[a]	OCCUPATION	NATIVITY[b]
2411 Indiana				
Julia Espe	25	S	stenographer—electrical company	NB–Iowa FP–Norwegian
Ida Fischer	22	S	steno—electrical company	NB–Iowa FP–German
Mary Goodman	20	S	steno teacher	NB–Missouri NP
Millie Thompson	22	S	steno—railroad office	NB–Illinois FP–Norwegian
Edith Reece	17	S	steno student	FB–Eng. Canadian
Mary Wilmar	36	S	steno—railroad co.	NB–Wisconsin FP–French
Mary Do(a)me	24	S	steno—woolen co.	NB—Connecticut FP—French
Blondina Strucke (s)	23	S	steno—railroad co.	NB–Illinois FP–German
Nellie Strucke (s)	20	S	steno—railroad co.	NB–Illinois FP–German

NAME	AGE	MARITAL STATUS[a]	OCCUPATION	NATIVITY[b]
2411 Indiana continued				
Lillian Koukelik (s)	19	S	bookkeeper—printing company	NB–Illinois FP–Austrian/Bohemian
Mario Dulzo	18	S	steno—hair company	NB–Illinois FP–French
Esther Abrams	19	S	steno—law office	NB–Illinois FP–German/Hebrew
Caroline Wilson	38	S	stenographer	NB–Indiana, NP
Elizabeth Arcus	30	S	business school teacher	NB–Illinois FP–Scot/English
Harriet Denhardt	19	S	steno—piano co.	FB–Canadian/Eng.
Beatrice Jackson	23	S	steno—physician's office	FB–Irish/Eng.
Florence Curran	17	S	steno student	NB–Illinois FP–Irish/Eng.
Adele Hannon	25	S	public stenographer	NB–Wisconsin NP
Clara Feupser	22	S	bookkeeper in grocery store	NB–Wisconsin FP–German
5658 South Wabash				
Helen Nunson	40	W	steno—horse dealer	NB–NY, NP
Elizabeth Morton	50	W	bookkeeper—railroad co.	NB–Penn., NP
Frances Charlebois	40	W	clerical work mail order house	NB–Michigan FP–Irish
Marguerite Kruner	22	S	steno—department store	NB–Mich., NP
Agnes Goodking	20	S	office work commission house	NB–Wisconsin FP–German and Irish/English
Johanna Dieck	18	S	public stenographer	FB–Russian/German
Bessie Dongol	27	S	steno—packing house	FB–English
Della Burns (s)	22	S	office work in department store	FB–Irish/English
Viola Jones	22	S	steno—telegraph supply	NB–Illinois, NP

NAME	AGE	MARITAL STATUS[a]	OCCUPATION	NATIVITY[b]
5658 South Wabash continued				
Jessie McGilvra	24	S	office work/ mail order house	NB–Michigan, NP
Margaret Kane	25	S	clerk/printing office	NB–Indiana FP–Irish/English
Anna Storz	23	S	bill clerk	NB–Illinois, NP
Elizabeth Dakers	35	S	steno—packing house	NB–NY, NP
Jennie Stevens	21	S	office work/ wholesale merchants	NB–Illinois FP–Irish
Kittie Moshenrose	21	S	office work/ mail order house	NB–Illinois, NP
Mary Schick	21	S	public stenographer	NB–Illinois, NP
Katherine Hoerler	22	S	steno—storage house	NB–Illinois FP–Swiss
Ethel Swartz	28	S	steno—sewing machine co.	NB–Illinois, NP
Frances Gibb	40	S	club stenographer	NB–NY, FP– English
Esther Mattson	18	S	stenographer	NB–Illinois FP–Swedish
Phoebe Baird	26	S	steno—mail order house	NB–Indiana FP–Irish
Nellie Spangler (s)	30	S	steno in instrument co.	NB–Illinois, NP
Thora Thorsmark	26	S	public stenographer	NB–Illinois FP–Danish
Celcilia Ludwig (s)	24	S	steno—druggists	NB–Iowa FP–German
Rose Ludwig (s)	22	S	steno—wholesale house	NB–Iowa FP–German
Margaret Ludwig (s)	20	S	bookkeeper— tailor's office	NB–Iowa FP–German
Elena Murray	39	S	office work—mail order house	FB–Irish
Fay Otis	21	S	clerk—stationery store	NB–Illinois, NP
Estelle Meir	34	S	bookkeeper operating clubs	NB–Iowa FP–German

NAME	AGE	MARITAL STATUS[a]	OCCUPATION	NATIVITY[b]
3111 Indiana				
Elva Downing	27	S	office work	NB–Illinois, NP
Ida V. Thompson	44	S	bookkeeper	NP–Penn., NP
Julia Mullen	34	S	clerical work—office	NB–Wisconsin FP–Irish
Katherine Evan	25	S	stenographer	FB–English
Anna King	27	S	stenographer	NB–[state not given], NP
Mary Watson	22	S	clerk in railroad office	NB–Illinois FP–Irish
Ida Oldman	29	S	bookkeeper—printing company	FB–English
Helen William	18	S	stenographer	NB–Illinois, NP
Barbara McClure	18	S	bookkeeper assistant	NB–Indiana, NP
Margaret Lindsay	NA	NA	stenographer	FB–Scots/English
C. C. Burns	40	W	clerk—club	FB–Canadian/Eng.
551 East 31st Street				
Lillian Hastings	20	S	deed recorder	NB–Illinois, NP

[a]S=single, M=married, W=widowed, D=divorced.
[b]NB=native-born; FP=one or both parents foreign; FB=foreign-born.

Notes, Bibliographic Essay, and Index

Notes

Preface

1. Cindy Sondik Aron, *Ladies and Gentlemen of the Civil Service: Middle-Class Workers in Victorian America* (New York: Oxford University Press, 1987).

2. Elyce J. Rotella, *From Home to Office: U.S. Women at Work, 1870–1930* (Ann Arbor, Mich.: UMI Research Press, 1981), p. 106. Nationally, women constituted 2.5 percent of the clerical labor force in 1870, 4.4 percent in 1880, 19.3 percent in 1890, 30.2 percent in 1900, 37.6 percent in 1910, 49.2 percent in 1920, and 52.5 percent in 1930. Rotella's figures are from Alba Edwards, *Comparative Occupational Statistics for the United States, 1870–1940* (Washington, D.C.: U.S. Government Printing Office, 1943), pp. 91, 100, except for 1900 which she calculated herself. See page 106.

3. Women did not constitute a majority of the clerical labor force until 1930, nationally. In Chicago, this occurred by 1920.

4. For works that have informed my definitions of the terms "sex" and "gender," see Joan W. Scott, "Gender: A Useful Category of Historical Analysis," *American Historical Review* 91 (December 1986), p. 1053; Gayle Rubin, "The Traffic in Women: Notes on the 'Political Economy' of Sex," in Rayna R. Reiter, ed., *Toward an Anthropology of Women* (New York: Monthly Review Press, 1975), pp. 157–210; and Gerda Lerner, *The Creation of Patriarchy* (New York: Oxford University Press, 1986), section on definitions, p. 238.

5. "Clerical work" is a general description of a number of occupations. During the fifty years under consideration, some clerical occupations vanished, while others came into existence. In addition, the work associated with certain clerical jobs changed over time. Clerical workers can include copyists, correspondents, stenographers, typists, secretaries, bookkeepers, cashiers, accountants, timekeepers, office helpers, office machine operators, and a wide variety of clerks, except retail clerks.

6. Margery Davies, *Woman's Place Is at the Typewriter: Office Work and Office Workers, 1870–1930* (Philadelphia: Temple University Press, 1982), pp. 59–62.

7. See Joanne J. Meyerowitz, *Women Adrift: Independent Wage Earners in Chicago, 1880–1930* (Chicago: University of Chicago Press, 1988); Margaret Gibbons Wilson, *The American Woman in Transition: The Urban Influence,*

1870–1920 (Westport, Conn.: Greenwood Press, 1979); and "The Girl Who Comes to the City," *Harper's Bazaar* (January 1908–January 1909).

8. Susan Carter and Mark Prus, "The Labor Market and the American High School Girl, 1890–1928," *Journal of Economic History* 42 (March 1982), pp. 163–171.

9. Leslie Woodcock Tentler, *Wage-Earning Women: Industrial Work and Family Life in the United States, 1900–1930* (New York: Oxford University Press, 1979).

10. This type of analysis uses the methodologies of two historians, E. P. Thompson and Gerda Lerner. In his study of the making of the English working class, Thompson argues against a mechanistic view of class, claiming that the working class "was present at its own making," and that "class is defined by men as they live their own history, and in the end, this is the only definition" (*The Making of the English Working Class* [London: Victor Gollancz, 1963], pp. 9, 11). Lerner, speaking of women in U.S. history, also asserts the primary importance of women as active participants in their own history. She asserts that "the true history of women is the history of their ongoing functioning in that male-defined work on their own terms." Women were not simply passive victims of an oppressive society; rather, "they always involved themselves in the world in their own way" (*The Majority Finds Its Past: Placing Women in History* [New York: Oxford University Press, 1979], pp. 148, 164).

11. My definition of patriarchy comes from Lerner, *Creation of Patriarchy,* pp. 238–239. According to Lerner, partriarchy is the institutionalization of male dominance over women and children in the family and society in general. "It does not imply," however, "that women are either totally powerless or totally deprived of rights, influence, and resources." Or, as Linda Gordon has recently written, "concepts of male supremacy" need also to explain "the power that women have managed to exert . . . and the extremely complex struggles, negotiations, and cooperation with which the sexes have faced each other and the social/cultural institutions that define gender relations." See Linda Gordon, *Heroes of Their Own Lives: The Politics and History of Family Violence* (New York: Viking Press, 1988), p. vi.

Chapter 1

1. Louisa May Alcott, *Work: A Story of Experience* (Boston: Roberts Brothers, 1873), p. 13.

2. Wesley G. Skogan, *Chicago Since 1840: A Time Series Data Handbook* (Urbana, Ill.: Institute of Government and Public Affairs, University of Illinois, 1976), table 1.

3. Bessie Louise Pierce, *A History of Chicago,* vol. 2 (New York: Alfred A. Knopf, 1937), p. 77; see also Elmer A. Riley, "The Development of Chicago and Vicinity as a Manufacturing Center Prior to 1880" (Ph.D. dissertation, University of Chicago, 1911); Allan Pred, *The Spatial Dynamics of United States*

Industrial Growth, 1800–1914: Interpretive and Theoretical Essays (Cambridge, Mass.: MIT Press, 1966), p. 54; Carl Abbott, *Boosters and Businessmen: Popular Economic Thought and Urban Growth in the Antebellum Middle West* (Westport, Conn.: Greenwood Press, 1981); David Ward, *Cities and Immigrants: A Geography of Change in Nineteenth Century America* (New York: Oxford University Press, 1971), pp. 36–37; Earl Shepard Johnson, "The Natural History of the Central Business District with Particular Reference to Chicago" (Ph.D. dissertation, University of Chicago, 1941), p. 9.

4. George E. Plumb, *Chicago: Its Natural Advantages as an Industrial and Commercial Center and Market* (Chicago: Civic and Industrial Committee of the Chicago Association of Commerce, 1910), p. 9.

5. Riley, "Development of Chicago," p. 37.

6. Quoted in Pierce, *History of Chicago,* vol. 3, p. 145.

7. Skogan, *Chicago Since 1840,* pp. 24–26.

8. Pierce, *History of Chicago,* vol. 3, p. 533.

9. *Ibid.;* Robert Higgs, "The Growth of Cities in a Midwest Region, 1870–1900," *Journal of Regional Science* no. 3 (1969), p. 369; and Pred, *Spatial Dynamics,* p. 54.

10. Pierce, *History of Chicago,* vol. 3, pp. 21–22.

11. Ward, *Cities and Immigrants,* p. 78.

12. Guiseppe Giacosa, "A City of Smoke," in Bessie Louise Pierce, *As Others See Chicago: Impressions of Visitors, 1673–1933* (Chicago: University of Chicago Press, 1933), p. 276.

13. Julian Ralph, "A Rapidly Moving and Business-Like City," in Pierce, *As Others See Chicago,* p. 289.

14. Rudyard Kipling, "How I Struck Chicago and How Chicago Struck Me," in Pierce, *As Others See Chicago,* p. 261.

15. Figures compiled from listings in city directories. See "Government Documents and Directories" in the Bibliographic Essay.

16. This analysis is from Margery Davies's chapter on the early office. She relied primarily upon novels and personal accounts. Margery Davies, *Woman's Place Is at the Typewriter: Office Work and Office Workers, 1870–1930* (Philadelphia: Temple University Press, 1982).

17. See Davies, *Woman's Place,* and C. Wright Mills, *White Collar* (New York: Oxford University Press, 1951).

18. Marcus T. C. Gould, *The Art of Shorthand Writing,* stereotype ed. (Philadelphia: n.p., 1830), p. 46.

19. See Ileen A. DeVault, "Sons and Daughters of Labor: Class and Clerical Work in Pittsburgh, 1870s–1910s" (Ph.D. dissertation, Yale University, 1985), pp. 51, 53. DeVault got this information from John Allen Rider, "A History of the Male Stenographer in the United States" (Ph.D. dissertation, University of Nebraska, 1966).

20. U.S. Bureau of the Census, *1890 Census of the Population* (Washington, D.C.: U.S. Government Printing Office), vol. 1, part 2.

21. R. V. Kennedy and Co., *D. B. Cooke and Company's City Directory for the Year 1859–1860* (Chicago: D. B. Cooke and Co., 1859).

22. Richard Sennett, *Families Against the City: Middle Class Homes of Industrial Chicago, 1872–1890* (New York: Vintage Books, 1974), p. 86.

23. *Ibid.*, pp. 126, 142.

24. See DeVault, "Sons and Daughters of Labor," p. 208. DeVault claims that 47 percent of all clerical workers in Pittsburgh in 1890 were native born with native-born parents. Thirteen percent were foreign born. Cindy Sondik Aron, *Ladies and Gentlemen of the Civil Service: Middle-Class Workers in Victorian America* (New York: Oxford University Press, 1987), p. 19. Aron states that between 88 percent and 92 percent of the government clerks she examines were from the ranks of the native born.

25. Pierce, *As Others See Chicago,* pp. 176–178.

26. *The Phonographic World* (January 1889), p. 89; Chicago city directories and manuscript census for Chicago, 1880. Please note that throughout the book, I will use *The Phonographic World* when referring to a publication that had many names over the course of several decades. Starting as *The Phonographic World* in 1885, the journal was called *The Illustrated Phonographic World* for one year in 1898, after which it was called *The Typewriter and Phonographic World* until 1908. Between 1909 and 1913, the journal was called *The Phonographic World and Commercial School Review.*

27. Janice Weiss, "Educating for Clerical Work: The Nineteenth Century Private Commercial School," *Journal of Social History* (Spring 1981), p. 407.

28. Edwin G. Knepper, *History of Business Education in the United States* (Ann Arbor, Mich.: Edwards Brothers, Inc., 1941), p. 54.

29. Albie Frances Mrazek, "Development of Commercial Education in Chicago's Public Schools" (M.A. thesis, University of Chicago, 1938), p. 50. Mrazek cites the *Chicago Journal,* January 16, 1849 for this information.

30. *Report of the Commissioner of Education* (Washington, D.C.: U.S. Government Printing Office, 1871–1892); hereafter abbreviated as *RCE*). See also Mrazek, "Development of Commercial Education," pp. 64, 69.

31. Aron, *Ladies and Gentlemen,* pp. 13–39.

32. DeVault, "Sons and Daughters of Labor," p. 143.

33. Angel Kwolek-Folland, "The Business of Gender: The Redefinition of Male and Female and the Modern Business Office in the United States, 1880–1930" (Ph.D. dissertation, University of Minnesota, 1987), pp. 73, 74. Kwolek-Folland's account was from Harry Braverman, *Labor and Monopoly Capital: The Degradation of Work in the Twentieth Century* (New York: Monthly Review Press, 1974), p. 305; and Priscilla Murolo, "White-Collar Women: The Feminization of the Aetna Life Insurance Company, 1910–1930," manuscript dated June 8, 1982, p. 8. Kwolek-Folland's chapter, "The 'Home Office' " was particularly helpful.

34. Perry R. Duis, *The Saloon: Public Drinking in Chicago and Boston, 1880–1920* (Urbana, Ill.: University of Illinois Press, 1983), pp. 186–187.

35. Alfred Trumble, "The Ancient Copyist," *The Phonographic World* (April 1889), p. 155.

36. See, in general, Roy Rosenzweig, *Eight Hours for What We Will: Workers and Leisure in an Industrial City, 1870–1920* (Cambridge: Cambridge University Press, 1983), and Kathy Peiss, *Cheap Amusements: Working Women and Leisure in Turn-of-the-Century New York* (Philadelphia: Temple University Press, 1986). See, specifically, Duis, *The Saloon*, p. 195, and Joanne Jay Meyerowitz, *Women Adrift: Independent Wage Earners in Chicago, 1880–1930* (Chicago: University of Chicago Press, 1988).

37. See, for example: Mills, *White Collar;* Braverman, *Labor and Monopoly Capital;* Richard Edwards, *Contested Terrain: The Transformation of the Workplace in the Twentieth Century* (New York: Basic Books, 1979); Alfred D. Chandler, *Strategy and Structure: Chapters in the History of American Industrial Enterprise* (Cambridge, Mass.: The M.I.T. Press, 1962).

38. Elyce J. Rotella, *From Home to Office: U.S. Women at Work, 1870–1930* (Ann Arbor, Mich.: UMI Research Press, 1981), pp. 66–67.

39. *Ibid.*, pp. 81–93.

40. U.S. Bureau of the Census. *1890 Census of the Population*, vol. 1, part 2.

41. Earl Shepard Johnson, "Natural History of the Central Business District," p. 213.

42. The McCormick Collection, the Wisconsin State Historical Society, Deering Harvester Company, *Record of Employees, 1896(?)* (1 volume). This book contains personnel records with varying degrees of information. The twenty-one men discussed represent 10 percent of the 210 male clerical employees listed in this book. It is impossible to determine why these men had complete forms while others had incomplete forms.

43. F. J. Squipp and I. S. Dement, "Our Courts," *The Phonographic World* (November 1887), p. 57; I. S. Dement, "State Stenographic Laws—Illinois," *The Phonographic World* (March 1889), p. 137; and *First Annual Dinner of Chicago Stenographers, Saturday, January 5, 1878* (Chicago: Beach, Barnard, and Co., 1878), p. 6.

44. *Second Annual Banquet of Chicago Stenographers, Saturday, January 11, 1879* (Chicago: Blakely, Brown, and March Printers, 1879), p. 17.

45. *Rules, Regulations, and Scales of Prices of the National Union of Stenographers* (Chicago, Illinois, adopted April 1, 1886), pp. 2, 6.

46. There is evidence of a Stenographers' Co-operative Association in *The Phonographic World* (July 1886), p. 208; a Chicago Stenographers' Association in issues of *The Phonographic World* for June 1889, p. 225; July 1889, pp. 240, 246; and September 1889, p. 5; and, finally, a Stenographer's Club of Chicago, *The Stenographer's Club of Chicago* (Chicago: Western Label Company Printers, 1892). This list is probably not complete.

47. Mr. Gurtler, "Plea for Business World's Recognition of High Status of the Accomplished Stenographer," *Chicago Commerce* (August 22, 1913), p. 32.

48. That male office workers could not exclude women through unions and professional associations has been mentioned in other works as reasons why women could more easily enter clerical jobs. See Samuel Cohn, *The Process of Occupational Sex-Typing: The Feminization of Clerical Labor in Great Britain* (Philadelphia: Temple University Press, 1985); and Ava Baron, "Contested Terrain Revisited: Technology and Gender Definitions of Work in the Printing Industry, 1850–1920," in Barbara Drygulski Wright, ed., *Women, Work, and Technology: Transformations* (Ann Arbor: University of Michigan Press, 1987), pp. 58–83. Baron's work in the printing industry provides an interesting contrast to the transformation of the clerical labor force. In the printing industry, male unionists were able to maintain control over their work even when technological changes had prompted management to attempt to replace male workers with cheaper, female workers.

Chapter 2

1. Letter from Isabel Wallace to her mother, November 23, 1885, the Wallace–Dickey Family Papers, Illinois State Historical Library.

2. During the last few years, there has been a blossoming of books on women's work during the nineteenth and twentieth centuries in the United States. Some that have informed my thinking are Alice Kessler-Harris, *Out to Work: A History of Wage-Earning Women in the United States* (New York: Oxford University Press, 1982); Thomas Dublin, *Women at Work* (New York: Columbia University Press, 1979); David Katzman, *Seven Days a Week: Women and Domestic Service in Industrializing America* (Urbana, Ill.: University of Illinois Press, 1978); Jacqueline Jones, *Labor of Love, Labor of Sorrow: Black Women, Work, and the Family From Slavery to the Present* (New York: Vintage Books, 1985); Barbara Melosh, *"The Physician's Hand": Work Culture and Conflict in American Nursing* (Philadelphia: Temple University Press, 1982); Susan Porter-Benson, *Counter Cultures: Saleswomen, Managers, and Customers in American Department Stores, 1890–1940* (Urbana, Ill.: University of Illinois Press, 1986); Christine Stansell, *The City of Women: Sex and Class in New York, 1789–1860* (New York: Knopf, 1986).

3. The issue of women's space in the business office was also considered in Angel Kwolek-Folland, "The Business of Gender: The Redefinition of Male and Female and the Modern Business Office in the United States, 1880–1930" (Ph.D. dissertation, University of Minnesota, 1987), esp. chapter II, "The 'Home Office,'" and Samuel Cohn, *The Process of Occupational Sex-Typing: The Feminization of Clerical Labor in Great Britain* (Philadelphia: Temple University Press, 1985), pp. 54–60.

4. On women and housing in Chicago, see Joanne J. Meyerowitz, *Women Adrift: Independent Wage Earners in Chicago, 1880–1930* (Chicago: University of Chicago Press, 1988).

5. John M. Coulter, *The Story of an Ideal: The Story of the Life and Work of Ina Law Robertson, 1867–1916* (Chicago: Eleanor Association, 1977).

6. Cindy Sondik Aron, *Ladies and Gentlemen of the Civil Service: Middle-Class Workers in Victorian America* (New York: Oxford University Press, 1987), p. 58.

7. This information comes from a survey of Sunday *Chicago Tribune* "help wanted" and "situation wanted" advertisements between 1870 and 1890. To account for seasonal variations, seasons were numbered from one to four. December, January, and February (winter) were season 1; March, April, and May (spring) were season 2; June, July, and August (summer) were season 3; and September, October, and November (fall) were season 4. Each month within a season was assigned a letter, A, B, or C, and each week in a month was assigned a number, 1, 2, 3, or 4. Starting with season 1, month A, and week 1, I picked Sunday, December 4, 1870, to start my search. My next selection, therefore, was season 2, month B, and week 2, or Sunday, April 10, 1870. I continued along, examining season 3, month C, and week 3 next, and season 4, month A, and week 4 after that. Therefore, as I started 1871, I began my examination with season 1, month B, and week 1, or January 8, 1871.

8. Of the 144 listings under the heading, "Situations Wanted—Female," during the 1870s, only twelve specified amaneunsis skills. Similarly, only one of the thirty-eight employers requesting female clerical help specified these skills. These quotes are from the listing of the *Chicago Tribune* of November 7, 1875.

9. For other examples, see the "Situation Wanted—Females" listings in the *Chicago Tribune* for March 21, 1875; November 7, 1875; September 10, 1876; May 6, 1877; June 10, 1877; April 20, 1879; and June 18, 1880.

10. The quote is from the *Chicago Tribune* listing, February 18, 1872. See also August 6, 1876, and April 6, 1873.

11. The quotes are from the *Chicago Tribune* listings from November 10, 1872, and March 10, 1878. See also August 6, 1876; August 10, 1873; June 21, 1874; April 20, 1879; and January 4, 1874.

12. The quote is from the *Chicago Tribune* listing from April 20, 1879. See also October 25, 1874; March 21, 1875; July 25, 1875; November 7, 1875; December 17, 1876; February 3, 1878; and March 10, 1878.

13. Margery Davies, *Woman's Place Is at the Typewriter: Office Work and Office Workers, 1870–1930* (Philadelphia: Temple University Press, 1982), pp. 53–54.

14. "The Typewriter and Women's Rights," *Gregg Writer* (April 15, 1913), p. 437.

15. "The First Typist," *Gregg Writer* (February 15, 1904), p. 233.

16. Quoted in Albie Frances Mrazek, "Development of Commercial Education in Chicago's Public Schools" (M.A. thesis, University of Chicago, 1938), p. 76, from *Annual Catalogue of Bryant and Stratton Business College and English Training School* (Chicago: H. B. Bryant, 1880), p. 31.

17. Although one cannot definitively prove that all employers made the

identification between pianos and typewriters and therefore assumed women would make the best operators, the association of pianos and typewriters was common enough. For some examples, see the following articles from *The Phonographic World:* "Women as Typewriters" (October 1887), p. 36; "The Piano and the Typewriter" (November 1896), p. 100; C. D. Dodge, "The Training of Stenographers" (March 1898), pp. 272–273; "Is a 'Rag-Time' Typewriter" (March 1900), p. 414; Frances Gillespie, "The Hand and Finger Training of Typewriter Operators" (March 1902), p. 63. In addition, scientific managers of the 1920s apparently also considered the transferability of these two skills. See Harry D. Kitson, "Determination of Vocational Aptitudes: Does the Tapping Test Measure Aptitude as Typist or Pianist?" *The Personnel Journal* (1927/8), pp. 192–198.

18. Margery Davies makes this argument in her book, *Woman's Place Is at the Typewriter.* She states, "Since many of these jobs, or at least their labels, had not existed before the growth of the office, they were not defined as men's jobs. Women who took such positions did not face the argument that they were taking over men's work" (p. 59).

19. Mrazek, "Development of Commercial Education," pp. 26, 60–61. Mrazek estimated that the average life span of the more established business colleges during these years was about three and one-half years. This was arrived at after an examination of 263 private schools gleaned from city directories, school censuses, the *Report of the Commissioner of Education* (hereafter RCE) (Washington, D.C.: U.S. Government Printing Office), telephone directories, and newspapers. See p. 38.

20. *RCE* (1881), pp. 397–411; and *RCE* (1882/1883), pp. 399–415. Other examples include the St. Ignatius Business School, which offered a ten-month course for $140.00 to 124 men whose average age was fifteen years; and Souder's Business School, which offered the same diverse courses as the Chicago Athenaeum Business School in a twelve-month course for $80.00. The average age of the students was nineteen years, and 84 percent of the student body was male.

21. *RCE* (1886/1887), pp. 804–813; and Mrazek, "The Development of Commercial Education," p. 27.

22. *RCE* (1892/3).

23. *RCE* (1897/1898), pp. 2441–2.

24. Because of the unreliability of the summarized city census data, it is difficult to characterize all of the domestic situations of these early clerical workers. In the late nineteenth century, however, the Bryant and Stratton Business College of Chicago highlighted the names of its students in some of the city's directories. This advertising technique has allowed me to glimpse the family backgrounds of some of these women by linking them with the manuscript census. Annie Ball's story was gleaned from city directories between 1868 and 1930, and the 1880 and 1910 manuscript censuses.

25. Included in this section are the stories of seven women who attended the Bryant and Stratton Business College in Chicago in 1880. These were the seven

names, out of the thirty-nine female students, whose names were highlighted in the Chicago city directory of 1880, that were linked to the manuscript census of 1880.

Chapter 3

1. "Women in the Professions," *The Phonographic World* (July 1892), p. 438.

2. Letter from Effie Jones to her father William Griffith Jones dated August 11, 1890, William Griffith Jones Papers, 1854–1925, Iowa State Historical Society. I would like to thank Mary Neth for bringing this material to my attention.

3. All labor force data came from the city censuses on these pages in the following U.S. Census Bureau volumes: U.S. Bureau of the Census, *1870 Census on Population Statistics*, vol. 1, p. 782; U.S. Bureau of the Census, *1880 Census of the Population of the United States*, vol. 1, p. 870; U.S. Bureau of the Census, *1890 Census of Population*, vol. 1, part 2, pp. 650–652; U.S. Bureau of the Census, *Special Report on Occupations, 1900*, pp. 516–523, 558–560; U.S. Bureau of the Census, *Statistics of Women at Work, Based on Unpublished Information Derived from the Schedules of the Twelfth Census* (Washington, D.C.: U.S. Government Printing Office, 1907), pp. 29, 228–233; U.S. Bureau of the Census, *Population—Occupational Statistics, 1910*, vol. 4, pp. 165, 544–547; U.S. Bureau of the Census, *Population—Occupations, 1920*, vol. 4, pp. 149, 1076–1080; U.S. Bureau of the Census, *Population—Occupations by States, 1930*, vol. 4, pp. 423–429, 447–450, 456–457, 463–465. Census classifications are not always comparable. The 1870 census of occupations for Chicago only included clerks and bookkeepers in manufacturing establishments. Therefore, this figure is low because it does not include clerical employees in trade and transportation or professional service. The 1880 census was somewhat more complete because it included nonspecific clerks and copyists. The 1890 census was the first census to classify clerical workers by function rather than by the type of establishment in which they worked. The classification included bookkeepers and accountants, clerks and copyists, stenographers and typists. There were a few problems with the 1890 census as well. No male stenographer–typists were listed in 1890. In addition, the special volume of *Statistics of Women at Work* reported that the census collectors included some saleswomen in the category of clerks and copyists in the 1890 census (p. 100). All three census schedules contain only *selected* occupations; therefore, 100 percent of Chicago's labor force is not included. I included all materials with these limitations in mind. Between 1900 and 1930, I used these three classifications: bookkeepers and accountants (and cashiers and auditors, when listed); clerks (not in stores); and stenographers and typists.

4. Elyce J. Rotella, *From Home to Office: U.S. Women at Work, 1870–1930* (Ann Arbor, Mich.: UMI Research Press, 1981), p. 119.

5. Ileen A. DeVault, "Sons and Daughters of Labor: Class and Clerical Work in Pittsburgh, 1870s–1910s" (Ph.D. dissertation, Yale University, 1985), p. 245.

6. Federal Works Agency Works Project Administration (Illinois), *The Chicago Foreign Language Press Survey* (Chicago, Ill., 1942). This project produced sixty-seven reels of articles translated from the newspapers of twenty-two foreign-language communities in Chicago between the 1850s and the 1930s. See, for example, "Advertisement for Commercial School at The Sisters of Nazareth," *Dziennik Chicagoski* (August 31, 1896), reel 49; "Advertisement for North Park College Mission Convent School," *Svenska Tribunen-Nyheter* (August 10, 1909), reel 63; an editorial in the Polish-language paper, *Dziennik Zwiaskowy*, entitled, "Mothers: Enroll your Daughters in High School and Universities" (June 29, 1917), reel 48. The writers of the editorial enjoined Polish mothers to encourage their daughters' education. "If the future of one's daughter is to be secured, she must be permitted to finish High School and then be sent to business college or normal school and so on."

7. See Kathy Peiss, *Cheap Amusements: Working Women and Leisure in Turn-of-the-Century New York* (Philadelphia: Temple University Press, 1986); and Joanne J. Meyerowitz, *Women Adrift: Independent Wage Earners in Chicago, 1880–1930* (Chicago: University of Chicago Press, 1988).

8. U.S. Bureau of the Census, *Statistics of Women at Work. Based on Unpublished Information Derived from the Schedules of the Twelfth Census* (Washington, D.C.: U.S. Government Printing Office, 1907), pp. 29, 228–233.

9. Oliver Smith Williams, "The Typewriter Girl in Chicago," *The Phonographic World* (September 1900), pp. 14–15.

10. The material presented in this section was derived from the female stenographers who advertised their services in the Chicago city directory of 1900 (pp. 2466, 2467), which I linked to the Federal Manuscript Census of 1900. Of the 118 listings of women, fifty-four were traceable in the census. See Appendix A for data base.

11. See note 8.

12. The same was true for Lottie B. Wooley, a twenty-seven-year-old widow who boarded. Lottie Wooley was a native-born woman whose father was German. She is listed as having one child living, but this child is not listed within the household.

13. The addresses of the four Eleanor Association residences in Chicago in 1900 were 2411 Indiana Ave., 3111 Indiana Ave., 551 East 31st Street, and 5658 Wabash Street. See Appendix B for data base.

14. Ileen DeVault has undertaken a similar comparison of clerical jobs with other options available to women at the time, particularly teaching. See DeVault, "Sons and Daughters of Labor," pp. 80–145, particularly pp. 97–99.

15. This information was taken from Illinois Bureau of Labor Statistics, *Seventh Annual Biennial Report: Part One: Working Women in Chicago* (Springfield, Ill.: 1892), pp. v–354.

16. The number of clerical workers was given by industry, not by establishment; therefore, the number of specific establishments employing clerical work-

ers is unknown. The industries that employed female clerical workers included tin can factories, suspender factories, shoe factories, uniform manufacturers, printing and publishing, dry goods, telephone service, department stores, bakeries, baking powder factories, book binderies, braid and embroidery works, cloak factories, electrical supply, envelope factories, fringe factories, lithography establishments, meat packing, neckware factories, paperbox factories, and a patent medicine laboratory. Information on wages and hours was calculated from information in table 1, "The Wages, Working Time, and Earnings of Women in Chicago." Information about expenses was calculated from table 5, "Income and Expenses of Those Reporting a Full Year's Experience, by Industry and Occupation." Although the Bureau of Labor Statistics provided summary information in the introduction to the survey, I calculated the numbers from the raw data in the tables myself. The survey statisticians grouped all non-operatives together, distorting the findings on clerical workers. Clerical workers in my group were stenographers and typists, bookkeepers, cashiers and cash girls, and clerks and office girls. Table 1 had 245 female clerical workers listed and table 5 had 155 female clerical workers listed. I did use the summary information for the operatives, despite some ambiguities about how these figures were calculated. The total number of female operatives in their sample was 4,681. Nevertheless, when the statisticians provided information about them, the number drawn upon was usually less, and varied depending upon the information provided. For example, they calculated the average yearly earnings of operatives, $297.00, from the earnings of 2,638 operatives.

17. Susan Porter-Benson, *Counter Cultures: Saleswomen, Managers, and Customers in American Department Stores, 1890–1940* (Urbana, Ill.: University of Illinois Press, 1986), pp. 183, 184.

18. *Proceedings of the Board of Education of the City of Chicago* (April 11, 1894), pp. 370–375.

19. National Education Association of the United States, *Teacher's Salaries and Salary Trends in 1923, Report of the Salary Committee* (Washington, D.C.: National Education Association of the United States, 1923), p. 83.

20. Alex Summers, *Salaries of Rural Teachers and Length of School Term in 1924* (Rural School Leaflet #39, U.S. Department of the Interior, Bureau of Education [Washington, D.C.: U.S. Government Printing Office, 1924]), p. 34.

21. Irene J. Graham, "Working Hours of Women and Girls in Chicago," *The Journal of Political Economy* (October 1915), p. 827.

22. Rotella, *From Home to Office*, p. 115.

23. Thomas Schelling, "The Process of Residential Segregation: Neighborhood Tipping," in Anthony H. Pascal, ed., *Racial Discrimination in Economic Life* (Lexington, Ky.: Lexington Books, 1972), pp. 157–184.

24. See Myra H. Strober and Carolyn L. Arnold, "The Dynamics of Occupational Segregation among Bank Tellers," in Claire Brown and Joseph A. Pechman, ed., *Gender in the Workplace* (Washington, D.C.: The Brookings Institute, 1987), pp. 109, 116–117.

Chapter 4

1. "New Words Sadly Needed," *The Phonographic World* (August 1896), p. 438.

2. This chapter owes a large debt to Margery Davies's chapter 5, "The Ideological Debate," from her book, *Woman's Place Is at the Typewriter: Office Work and Office Workers, 1870–1930* (Philadelphia: Temple University Press, 1982). Much of the material I use, although from different sources, is strikingly similar. I believe that my analysis both builds upon and moves in a different direction from Davies's. She claims on page 96 that "the ideological assumptions about the natural characteristics of males and females were made to mesh very neatly with the way in which clerical work was organized. Assumptions about women helped to justify not only a situation in which women were clustered in the lower levels of a work organization, but also the very fact that such positions, devoid of much chance of substantial promotion, existed at all." I agree that the assumptions about natural characteristics were important. I am interested in how these assumptions came into being and how they functioned to facilitate women's entrance into clerical occupations.

3. See, for example, Alice Kessler-Harris, *Out to Work: A History of Wage Earning Women in the United States* (New York: Oxford University Press, 1982); Nancy Cott, *The Bonds of Womanhood: "Woman's Sphere" in New England, 1780–1835* (New Haven, Conn.: Yale University Press, 1977); Kathryn Kish Sklar, *Catharine Beecher: A Study in American Domesticity* (New York: Norton, 1973); Carroll Smith-Rosenberg, "The Female World of Love and Ritual: Relations Between Women in Nineteenth-Century America," *Signs* (Autumn 1975), p. 19.

4. These ideas were informed by my general reading in the literature on the sex-typing of occupations. See, for example, Valerie Kincade Oppenheimer, "The Sex-Labeling of Jobs," *Industrial Relations* (May 1968), p. 219; Sam Cohn, *The Process of Occupational Sex-Typing: The Feminization of Clerical Labor in Great Britain* (Philadelphia: Temple University Press, 1985), particularly chapter 1, "Thinking about Occupational Sex Typing," p. 3; Barbara Reskin, ed., *Sex Segregation in the Workplace: Trends, Explanations, Remedies* (Washington, D.C.: National Academy Press, 1984); Shirley Dex, *The Sexual Division of Work: Conceptual Revolutions in the Social Sciences* (New York: St. Martins Press, 1985); Julie A. Matthaei, *An Economic History of Women in America* (New York: Schocken Books, 1982); Barbara Reskin and Heidi Hartmann, eds., *Women's Work and Men's Work: Sex Segregation on the Job* (Washington, D.C.: National Academy Press, 1986); Martha Blaxall and Barbara Reagan, eds., *Women and the Workplace: The Implications of Occupational Segregation* (Chicago: University of Chicago Press, 1976).

5. "The Preachers' Survey," *The Phonographic World* (November 1889), pp. 84–85. The rest of the survey appeared in the issues of December 1889, pp. 100–102; January 1890, pp. 134–135; February 1890, pp. 172–174; March 1890, pp. 206–207; and April 1890, pp. 245–247.

6. William H. Slocum, "Why Some Women Fail of Success in the Court Reporter's Office," *The Phonographic World* (November 1887), p. 53. See also the following articles in that magazine's issues: "The Typewriter vs. Saleswomen and Governesses," October 1886, p. 34; "Women vs. Male Stenographers," January 1892, p. 204; "Would Bar Women as Court Stenographers!" August 1904, pp. 112–113; and "U.S. Government in Need of Good Male Stenographers," December 1902, pp. 462–465.

7. "The Typewriter vs. Saleswomen and Governesses," *The Phonographic World* (October 1886), p. 34; "Typewriter Talk," *The Phonographic World* (June 1887), p. 196; "Chicago's Typewriter Operators," *The Phonographic World* (July 1889), p. 261.

8. "Male and Female Stenographers Compared," *The Phonographic World* (September 1889), p. 15.

9. "The Return of the Business Woman," *The Ladies' Home Journal* (March 1900), p. 16.

10. Hattie A. Shinn, "In Defense of the 'Pretty Type-Writer'," *The Phonographic World* (July 1889), p. 253.

11. Mrs. R. F. Allie, "Why Some Women Fail of Success in the Court Reporter's Office," *The Phonographic World* (November 1887), p. 53.

12. Jane Addams, *A New Conscience and an Ancient Evil* (New York: The MacMillan Company, 1912), pp. 213–214.

13. Clara E. Laughlin, *The Work-A-Day Girl: A Study of Present Day Conditions* (Chicago: Fleming H. Revill, Co., 1913), p. 52.

14. *Ibid.*, pp. 107–124.

15. Janette Egmont, "The Women Stenographer as a Moral Factor," *The Phonographic World* (July 1890), p. 341.

16. See, "Uncle Sam Prefers Male Stenographers," *The Phonographic World* (November 1911), p. 222; and "Women in Government Service," *Gregg Writer* (November 15, 1911), p. 157.

17. Fessenden N. Chase, *Women Stenographers* (Portland, Me.: Southworth Printing Co., 1910), pp. 1, 11–12, 14, 19–20.

18. See these articles in *The Phonographic World:* Hattie A. Shinn, "In Defense of the 'Pretty Type-writer,' " (July 1889), p. 253; "Are Young Men Scared?" (March 1913), p. 430; "Would Censor Movies," (May 1913), p. 551; and "The Typewriter Girl," (March 1906), pp. 203–204.

19. Kathryn Chatoid, "Does Business Contaminate Women?" *The Phonographic World* (November 1900), pp. 140–141.

20. *Ibid.*

21. "The Efficiency of Women Stenographers," *The Phonographic World* (May 1900), p. 529.

22. S. S. Packard, "The Girl Amanuensis," *The Phonographic World* (October 1888), pp. 40–41; see also "The Efficiency of Women Stenographers," p. 529.

23. W. N. Ferris, "The Old Education and the New," *The Phonographic*

World (November 1902), pp. 398–401; see also "Girl Stenographers and Their Employers," *The Phonographic World* (February 1891), p. 184.

24. Egmont, "The Woman Stenographer as a Moral Factor," p. 341.

25. Cromwell Childe, "How To Select a Stenographer," *System* (April 1912), pp. 340–341.

26. This change in the appearance of the clerical worker was advocated or noted in Packard, "The Girl Amanuensis," pp. 40–41; "The Ideal Stenographer," *The Phonographic World* (March 1896), p. 261; Chatoid, "Does Business Contaminate Women," pp. 140–141; "Women Who Do Eat With Their Employers," *The Phonographic World* (November 1901), pp. 252–253; E. F. Jones, "Plain Talk from a Business Man," *The Phonographic World* (July 1901), pp. 490–491; "Personal Appearance," *Gregg Writer* (December 15, 1903), pp. 135–137; "The Dress of the Female Stenographer," *The Phonographic World* (November 1904), pp. 334–335; "Girls Seeking Positions," *Gregg Writer* (October 15, 1906), pp. 60–61; "Office Etiquette for Business Women," *Gregg Writer* (September 15, 1909), p. 4.

27. Jeanette Ballantyne, "Why Some Women Fail of Success in Court Reporter's or Business Office," *The Phonographic World* (September 1887), pp. 16–17.

28. "Wanted—One Hundred Girls as Stenographers," *The Phonographic World* (April 1910), p. 224 (reprinted from the *Chicago Journal*). These kinds of õbjections were fairly common. See "U.S. Government in Need of Good Male Stenographers," pp. 462–465; "Women Stenographers Don't Please the United States Government," *The Phonographic World* (May 1906), p. 285; "Women Stenographers Barred," *The Phonographic World* (October 1903), pp. 338–339; "She's Only a Woman," *The Phonographic World* (August 1903), p. 150; "Women vs. Male Stenographers," p. 204; Charles R. Barrett, "Good Outlook for Women," pp. 321–322; "Girl Stenographers and Their Employers," p. 184; "Young Men Wanted in the Stenographic Profession," *The Phonographic World* (February 1904), pp. 161–166; "A Hint to Women Amanuensis," *The Phonographic World* (September 1903), p. 293.

29. This section on the feminine work ethic was informed by the chapter "Idle Womanhood: Feminist Versions of the Work Ethic," in Daniel T. Rodgers's *The Work Ethic in Industrial America, 1850–1920* (Chicago: University of Chicago Press, 1978).

30. "The Typewriter Girl," pp. 203–204.

31. "Young Women Who Do Eat With Their Employers," pp. 252–253; "Office Etiquette for Business Women," pp. 4–5; Clara Preston Wright, "Points for the Business Woman," *Gregg Writer* (August 15, 1907), p. 454.

32. Chatoid, "Does Business Contaminate Women," p. 140.

33. "Women Stenographers Don't Please," p. 285; "Women Stenographers Barred," pp. 338–339.

34. Barrett, "Good Outlook for Women," p. 321. These kinds of sentiments are also found in "She's Only a Woman," p. 150; "Women vs. Male Stenographers," p. 204; "Young Men Wanted in the Stenographic Profession," pp. 161–

166; and Elbert Hubbard, "The Stenographer," *Gregg Writer* (January 15, 1915), p. 238.

35. "Girl Stenographers and Their Employers," p. 184.

36. "Wanted—One Hundred Girls As Stenographers," p. 224; and Stanley R. Osborn, "Stenography as a Stepping Stone to Fortune for Young Men," *Gregg Writer* (November 15, 1911), p. 125 (reprinted from the *Chicago Tribune*).

37. "Women's Work," *The Phonographic World* (May 1888), p. 197.

38. "Women vs. Male Stenographers," p. 204.

39. Quotes from "Stenographers as Wives," *The Phonographic World* (August 1911), p. 55, and "Why Business Girls Make the Best Wives," *The Phonographic World* (August 1907), p. 73. See also "The Typewriter Girl as Wife Material," *The Phonographic World* (June 1896), p. 381; Fredric Irland, "Opportunities of the Shorthand Beginner," *The Phonographic World* (January 1903), p. 96; "To Marry or Not to Marry: That is the Question," *The Phonographic World* (November 1905), pp. 319–320, and (December 1905), pp. 399–400; and "Women's Sphere in the Business World," *The Phonographic World* (March 1902), pp. 14–23.

40. Mrs. Frank Learned, "The Young Woman in Business," *Gregg Writer* (July 15, 1915), p. 656.

41. I have found Cathy Davidson's personal comments as well as her introduction to *Revolution and the Word: The Rise of the Novel in America* (New York: Oxford University Press, 1986) extremely helpful for understanding the ways literary works have been and can be used for understanding the past. See also James Smith Allen, "History and the Novel: *Mentalité* in Modern Popular Fiction," *History and Theory* 22 no. 3 (1983), p. 249; Janice Radway, "The Utopian Impulse in Popular Literature: Gothic Romance and 'Feminine Protest'," *American Quarterly* 33 (Summer 1981); John G. Cawelti, *Adventures, Mystery, and Romance: Formula Stories as Art and Literature* (Chicago: University of Chicago Press, 1976); Stanley Fish, "Literature in the Reader: Affective Stylistics," *New Literary History* 2 (Autumn 1970), pp. 123–162.

A note on methodology is appropriate. Obviously, one does not interpret and use short stories, novels, and movies as one uses more conventional manuscript sources. Even more so than with the traditional sources of historical inquiry, the intentionality of the writer and the response of the reader merits serious attention. And in recent years, the scholarship concerning the appropriate interpretation of literary works for historical analysis has flowered with numerous competing schools. Rather than latching on to a specific school and engaging in an analysis that would serve to more forcefully validate an interpretative framework than to illuminate the past, let me describe the types of questions, informed by a general reading, that I have brought to my analysis of all literary and cinematic sources in this book. First, by describing the depictions of the female clerical worker in light of the larger historical context and the specific debates previously described, one can deduce the meaning of the author or film maker and, in some instances, the intended impact on the readers and viewers. To accomplish this, I surveyed the literature and films for repeated images, characters, and plots, paying special attention to the female clerical workers' attributes. Did she conform to the norms of feminine behavior and with what reward, or did she deviate and at what price? Does any aspect of the story allow for the empowerment of the reader or the viewer, or does the story, as Janice Radway believes is the case with gothic romances, "engage individuals in a dynamic process of meaning-production through which potentially subversive dissatisfactions are initially expressed, and then managed, recontained, and temporarily explained away by subsequent constructions" (see Radway, "The Utopian Impulse," p. 141).

In addition, all of the cultural sources examined—movies, novels, short stories, photos, and plays—can reveal less intended meanings. Many of these sources functioned not only as outlets of artistic expression, but also, because they were created with an audience (and profit) in mind, tapped "shared cultural conventions." These amorphous assumptions that a "society" maintains at any given point in time scholars also called mentalities or "community assumptions" or the "collective unconscious" (see Allen, "History and the Novel," p. 249; and Davidson, *Revolution and the Word*, pp. 4–5). What was funny, sad, poignant, shocking, appealing, or mysterious about a particular character or situation can reveal the assumptions shared by both the writer or film maker and his or her audience. In fact, I find it significant that the female clerical worker in her work setting appeared so often in the popular culture and in such a varied way before 1930, whereas it is very difficult to find her the focus of any movies, books, or short stories today. To put the matter perhaps a bit simplistically, the female clerical worker, as a character, was interesting to the larger society. Her place within the world of work, the city, and her relationship to marriage was not yet firmly established.

42. "The Typewriter Girl," pp. 203–204; and "Young Women Who Do Eat with Their Employers," pp. 252–253. I will examine this image in the media in more depth in the second half of this chapter.

43. The stories from *The Phonographic World* are listed in chronological order. If the story came from another source, this is indicated. "Bidlington's Miss Stubbs," *Boston Transcript* (August 1887), p. 245; "Typewritten," *London Idler* (January 1894), pp. 181–183; Lillian M. Gowdy, "The Amanuensis Girl: Being a Truthful Narrative of How She Brought Order, Neatness, Efficiency and Comfort in Her Train" (July 1896), pp. 412–413; Martha Ellsbeth, "For the Sake of the Office" (May 1902), pp. 249–253; "Women and Their Work," *New York Evening Post* (August 1902), pp. 94–98; E. K. Stevens, "The Little Typist" (October 1902), pp. 288–295; Anne Guilbert Mahon, "A Stenographer's Compensation" (November 1902), pp. 369–371; Anne Guilbert Mahon, "The New Stenographer" (October 1903), pp. 311–314; Ellis Wood, "The Mighty Atom" (January 1904), pp. 3–6; Ethyl B. Palmer, "A Telephone Proxy" (February 1904), pp. 111–114; Edith Azalia Adams, "A Flash in the Night" (March 1904), pp. 205–207; Jennie Cook, "True Blue" (April 1904), pp. 271–276; Mrs. E. C. Washabaugh, "Eleanor's Investment" (May 1904), pp. 335–338; Anne Guilbert

Mahon, "The Too Obliging Miss Blake" (June 1904), pp. 407–410; Hattie Witherington Sutton, "The Will and the Way" (August 1905), pp. 77–80; Marion Mitchell Barr, "A Mistake in Identity" (October 1905), pp. 203–207; Robert Barr, "The Typewritten Letter" (November 1905), pp. 267–272; Edith Azalia Adams, "The One Thing Needful" (February 1906), pp. 73–77; Edith Azalia Adams, "C.S.—Competent Stenographer" (March 1906), pp. 141–145; Emily Ruth Calvin, "Laura's Mother" (June 1906), pp. 361–362; "Wanted—A Stenographer" (November 1906), pp. 344–346; Elizabeth Colbert Washabaugh, "The Confidences of Annie" (December 1906), pp. 402–405; Hattie Witherington Sutton, "The 'Air' of Meggy" (May 1907), pp. 318–322; Edith Azalia Adams, "Her Independent Touch" (October 1907), pp. 262–254.

44. The fifteen stories that are not resolved with some kind of romantic interaction are in chronological order. "Bidlinton's Miss Stubbs," p. 245; Gowdy, "The Amanuensis Girl," pp. 412–413; "Women and Their Work," pp. 94–98; Stevens, "The Little Typist," pp. 288–295 (Stevens' story ends ambiguously. The little typist of the title ends up as a stenographer with a man whom she respects and who, presumably, will teach her the law, which she longs to study. But there are romantic overtones, as well. It is unclear whether she will end up as a lawyer or a wife); Mahon, "A Stenographer's Compensation," pp. 369–371; Mahon, "The New Stenographer," pp. 311–314; Wood, "The Mighty Atom," pp. 3–6; Adams, "A Flash in the Night," pp. 205–207; Cook, "True Blue," pp. 271–276; Mahon, "The Too Obliging Miss Blake," pp. 407–410; Hattie Witherington Sutton, "The Will and the Way," pp. 77–80; Adams, "C.S.— Competent Stenographer," pp. 141–145; Calvin, "Laura's Mother," pp. 361–362; Sutton, "The 'Air' of Meggy," pp. 318–322; and Adams, "Her Independent Touch," pp. 262–264.

45. See "Typewritten," p. 181; Barr, "The Typewritten Letter," p. 207. See also Washabaugh, "Eleanor's Investment," p. 335; Ellsbeth, "For the Sake of the Office," pp. 249–253; and Palmer, "A Telephone Proxy," pp. 111–114.

46. See Adams, "The One Thing Needful," p. 73; Barr, "A Mistake in Identity." See also Washabaugh, "The Confidences of Annie," p. 402; and "Wanted—A Stenographer," p. 344.

47. Henry Blake Fuller, *The Cliff Dwellers* (Ridgewood, N.J.: The Gregg Press, 1968), p. 70.

48. *Ibid.*, pp. 187–188.

49. David Graham Phillips, *The Grain of Dust* (New York: D. Appleton and Co., 1911), p. 63.

50. *Ibid.*, p. 152.

51. *Ibid.*, p. 246.

52. *Ibid.*, p. 309.

53. Kathy Peiss, *Cheap Amusements: Working Women and Leisure in Turn-of-the-Century New York* (Philadelphia: Temple University Press, 1986), pp. 139–162. I found this section on the gender images in the early films extremely helpful. See also Lary May, *Screening Out the Past: The Birth of Mass Culture and the Motion Picture Industry* (New York: Oxford University Press, 1980), pp.

147–148; and Roy Rosenzweig, *Eight Hours for What We Will: Workers and Leisure in an Industrial City, 1870–1920* (Cambridge: Cambridge University Press, 1983), pp. 191–208.

54. Peiss, *Cheap Amusements,* p. 156.

55. I screened these early films at the Motion Picture, Broadcasting, and Recorded Sound Division of the Library of Congress. For summaries of these motion pictures, see Kemp R. Niver, *Motion Pictures from the Library of Congress Paper Print Collection, 1894–1912* (Berkeley: University of California Press, 1962), and Rita Horwitz and Harriet Harrison, *The George Kleine Collection of Early Motion Pictures in the Library of Congress: A Catalogue* (Washington, D.C.: Library of Congress, 1980).

56. Peiss, *Cheap Amusements,* p. 158. Peiss cites Elizabeth Ewen, "City Lights: Immigrant Women and the Rise of the Movies," *Signs* 5, supp. (Spring 1980), pp. S45–S65.

Chapter 5

1. Scholars who have analyzed the impact of Taylorism on work and workers in U.S. history include: Alfred D. Chandler, *Strategy and Structure: Chapters in the History of American Industrial Enterprise* (Cambridge, Mass.: M.I.T. Press, 1962), pp. 19–51; C. Wright Mills, *White Collar* (New York: Oxford University Press, 1951), pp. 68–69; Harry Braverman, *Labor and Monopoly Capital: The Degradation of Work in the Twentieth Century* (New York: Monthly Review Press, 1974), p. 300; Margery Davies, *Woman's Place Is at the Typewriter: Office Work and Office Workers, 1870–1930* (Philadelphia: Temple University Press, 1982), pp. 97–128.

2. Angel Kwolek-Folland, "The Business of Gender: The Redefinition of Male and Female and the Modern Business Office in the United States, 1880–1930" (Ph.D. dissertation, University of Minnesota, 1987), p. 75. Folland provocatively asserts that "while office employees continued to maintain some control over their relations with management and their work experience, the buildings they worked in began to institutionalize Taylor's ideas in physical form at least ten years before public discussion of 'scientific management.' "

3. Heidi Hartmann, "The Unhappy Marriage of Marxism and Feminism: Towards a More Progressive Union," in Lydia Sargent, ed., *Women and Revolution: A Discussion of the Unhappy Marriage of Marxism and Feminism* (Boston: South End Press, 1981), p. 18.

4. Alan Spear, *Black Chicago: The Making of a Negro Ghetto, 1890–1920* (Chicago: University of Chicago Press, 1967), p. 34.

5. See Richard C. Edward, Michael Reich, and David M. Gordon, eds., *Labor Market Segmentation* (Lexington, Mass.: D.C. Heath and Co., 1975); and David M. Gordon, Richard C. Edwards, and Michael Reich, *Segmented Work, Divided Workers: The Historical Transformation of Labor in the United States* (Cambridge: Cambridge University Press, 1982).

6. See Davies, *Woman's Place Is at the Typewriter*, pp. 163–175; Elyce J. Rotella, *From Home to Office: U.S. Women at Work, 1870–1930* (Ann Arbor, Mich.: UMI Research Press, 1981), p. 168. See also Valerie Kincade Oppenheimer, "The Sex-Labeling of Jobs," *Industrial Relations* 7 (May 1968), p. 219; Heidi Hartmann, "Capitalism, Patriarchy, and Job Segregation by Sex," in Martha Blaxall and Barbara Reagan, eds., *Women and the Workplace: The Implications of Occupational Segregation* (Chicago: University of Chicago Press, 1976), p. 139.

7. N. S. B. Gras, "Development of a Metropolitan Economy in Europe and America," *American Historical Review* 27 (1922), pp. 702–705; James Heilbrun, *Urban Economics and Public Policy* (New York: St. Martins Press, 1974), p. 33; David Ward, *Cities and Immigrants: A Geography of Change in Nineteenth Century America* (New York: Oxford University Press, 1971), p. 94.

8. As quoted in Harold Mayer and Richard Wade, *Chicago, Growth of a Metropolis* (Chicago: University of Chicago Press, 1969), p. 226.

9. Frank A. Randall, *History of the Development of Building Construction in Chicago* (Urbana, Ill.: University of Illinois Press, 1949), p. 11; S. Ferdinand Howe, *Chicago: Commerce, Manufacturing, Banking, and Transportation Facilities* (Chicago: S. Ferdinand Howe and Co., 1884), p. 8; Heilbrun, *Urban Economics*, p. 32.

10. Randall, *History of the Development*, p. 11; Carl W. Condit, *Chicago, 1910–1929: Building, Planning and Urban Technology* (Chicago: University of Chicago Press, 1973), p. 89.

11. Mayer and Wade, *Chicago*, p. 214.

12. A. T. Andreas, *History of Chicago* (Chicago: A. T. Andreas Publishers, 1884), p. 554.

13. Bessie Louise Pierce, *A History of Chicago*, vol. 3 (New York: Alfred A. Knopf, 1937), pp. 224–230.

14. Earl Shepard Johnson, "The Natural History of the Central Business District with Particular Reference to Chicago" (Ph.D. dissertation, University of Chicago, 1941), pp. 259, 376.

15. Braverman, *Labor and Monopoly Capital*, p. 300.

16. Johnson, "Natural History," pp. 354–355.

17. Chicago Association of Commerce, *Chicago: The Great Central Market* (Chicago: R. L. Polk and Company, 1923), p. 50.

18. *Ibid.*, pp. 60, 74.

19. See Boris Emmet and John E. Jeuck, *Catalogues and Counters: A History of Sears, Roebuck, and Company* (Chicago: University of Chicago Press, 1950); and Louis E. Asher and Edith Neal, *Send No Money* (Chicago: Argus Books, 1942).

20. Chicago Association of Commerce, *Chicago*, p. 74.

21. This information for bookkeepers, cashiers, and accountants in Chicago is strikingly different from that for Boston during this period. See Carole Srole, " 'A Position That God Has Not Particularly Assigned to Men': The Feminiza-

tion of Clerical Work, Boston, 1860–1915" (Ph.D. dissertation, University of California, Los Angeles, 1984), p. 227.

22. There has been a flowering of primarily sociological literature concerning women's participation in the labor force. See, for example, Blaxall and Reagan, eds. *Women and the Workplace,* Barbara Reskin, ed., *Sex Segregation in the Workplace: Trends, Explanations, Remedies* (Washington, D.C.: National Academy Press, 1984); Barbara Reskin and Heidi Hartmann, eds., *Women's Work and Men's Work: Sex Segregation on the Job* (Washington, D.C.: National Academy Press, 1986); Clair Brown and Joseph A. Pechman, eds., *Gender in the Workplace* (Washington, D.C.: The Brookings Institute, 1987). In this last volume see, in particular, Myra H. Strober and Carolyn L. Arnold, "The Dynamics of Occupational Segregation Among Bank Tellers," pp. 107–158; Barbara Drygulski Wright et al., eds., *Women, Work, and Technology: Transformations* (Ann Arbor, Mich.: The University of Michigan Press, 1987).

23. Shirley Dex, *The Sexual Division of Work: Conceptual Revolutions in the Social Sciences* (New York: St. Martins Press, 1985), p. 192.

24. Samuel Cohn, *The Process of Occupational Sex-Typing: The Feminization of Clerical Labor in Great Britain* (Philadelphia: Temple University Press, 1985), p. 220.

25. Ava Baron, "Contested Terrain Revisited: Technology and Gender Definitions of Work in the Printing Industry, 1850–1920," in Wright et al., eds., *Women, Work, and Technology,* p. 61.

26. Letter from Isabel Wallace to her mother, November 24, 1885, the Wallace-Dickey Family Papers, Illinois State Historical Library.

27. Letter from Effie Jones to her father William Griffith Jones, August 11, 1890, William Griffith Jones Papers, 1854–1925, Iowa State Historical Society.

28. Letter from Effie Jones to her mother, October 27, 1892, William Griffith Jones Papers.

29. Letter from Effie Jones to her mother, September 21, 1892, William Griffith Jones Papers.

30. Information on specific departments in Sears, Roebuck, and Company was obtained from captions under a series of stereoscoptic pictures produced by the company for public relations in 1906–1907. In this instance, I relied on picture number 48, "The Training School."

31. Emmet and Jeuck, *Catalogues and Counters,* p. 137.

32. *Sears, Roebuck, and Company and Their Employees* (Chicago, 1906), p. 49. This was an employee manual.

33. Stereoscoptic picture number 26, "The Stenographic Department," Sears, Roebuck, and Company, Chicago, 1906–1907.

34. *Manual of Information for Correspondents and Letter Inspectors* (Chicago: Sears, Roebuck, and Company, 1907), pp. 120–121.

35. *Ibid.,* pp. 120–124; Emmet and Jeuck, *Catalogues and Counters,* p. 133; *The Skylight,* selected numbers between August 20, 1901, and December 8, 1908.

36. *Manual of Information,* pp. 120–124; Emmet and Jeuck, *Catalogues and Counters,* p. 148.

37. Davies, *Woman's Place,* pp. 97–128.

38. I would like to thank series editor Ronnie Steinberg for this insight.

39. M. E. Chase, "From Stenographer to the Ownership of a $100,000 Business," *Fort Dearborn Magazine* (December 1921), p. 8; see also *Chicago Central Business Directory, 1908* (Chicago: The Winter's Publishing Co., 1908). In this book, stenographers' offices are listed in office buildings.

40. Margaret Hedstrom, "Automating the Office: Technology and Skill in Women's Clerical Work, 1940–1970" (Ph.D. dissertation, University of Wisconsin, 1988), p. 22. Hedstrom refers to those who attempted to rationalize the office before Taylor's ideals as "systematizers."

41. See Hedstrom, "Automating the Office," particularly chapter 1, " 'The Office Is Management': Management Ideology and Practice, 1900–1940," pp. 12–74; Mills, *White Collar;* Braverman, *Labor and Monopoly Capital;* Davies, *Woman's Place.*

42. "Shall I Have a Central Typing Department," *System* (February 1919), pp. 231–232.

43. For information on bookkeeping, see: Sharon Hartman Strom, " 'Machines Instead of Clerks': Technology and the Feminization of Bookkeeping, 1910–1950," in Heidi Hartmann, ed., *Computer Chips and Paper Clips: Technology and Women's Employment,* vol. II (Washington, D.C.: National Academy Press, 1987), pp. 63–97.

44. Carole Srole, in her dissertation, " 'A Position,' " believes that the depression in the 1870s contributed to changes in the clerical labor force in Boston. See pp. 122, 650–653.

45. *Report of the Commissioner of Education* (Washington, D.C.: U.S. Government Printing Office, 1897/8), pp. 2,441–2,442.

46. "School of Commerce Announces Broadened Course to Prepare Students for Business Careers," *Chicago Commerce* (July 21, 1911), p. 21.

47. *System* (December 1902), p. 1.

48. Kendall Banning, "Making Partners of Employers," *System* (January 1910), p. 24.

49. Kendall Banning, "Machines Instead of Clerks," in *Accounting and Office Methods* (Chicago: A. W. Shaw Co., 1914), p. 40.

50. See Strom, "Machines Instead of Clerks" in Hartmann, *Computer Chips and Paper Clips,* pp. 63–97; Hedstrom, "Automating the Office," p. 47; Priscilla Murolo, "White-Collar Women: The Feminization of the Aetna Life Insurance Company, 1910–1930" (unpublished paper, Yale University, 1982), cited in Strom, "Machines Instead of Clerks," p. 74.

51. Cindy Sondik Aron, *Ladies and Gentlemen of the Civil Service: Middle-Class Workers in Victorian America* (New York: Oxford University Press, 1987), pp. 124–126. Hedstrom in "Automating the Office" states that "the structure of office work was not that clearly divided between women's jobs at the bottom and

men's jobs at the top. Rather, two overlapping, but sexually differentiated career ladders were in place" (p. 20).

52. "Will Discharge Women Clerks," *The Phonographic World* (January 1899), p. 223.

53. "Women Stenographers Barred," *The Phonographic World* (October 1903), pp. 338–339. See also "Women Stenographers Must Go," *The Phonographic World* (August 1903), p. 201.

54. "Fine Changes for Men Stenographers," *The Phonographic World* (October 1902), p. 251. See also "Women versus Male Stenographers," *The Phonographic World* (January 1892), p. 204; "A Great Mistake," *The Phonographic World* (October 1902), p. 250; "Women in Government Service," *Gregg Writer* (November 15, 1911), p. 157; "Male versus Female Stenographers," *The Phonographic World* (December 1911), p. 276.

55. See "Advancement," *Gregg Writer* (October 15, 1905), p. 46; H. G. Kidd, "The Possibilities of the Male Stenographer," *Gregg Writer* (August 15, 1905), p. 453; "Wanted—Young Men," *Gregg Writer* (October 15, 1908), p. 79; "More Male Stenographers Needed," *Gregg Writer* (February 15, 1914), p. 297; Henry J. Holm, "Shorthand is a Field Which Seeks Workers," *Chicago Commerce* (October 27, 1923), p. 98; "Young Men Wanted," *The Phonographic World* (September 1892), p. 15; "Male Stenographers," *The Phonographic World* (October 1902), p. 260; "Editorial," *The Phonographic World* (March 1903), p. 201; "Young Men Wanted in Stenographic Profession," *The Phonographic World* (February 1904), pp. 161–166; "The Young Man Stenographer," *The Phonographic World* (August 1908), p. 77.

56. See "On the Threshold," *Gregg Writer* (September 15, 1908), p. 1; John Robertson, "What Becomes of Stenographers," *The Phonographic World* (March 1889), p. 145; "James Abbott of Chicago," *The Phonographic World* (March 1891), p. 217; "Arthur Reid of Chicago," *The Phonographic World* (May 1891), p. 283; "Women Versus Male Stenographers," p. 204; John F. Soby, "Male Stenographers Required," *The Phonographic World* (July 1902), pp. 38–41; "A Great Mistake," p. 250; "Young Men Wanted in the Stenographic Profession," pp. 161–166; "The Young Man Stenographer," p. 77.

57. "On the Threshold," p. 1.

58. Quoted in *Bryant and Stratton Business College Bulletin* (Chicago: H. B. Bryant, 1939), p. 1.

59. "Women Stenographers Barred," pp. 338–339.

60. F. C. Henderschott and F. E. Weakly, *The Employee Department and Employee Relations* (Chicago: LaSalle Extension University, 1918), pp. 20–25.

61. National Industrial Conference Board, Inc. *Clerical Salaries in the United States, 1926* (New York: National Industrial Conference Board, 1926). Even though the number of clerical workers in Chicago is reported as 2,705 in the text of the report, the appendixes with the data contain 2,699 clerical workers in Chicago, 952 males and 1,747 females. These were reportedly in 32 establishments in Chicago.

62. *Ibid.*, p. 14.

Chapter 6

1. See Jane Addams, *A New Conscience and an Ancient Evil* (New York: The MacMillan Co., 1912); William Stead, *If Christ Came to Chicago!* (London: The Review of Reviews, 1894); Joanne Jay Meyerowitz, *Women Adrift: Independent Wage Earners in Chicago, 1880–1930* (Chicago: University of Chicago Press, 1988).

2. Addams, *A New Conscience*, pp. 213–214.

3. On Chicago, see Julia Wrigley, *Class Politics and Public Schools: Chicago, 1900–1950* (New Brunswick, N.J.: Rutgers University Press, 1982). For a general discussion, see Joel Spring, *Educating the Worker–Citizen: The Social, Economic, and Political Foundation of Education* (New York: Longman, Inc., 1980).

4. On Chicago, see David John Hogan, *Class and Reform: School and Society in Chicago, 1880–1930* (Philadelphia: University of Pennsylvania Press, 1985). For a general discussion, see Michael W. Apple, *Ideology and Curriculum* (London: Routledge and Kegan Paul, 1979).

5. See Elisabeth Hansot and David Tyack, "Gender in American Public Schools: Thinking Institutionally," *Signs* 13 (Summer 1988), p. 741.

6. George Counts, *School and Society in Chicago* (New York: Harcourt, Brace, and Co., 1928), pp. 49–50; Wrigley, *Class Politics;* and Mary Herrick, *The Chicago Schools: A Social and Political History* (Beverly Hills, Ca.: Sage Publications, 1971).

7. John L. Rury, "Vocationalism for Home and Work: Women's Education in the United States, 1880–1930," *History of Education Quarterly* 24 (Spring 1984), pp. 33–34. Rury states that "if business educators were aware of the preponderance of women in their classes they rarely made reference to it." In fact, he claims that there was little explicit segregation of men and women in commercial programs. "Whether for reasons of economy or principle, men and women continued to pursue the same course of commercial study in high schools throughout this period. The impact of the marketplace upon the development of commercial education was substantial, but it was not strong enough to bring educators to differentiate formally the business course by sex."

8. And they did for good economic reasons. See Susan Carter and Mark Prus, "The Labor Market and the American High School Girl, 1890–1928," *Journal of Economic History* 42 (March 1982), p. 164.

9. Albie Frances Mrazek, "Development of Commercial Education in Chicago's Public Schools" (M.A. thesis, University of Chicago, 1938), p. 113.

10. *Ibid.;* and William P. Wilson, "The History and Development of the Public Education Program in Chicago" (Ph.D. dissertation, University of California–Los Angeles, 1948), pp. 202–203.

11. *41st Annual Report of the Board of Education of the City of Chicago* (Chicago: Hack and Anderson, 1895), p. 149 (hereafter abbreviated as *AR*).

12. John E. Stout, "The Development of the High School Curricula in the

North Central States from 1860–1918" (Ph.D. dissertation, University of Chicago, 1921), p. 109.

13. 38th *AR* (1892), p. 50; and 40th *AR* (1894), p. 43.

14. *Proceedings of the Board of Education of the City of Chicago* (August 17, 1892), p. 75 (hereafter abbreviated as *Pro*).

15. *Report of the Commissioner of Education* (Washington, D.C.: U.S. Government Printing Office, 1897/8), p. 2460 (hereafter abbreviated as *RCE*).

16. 41st *AR* (1895), p. 230; Mrazek, "Development of Commercial Education," p. 112.

17. On these developments generally, see Edwin Knepper, *History of Business Education in the United States* (Ann Arbor, Mich.: Edwards Brothers, Inc., 1941), pp. 106–124.

18. 44th *AR* (1898), p. 24.

19. 45th *AR* (1899), p. 165.

20. *Ibid.*, p. 148. Hansot and Tyack report that the belief that girls were better trained than boys was common. See Hansot and Tyack, "Gender in American Public Schools," p. 758.

21. 49th *AR* (1903), p. 14. The debate about the Cooley plan was featured prominently in Wrigley, *Class Politics* (chapter 3), and in Hogan, *Class and Reform* (chapter 4).

22. *Pro* (September 23, 1908), p. 185.

23. Board of Education of the City of Chicago, *Course of Study for the High Schools of Chicago* (June 1909).

24. 47th *AR* (1901), p. 88.

25. Mrazek, "Development of Commercial Education," p. 141.

26. 55th *AR* (1909), p. 128 (470 men and 457 women).

27. 56th *AR* (1910), p. 83.

28. 58th *AR* (1912), p. 107.

29. Board of Education of the City of Chicago, *Course of Study for the High Schools of Chicago* (June 1915 and August 1917).

30. Mrazek, "Development of Commercial Education," p. 141.

31. City Club of Chicago's Subcommittee of the Committee on Public Education, *A Report on Vocational Training in Chicago and other Cities* (Chicago: City Club of Chicago, 1912), pp. 238–243.

32. *Ibid.*, p. 358.

33. 59th *AR* (1913), p. 114; Counts, *School and Society,* pp. 159–160.

34. 59th *AR* (1913), p. 204; John W. Bell, "The Development of the Public High School in Chicago" (Ph.D. dissertation, University of Chicago, 1939), pp. 51–52.

35. *Pro* (December 19, 1917), p. 780. These courses were at Phillips, Medill, Lakeview, Schurz, and Austin high schools.

36. 65th *AR* (1919), p. 8.

37. I. L. Roberts, "The Swift Continuation School," *Chicago Schools Journal* (October 1923), p. 57.

38. 57th *AR* (1911), p. 22.

39. 57th *AR* (1911), p. 91.

40. *Handbook of the Lucy Flower Technical High School* (Chicago, 1937).

41. 59th *AR* (1913), p. 319. Some 181 students were enrolled in the four-year courses at the start of the school year. Some 1,790 students were enrolled in both of the two-year courses, 573 in accounting and bookkeeping, and 1,217 in stenography and typing (*AR*, 1937), p. 118; Mrazek, "Development of Commercial Education," p. 141.

42. In 1913, women constituted 43.6 percent of the enrollment in the four-year course. Although only 37 percent of the students enrolled in the two-year accounting course were women, they accounted for 86.1 percent of those enrolled in the two-year stenography course. Overall, women made up 70.3 percent of those enrolled in the two-year commercial courses and 68 percent of all students enrolled in all commercial courses. They maintained similar percentages until by 1925, women made up 87 percent of all students enrolled in commercial courses. See 59th *AR* (1913), p. 319; *RCE* (1914), p. 450; *RCE* (1915), p. 553; *RCE* (1916), p. 530; *AR* (1924), p. 22.

43. Rury, "Vocationalism for Home and Work," pp. 32–33.

44. Charles Boyd, "What Schools Might Learn from the Employment Agency," *Proceedings from the Second Annual Convention of the Vocational Education Association of the Midwest* (March 30, 31, and April 1, 1916), p. 119.

45. Scholarship and Guidance Association Records, *Annual Report* (February 15, 1924), p. 5. (Scholarship and Guidance Association was the most recent name of both the Joint Committee on Vocational Training of Girls and the Vocational Supervision League. The collection at the Midwest Women's Historical Collection at the University of Illinois at Chicago Circle Campus has all of this organization's materials under this name.)

46. Sophonisba Breckinridge and Edith Abbott, "Finding Employment for Children Who Leave School to go to Work: Report to the Chicago Women's Club, the Chicago Association of Commerce, the Chicago Association of Collegiate Alumnae, and the Women's City Club" (Chicago: Chicago School of Civics and Philanthropy, Department of Social Investigation).

47. "A Brief Statement of the Work of the Vocational Bureau and the Joint Committee for Vocational Supervision" (1914), p. 2. Vocational Supervision League of Chicago archives, Scholarship and Guidance Association Records.

48. "Report of the Scholarship Work," *General Report for 1920–1921* (September 1920–June 1921), p. 3. Scholarship and Guidance Association Records.

49. *Committee for Scholarship for Jewish Children* (1917), p. 2. Scholarship and Guidance Association Records.

50. See, for example, Chicago Women's Club, "Report of Education Department," *Minutes* (April 24, 1907), p. 171; Chicago Women's Club, "Education Department," *Annual Report* (April 27, 1912), p. 2.

51. Association of Collegiate Alumnae of Chicago, *Minutes* (October 17, 1908), p. 222.

52. Association of Collegiate Alumnae of Chicago, *Minutes* (December,

1910), p. 229; Chicago Women's Club, "Department of Education," *Minutes* (April 24, 1907), p. 171; Emma Gilbert Shorey, "The Collegiate Alumnae and the Public Schools in Chicago," *Journal of the Association of Collegiate Alumnae* (December 1898), p. 66.

53. "Corrective Forces at Work in Chicago on the Educational and Industrial Problem of Hiring and Firing," *Chicago Commerce* (May 22, 1914), pp. 8–9.

54. "Back To School," *Chicago Commerce* (August 28, 1914), p. 46.

55. American Association of University Women–Chicago Branch Collection, "The AAUW: Chicago Branch, 1889–1914" (unpublished history, no author given), p. 2; *Announcement to Members of the Chicago Association of Collegiate Alumnae* (1916). (The American Association of University Women is the same organization as the Association of Collegiate Alumnae.)

56. "News Notes from the Bureau of Occupations," *Journal of the Association of Collegiate Alumnae* (December 1916), pp. 279–280.

57. "News Notes from the Bureau of Occupations," *Journal of the Association of Collegiate Alumnae* (January 1917), p. 349.

58. "News Notes from the Bureau of Occupations," *Journal of the Association of Collegiate Alumnae* (October 1918), p. 50.

59. Mary S. Sims, *The Natural History of a Social Institution–the Young Women's Christian Association* (New York: The Woman's Press, 1936), p. 31.

60. YWCA of Chicago Collection, J. Quincy Ames, *Cooperation Between the Young Women's Christian Association and the Young Men's Christian Association* (Chicago: YMCA College, 1929), p. 17.

61. YWCA of Chicago Collection, *19th Annual Report* (1895), p. 30; *22nd Annual Report* (1898), p. 35; *23rd Annual Report* (1899), p. 36; *24th Annual Report* (1900), p. 33; *25th Annual Report* (1901), p. 43; *26th Annual Report* (1902), p. 30; *28th Annual Report* (1904), p. 22; *29th Annual Report* (1905), p. 23; *30th Annual Report* (1906), p. 28; *32nd Annual Report* (1908), pp. 24–25; *33rd Annual Report* (1909), p. 24; *34th Annual Report* (1910), p. 26; *35th Annual Report* (1911), p. 22; *36th Annual Report* (1912), p. 23; *37th Annual Report* (1913), p. 23; *38th Annual Report* (1914), p. 18; *39th Annual Report* (1915), p. 21; *40th Annual Report* (1916), p. 23; *41st Annual Report* (1917), p. 21.

62. YWCA of Chicago Collection, *31st Annual Report* (1907), p. 22.

63. Kittie Van Bodengraven, "Stenographers' and Typists' Association," *Gregg Writer* (March 15, 1910), p. 356.

64. *Union Labor Advocate* (June 1905), p. 31.

65. Letter from Lillian M. Bransfield to Agnes Nestor, October 31, 1908, in the Agnes Nestor Papers, Chicago Historical Society (microfilm edition of *Papers of the Women's Trade Union League and its Principal Leaders, Agnes Nestor Papers,* reel 1); "Stenographers' and Typists' Association of Chicago," *Union Labor Advocate* (June 1909), p. 14; "Stenographers' Union," *Gregg Writer* (March 15, 1910), p. 381.

66. "Stenographers' and Typists' Association of Chicago," p. 14.

67. The *Chicago Daily Tribune* and the *Chicago Record-Herald* reported different membership numbers. "Miss Van Bodengraven who Leads Stenogra-

phers," *Chicago Record-Herald*, October 28, 1911, p. 14; "Typists Fix City Wage Scale," *Chicago Daily Tribune*, October 28, 1911, p. 4.

68. "Organization Committee," *1911/1913 Bienniel Report*, p. 10, in *Papers of the Women's Trade Union League: Publications of the Chicago Branch*, reel 9.

69. "Mail Bag," *Life and Labor* (April 1912), p. 128.

70. *Ibid.*

71. "Are You a Stenographer?" *Bulletin of the Chicago Branch of the Women's Trade Union League* (June 1912), p. 4, in *Papers of the Women's Trade Union League: Publications of the Chicago Branch*, reel 9.

72. "Organization Committee," *1911/1913 Bienniel Report*, p. 14, in *Papers of the Women's Trade Union League: Publications of the Chicago Branch*, reel 9.

73. Emily Barrows, "Trade Union Organizing Among Women in Chicago," (M.A. thesis, University of Chicago, 1927), pp. 63–64.

74. There are conflicting data concerning when this union started. James Errant, in "Trade Unionism in the Civil Service in Chicago, 1895–1930" (Ph.D. dissertation, University of Chicago, 1939) claims that it started in 1907. Emily Barrows writes that it started in 1912. I have sided with Barrows because the union appears in the WTUL Reports in 1912.

75. Barrows, "Trade Union Organizing," p. 42; Errant, "Trade Unionism in the Civil Service," p. 167.

76. Errant, "Trade Unionism in the Civil Service," p. 167; *Chicago Daily News*, June 30, 1919, p. 1; *Chicago Daily News*, March 30, 1920, p. 1.

77. Ethel Geneva Ellison, "The Status of Women in Chicago's City Service," (M.A. thesis, University of Chicago, 1927), p. 82.

78. Bodengraven, "Stenographers' and Typists' Association," p. 357.

79. *Life and Labor* (January 1915), p. 6, cited in Roslyn Feldberg, " 'Union Fever': Organizing Among Clerical Workers, 1900–1930," *Radical America* (May/June 1980), p. 59.

80. Feldberg, "Union Fever," p. 53.

Chapter 7

1. *Eleanor Record* (January 1919), p. 13 (hereafter abbreviated as *ER*).

2. See James McGovern, "The American Woman's Pre–World War I Freedom in Manners and Morals," *Journal of American History* 55 (September 1968), pp. 315–333; Paula Fass, *The Damned and the Beautiful: American Youth in the 1920s* (New York: Oxford University Press, 1977). Estelle Freedman, "The New Woman: Changing Views of Women in the 1920s," *Journal of American History* 61 (September 1974), pp. 372–393; Elaine Tyler May, *Great Expectations: Marriage and Divorce in Post–Victorian America* (Chicago: University of Chicago Press, 1980); Lary May, *Screening Out the Past: The Birth of Mass Culture and the Motion Picture Industry* (New York: Oxford University Press, 1980).

3. Betty Friedan, in *The Feminine Mystique* (New York: Dell Books, 1963), p. 47, discusses how the writers and subjects of women's magazine fiction changed after World War II. The career-woman heroine who was created by career women had changed to the "happy housewife" created primarily by men.

4. Sumiko Higashi, *Virgins, Vamps, and Flappers: The American Silent Movie Heroine* (Montreal: Eden Women's Press, 1978), pp. 170–171.

5. I viewed excerpts of the film *The Stenog* (1918) at the Library of Congress Film Archive. The entire plot was in the Library of Congress Film Archive's collection of copyrighted screenplays.

6. Mary Carolyn Davies, "A Bite of the Lotus," *Woman's Weekly* (June 15, 1918), p. 1. *Woman's Weekly* was a woman's magazine published in Chicago.

7. I only considered those films from the 1920s that were both listed in the American Film Institute Catalogue and reviewed in *Variety* when released. This assured me that the film was actually seen by the public, and gave me some idea regarding the nature of the movie house in which it was shown and how it was received by reviewers and the public. See Kenneth W. Munden, ed., *The American Film Institute Catalogue of Motion Pictures Produced in the United States, 1921–1930* (New York: R. R. Bowker Co., 1971); *Variety Film Reviews,* vols. 1–4 (New York: Garland Publishing Co., 1983); Max Joseph Alvaroz, *Index to Motion Pictures Reviewed in Variety* (Metuchen, N.J.: Scarecrow Press, 1982).

8. This theme was also found in other films. See *Fair Play* (1925), *The Bachelor Girl* (1929), *Lights of the Desert* (1922), *Luring Lips* (1921), *Man to Man* (1930), *Over the Wire* (1921), *Ladies Beware* (1927), *Appearances* (1921), *Any Woman* (1925), *The Clean Up* (1923), *The Curse of Drink* (1922), *Daytime Wives* (1923), and *Salome of the Tenements* (1925).

9. George Ethelbert Walsh, "The Little Petticoat Patriot," *Woman's Weekly* (October 19, 1918), pp. 6, 11; (October 26, 1918), pp. 7, 12; (November 2, 1918), pp. 6, 11; (November 9, 1918), pp. 5–6, 10.

10. See also *The Locked Door* (1929), *The Tie That Binds* (1923), *Lying Wives* (1925), *Man and Maid* (1925), *Ladies Must Play* (1930), *Beyond the Rainbow* (1922), and *Hell's High Road* (1925).

11. I viewed *The Office Wife* at the Film Collection at the Wisconsin State Historical Society.

12. See *The Splendid Lie* (1922), *Chickie* (1925), *The Better Way* (1926), *Thumbs Down* (1927), and *The Bachelor Girl* (1929).

13. See also William Fleming French, "Making a Way," *Woman's Weekly* (October 20, 1917), p. 3; and R. O'Grady, "Her Own Pill," *Woman's Weekly* (August 10, 1922), pp. 3–4, 16–17.

14. C. Wright Mills, *White Collar* (New York: Oxford University Press, 1967), p. xiii.

15. *Ibid.,* p. 204.

16. The novels under consideration in this section are Nathan Asch, *The Office* (New York: Harcourt, Brace and Co., 1925); John Dos Passos, *U.S.A.* (New York: Random House, 1937); Sinclair Lewis, *The Job* (New York: Har-

court, Brace and Co., 1917); Christopher Morley, *Human Being* (New York: Doubleday, Doran, and Co., 1933); Christopher Morley, *Kitty Foyle* (Philadelphia: J. P. Lippincott Co., 1939); Booth Tarkington, *Alice Adams* (New York: Doubleday, Page, and Co., 1921); Ruth Suckow, *Cora* (New York: Alfred A. Knopf, 1929).

17. Lewis, *The Job*, p. 47.

18. Tarkington, *Alice Adams*, pp. 433–434.

19. *Ibid.*

20. Lewis, *The Job*, p. 159.

21. Morley, *Human Being*, p. 283.

22. Lewis, *The Job*, p. 270.

23. According to the biographical information provided by Knopf, Suckow was a self-described Midwesterner who appears to have been a self-supporting woman throughout her life.

24. Suckow, *Cora*, pp. 333, 334.

25. Monthly occupational reports of the central Eleanor club, 1919–1934, Parkway Eleanor Association, Chicago; and *ER* (January 1915), pp. 7–12.

26. Reprinted in *ER* (April 1916), p. 6.

27. John M. Coulter, *The Story of an Ideal: The Story of the Life and Work of Ina Law Robertson, 1867–1916* (Chicago: The Eleanor Association, 1977), p. 34.

28. *ER* (December 1928), p. 5.

29. Coulter, *The Story of an Ideal*, p. 54.

30. Letter from Miss Alma Babb to Lisa M. Fine, June 21, 1983.

31. *ER* (September 1920), p. 15.

32. *ER* (August 1915), p. 12.

33. *ER* (October 1927), p. 15.

34. *ER* (February 1923), p. 11.

35. *ER* (August 1920), p. 14.

36. In 1913, women in Illinois were permitted to vote in certain elections, including Presidential elections.

37. *ER* (December 1916), pp. 12–14.

38. Coulter, *The Story of an Ideal*, p. 56.

39. *ER* (May 1915), p. 3.

40. *ER* (July 1921), pp. 4–5.

41. *ER* (January 1917), p. 5.

42. *ER* (September 1915), p. 11.

43. Barbara Myerhoff, "Rites of Passage: Process and Paradox," in Victor Turner, ed., *Celebration: Studies in Festivity and Ritual* (Washington, D.C.: Smithsonian Institution Press, 1982), p. 129. Other works in anthropology have also informed my thoughts on rituals. See Judith K. Brown, "A Cross-Cultural Study of Female Initiation Rites," *American Anthropologist* 65 (August 1963), p. 837; Mary Douglas, *Implicit Knowledge: Further Essays in Anthropology* (London: Routledge and Kegan Paul, 1975); Clifford Geertz, *The Interpretation of Culture* (New York: Basic Books, 1973); Clifford Geertz, *Local Knowledge:*

Further Essays in Interpretive Anthropology (New York: Basic Books, 1983); Claude Lévi-Strauss, *Structural Anthropology* (New York: Basic Books, 1963); Victor Turner, *The Ritual Process* (Chicago: Aldine Press, 1969); Arnold Van Gennep, *The Rites of Passage* (Chicago: University of Chicago Press, 1960). Historians have also described similar behavior as ritual. Helen Lefkowitz Horowitz, in her *Alma Mater: Design and Experience in Women's Colleges from their Nineteenth Century Beginnings to the 1930s* (New York: Alfred A. Knopf, 1984), p. 162, claims that "students resorted to role-playing and costumes in their parties and rituals, as well as in their dramatic productions. At the all-female dances, upper-class students took the part and sometimes the attire of men." Mary Christine Anderson, in her "Gender, Class, and Culture: Women Secretarial and Clerical Workers in the United States, 1925–1955" (Ph.D. dissertation, Ohio State University, 1986), devotes an entire chapter to this kind of ritualistic behavior among women living at YWCA residences. See chapter 5, "After Work: The Homosocial Culture of Young Women Office Workers, 1920–1948."

44. *ER* (December 1916), p. 15. Other kid parties with club number provided were reported in the *Eleanor Record*. See *ER* (July 1916), club 1, p. 12; (March 1917), club 5, pp. 18–19; (December 1917), club 5, p. 15; (October 1921), club 1, p. 15; (August 1921), club 1, p. 10; (November 1921), club 6, p. 16; (January 1922), club 1, p. 10; (May 1922), club 4, p. 13; (March 1924), club 4, p. 13; (May 1924), clubs 1 and 3, pp. 10, 11.

45. *ER* (January 1922), p. 10.
46. *ER* (May 1924), p. 10.
47. *ER* (August 1921), p. 10.
48. *ER* (June, July, and August 1924), p. 14.
49. *ER* (May 1916), p. 21.
50. *ER* (June 1922), p. 10.
51. *ER* (June 1923), p. 11.
52. *ER* (July 1916), p. 14.
53. *ER* (May 1923), p. 11.

54. Carroll Smith-Rosenberg has documented the importance of female friendships in her article, "The Female World of Love and Ritual: Relations Between Women in Nineteenth-Century America," *Signs* 1 (Autumn 1975), p. 19. Women in the Eleanor clubs also found this support essential in their own lives.

55. *ER* (January 1917), p. 5.

56. See, for example, *ER* (January 1917), p. 5; *ER* (October 1917), p. 4; *ER* (June 1917), p. 4; *ER* (July 1921), pp. 4, 5; *ER* (February 1927), pp. 4, 5; *ER* (April 1927), p. 5; *ER* (June, July, and August 1927), pp. 6, 7, and 8; and *ER* (March 1931), pp. 5–7. A "Business Woman's Creed," printed in the *Eleanor Record* in May 1915, echoes the work ethic embraced by these women: "I believe in the firm I am working for, in the goods I am selling and in my ability to get results. I believe that honest work can be done by honest women, by means of honest methods; that in this world of competition, one gets just what she goes

after, and that earnest, zealous effort is never entirely lost. I believe in working, not weeping; in boosting, not knocking, and in the joy and satisfaction of labor well done" (*ER* [May 1915]), p. 3.

57. I would like to thank Steve Feierman for this as well as other insights into these rituals. Although it is beyond the scope of my analysis here, I would like to suggest that kid parties may have been a particularly female response to work discipline. Much has been written about the response of male industrial workers to the imposition of work timed by the clock and regulated by scientific management. Like pre-industrial workers, many of the Eleanor women were from small towns and rural areas and may have had no prior exposure to time discipline before coming to work in the city.

58. *ER* (September 1920), p. 12.

59. *ER* (April 1921), p. 13.

60. *ER* (May 1922), p. 10.

61. *ER* (May 1921), p. 13.

62. Myerhoff, "Rites of Passage," p. 129. She claims, "A view of reality and a corresponding view of self are thus established through ritual, creating a subjective psychological state that restructures meaning. This is the work of ritual and the way it provides solutions to problems."

63. "Crinoline Days" is perhaps understandable on both personal and historical levels. A crinoline is both the undergarment of an earlier time and an undergarment from childhood.

64. *ER* (April 1924), p. 10.

65. "Our Famous Women," *ER* (March 1923), p. 2.

Chapter 8

1. "Will Celebrate Jubilee of Typewriter," *Chicago Commerce* (July 21, 1923), pp. 13–14.

2. Ruth Shonle Cavan, *Business Girls: A Study of Their Interests and Problems,* Religious Education Monograph no. 3 (Chicago: The Religious Education Association, 1929), pp. 56–57.

3. Ethel Erickson, *The Employment of Women in Offices,* Bulletin of the Women's Bureau no. 120, U.S. Department of Labor (Washington, D.C.: U.S. Government Printing Office, 1934), p. 70.

4. *Ibid.,* pp. 86–88.

5. Since Harry Braverman's *Labor and Monopoly Capital: The Degradation of Work in the Twentieth Century* (New York: Monthly Review Press, 1974), most historians have been careful not to overstate the amount of scientific management techniques applied to all types of workplaces during the first four decades of the twentieth century; recent historians of the labor process in white-collar sectors have maintained that cautious stance. See Mary Christine Anderson, "Gender, Class, and Culture: Women Secretarial and Clerical Workers in the United States, 1925–1955" (Ph.D. dissertation, Ohio State University, 1986), and Margaret Lucille Hedstrom, "Automating the Office: Technology and

Skill in Women's Clerical Work: 1940–1970" (Ph.D. dissertation, University of Wisconsin–Madison, 1988).

6. Erickson, *Employment of Women,* p. 91.

7. *Ibid.,* pp. 16, 17.

8. *Ibid.,* p. 90, and see also Sharon Hartman Strom, " 'Machines Instead of Clerks': Technology and the Feminization of Bookkeeping, 1910–1950," in Heidi Hartmann, ed., *Computer Chips and Paper Clips: Technology and Women's Employment,* vol. II (Washington, D.C.: National Academy Press, 1987), pp. 63–97.

9. Erickson, *Employment of Women,* p. 75.

10. "These Days: Crusading for Human Efficiency" (Chicago: Montgomery Ward and Co., January 9, 1920), p. 9, from the Archival Organization File, part 1, box 82, at the Labor–Management Documentation Center, Martin P. Catherwood Library, New York State School for Industrial and Labor Relations, Cornell University.

11. "These Days," p. 6.

12. "Sears Jobs for Sears Men" (Chicago: Sears, Roebuck and Co., 1930), from Archival Organization File, part 4, box 113, at the Labor–Management Documentation Center, Martin P. Catherwood Library.

13. Erickson, *Employment of Women,* p. 17.

14. *Ibid.,* p. 14.

15. Margery Davies, *Woman's Place Is at the Typewriter: Office Work and Office Workers, 1879–1930* (Philadelphia: Temple University Press, 1982), Chapter 7, "The Private Secretary," pp. 129–162, and in particular pages 154 and 155; and Anderson, "Gender, Class, and Culture," section entitled "The Secretary's Job," pp. 372–381.

16. Erickson, *Employment of Women,* p. 92.

17. *Ibid.,* p. 85.

18. Cavan, *Business Girls,* p. 62.

19. See Alfred L. Severson, "Discrimination Against Jews in Employment in Chicago Offices" (M.A. thesis, University of Chicago, 1934).

20. Theodore T. Cowgill, "The Employment Agencies of Chicago" (M.A. thesis, University of Chicago, 1928), p. 85.

21. Letitia F. Merrill, "Children's Choice of Occupation," *Chicago Schools Journal* (December 1922), pp. 157–158.

22. *Ibid.*

23. Vocational Guidance Bureau, *A Study of Beginning Office Positions for Young Women* (Chicago: Board of Education of the City of Chicago, 1925), p. 18.

24. *Proceedings of the Board of Education of the City of Chicago* (July 9, 1924), p. 13; and *Proceedings of the Board of Education of the City of Chicago* (September 3, 1924), pp. 168–169.

25. *Annual Report of the Board of Education of the City of Chicago* (June 30, 1925), p. 103.

26. Edwin C. Cooley, *Second Annual Report on Chicago's Continuation Schools* (Chicago: Board of Education of the City of Chicago, 1920), pp. 3, 12.

NOTES TO CHAPTER 8

27. Nona Goodwin, "Socializing Influences in a Part-Time School for Girls," *Chicago Schools Journal* (September 1922), p. 8.

28. *Ibid.*, p. 5.

29. *Ibid.*, p. 7.

30. Scholarship and Guidance Association Records, *Annual Office Report* (1923–1924), pp. 8–9.

31. *Office Report for the Director's Meeting* (October 19, 1920), p. 7. Vocational Supervision League of Chicago archives, Scholarship and Guidance Association Records. See also in Scholarship and Guidance Association Records, *Report of the Director's Meeting* (November 15, 1921), p. 6; *Scholarship and Guidance Director's Meeting, Office Report* (March 15, 1921); *Annual Office Report of the Scholarship Association for Jewish Children* (May 1, 1919–May 1, 1920), p. 3; *Annual Office Report* (1921–1922); *Annual Office Report of the Scholarship Association for Jewish Children* (April 1927), pp. 9–10; *Annual Office Report* (1929), p. 7.

32. *Annual Office Report of the Scholarship Association for Jewish Children* (April 1927), pp. 9–10. Scholarship and Guidance Association Records.

33. Cavan, *Business Girls*, pp. 2–3.

34. Joanne J. Meyerowitz, *Women Adrift: Independent Wage Earners in Chicago, 1880–1930* (Chicago: University of Chicago Press, 1988). Meyerowitz also described this shift in the focus of reformers.

35. Meyerowitz, *Women Adrift*, pp. 46, 47.

36. Ann Elizabeth Trotter, *Housing for Non-Family Women in Chicago: A Survey* (Chicago: Chicago Community Trust, 1921), p. 15.

37. *Ibid.*, p. 38.

38. *Ibid.*, p. 15.

39. In the mid-1910s, the Eleanor club issued this list of boarding-houses for women. Superintendents of the club were instructed to provide girls leaving the Eleanor club with a list of suitable accommodations. They were as follows. Jewish homes: Josephine club (for immigrant girls), Miriam club (for working girls), Ruth club; Roman Catholic homes: Mercy Home (for working girls), St. Joseph Home; Non-Catholic Homes: Augustana Central Home, Immanuel Women's Home Association (Swedish), Mission Home (Swedish Lutheran), Indiana House, McKinley (for working girls), Susanna Wesley Home (for Scandinavian clerks and domestics), Y.W.C.A., Home of the Friendless, Women's Model Lodging House; "Colored People": The Phyllis Wheatley Home; Miscellaneous homes: Baptist Deaconesses and Girls Home, Cooperative League of Chicago, Free Kindergarten Association Dormitory, Hobbs House, House of Providence, The Jane club, Martha Washington Home (for drunkards), Mespa Swedish Home, Monette Hall, Norwegian–Danish Young Women's Christian Home, Salvation Army Home for Young Women.

40. Meyerowitz, *Women Adrift*, p. 89.

41. *Eleanor Record* (March 1918), p. 14.

42. *Bulletin* (February 1917), p. 1. Women's City Club of Chicago Collection.

43. "Club Privileges for the Business Woman," *Bulletin* (June 1922), p. 41.

44. Esther J. Wanner, "News of the Young Woman's Auxilliary," *Bulletin* (July/August, 1922), p. 63.

45. Margaret E. O'Connell, "Business Women and the YWCA," *The Association Monthly* (January 1917), p. 529.

46. "Business and Professional Women's Conference," *The Association Monthly* (July 1922), p. 354; YWCA of Chicago, *47th Annual Report* (1924), p. 25; YWCA of Chicago, "Business And Professional Women," *Report of the National Board of the YWCA of USA, 9th Annual Convention at Milwaukee, Wisconsin* (April 21–28, 1926), p. 59.

47. YWCA of Chicago, *8th Annual Convention of the National Board of the YWCA* (New York, April 30–May 6, 1924), p. 318. The national board reported that there were 18,000 girls in the industrial clubs and about 31,000 girls in their business girls clubs.

48. YWCA of Chicago, "The Interests and Concerns of Membership Groups: Business and Professional," *Report of the National Board of the YWCA of USA to the 10th National Convention* (Sacramento, Calif., April 14–21, 1928), p. 30.

49. YWCA of Chicago, "Young Business Women's Clubs," *47th Annual Report* (1924), p. 17. This criticism of business women also appeared in Ethel Mae Lindelof, "A Business Woman's Attitude Toward Legislation," *The Woman's Press* (September 1923), p. 577.

50. YWCA of Chicago, "Young Business Women," *Minutes of the Regular Meeting* (November 10, 1927), p. 3.

51. YWCA of Chicago, *47th Annual Report* (1924), p. 25.

52. YWCA of Chicago, *Minutes of the Board of Director's Meeting* (November 9, 1922), p. 2.

53. YWCA of Chicago, *46th Annual Report* (1923), p. 21.

54. YWCA of Chicago, "The Girl and the Job," *The Tiny Y* (December 1922), p. 3.

55. YWCA of Chicago, *Board of Director's Meeting* (December 13, 1923), p. 2.

56. YWCA of Chicago, *47th Annual Report* (1924), p. 17.

57. YWCA of Chicago, "Education," *44th Annual Report* (1921), p. 10.

58. YWCA of Chicago, "Central Branch," *45th Annual Report* (1922), p. 8; *Board of Director's Meeting* (April 12, 1923), p. 4; "Business Courses," *The Tiny Y* (January 1925), p. 2; "Young Business Women's Club," *47th Annual Report* (1924), p. 25.

59. Gladys Gardner Jenkins, "The Business Girl Looks at Marriage: The Chicago YWCA Studies an Old Institution in a New Way," *The Woman's Press* (June 1929), pp. 406–407.

60. Cavan, *Business Girls*, pp. 84–86.

61. Grace Coyle, "The Clerical Worker and Her Job," *The Woman's Press* (July 1928), p. 460.

Bibliographic Essay

*T*HIS STUDY required the use of a wide variety of archival, manuscript, and other primary sources, many of which were found in the rich collections of the Chicago area. Below is a selected list of the primary sources used in this book, grouped together by type.

Government Documents and Directories

The five major government documents used were manuscript census schedules, summary census material, reports of the Illinois Bureau of Labor Statistics, the Reports of the Commissioner of Education, and the Bulletins of the Women's Bureau of the U.S. Department of Labor. The hand-written manuscript census schedules of 1880, 1900, and 1910 provided much of the household information on clerical workers throughout the book. Demographic data on the clerical labor force in Chicago came from the summarized census material issued from the U.S. Bureau of the Census in 1870, 1880, 1890, 1900, 1910, 1920, and 1930, and in particular, U.S. Bureau of the Census, *Statistics of Women at Work Based on Unpublished Information Derived from the Schedules of the Twelfth Census* (Washington, D.C.: U.S. Government Printing Office, 1907). Additional information about the working conditions and budgets of female clerical workers came from the *Seventh Annual Bienniel Report: Part One: Working Women in Chicago* (Springfield, Ill.: Illinois Bureau of Labor Statistics, 1892), as well as from other bulletins and reports of the Illinois Bureau of Labor Statistics. The *Report of the Commissioner of Education* (Washington, D.C.: U.S. Government Printing Office) from the 1870s through the 1910s provided information about private business colleges in Chicago. The U.S. Department of Labor's Women's Bureau studies, particularly Ethel Erickson's *The Employment of Women in Offices*, Bulletin of the Women's Bureau no. 120 (Washington, D.C.: U.S. Government Printing Office, 1934) was also helpful in piecing together information about wages, hours, and working conditions of female clerical workers.

The information supplied in the Chicago city directories was used in a variety of ways. I used directories from the earlier years to get a crude sense of the labor force. I used directories after 1870 to generate names of small groups of clerical workers (public stenographers and business school students), to check addresses for manuscript census searches, and to determine the length of time clerical workers spent in the labor force in Chicago. Directories used were:

Fergus' 1839 Directory of the City of Chicago. Chicago: Fergus Printing Co., 1879.

Norris, J. W. *General Directory and Business Advertiser of the City of Chicago.* Chicago: Ellis and Fergus Printers, 1844.

Norris, J. W. *A Business Advertiser and General Directory of the City of Chicago.* Chicago: J. Campbell and Co., 1845.

Norris' Chicago Directory for 1846 and 1847. Chicago: Geer and Wilson, 1846.

Hathaway, O. P., and Taylor, J. H. *Chicago City Directory and Annual Advertiser for 1849–1850.* Chicago: Jas. J. Langdon Book and Job Printer, 1849.

Kennedy, R. V., and Company. *D. B. Cooke and Company's City Directory for the Year 1859–1860.* Chicago: D. B. Cook and Company, 1859.

John C. W. Bailey's Chicago City Directory for 1864–1865. Chicago: John C. W. Bailey, 1864.

Edward's Chicago Business Directory, 1866–1867. Chicago: Edwards, Greenough, and Deved, 1866.

John C. W. Bailey's City Directory. Chicago: John C. W. Bailey, 1867.

Edward's Annual Directory to the City of Chicago, 1868–1869. Chicago: Edward and Co., 1868.

Edward's Annual Directory to the City of Chicago, 1869–1870. Chicago: Edward and Co., 1869.

Directory of the Inhabitants, Institutions, Incorporated Companies and Manufacturing Establishments of the City of Chicago, 1870. Chicago: Richard Edward Publisher, 1870.

Edward's Annual Directory. Chicago: Edward's Publishing Co., 1872.

Edward's 16th Annual Directory of the City of Chicago. Chicago: Richard Edward Publisher, 1873.

The Lakeside Annual Directory of the City of Chicago. Chicago: William Donnelley and Co., 1874 and 1875.

The Lakeside Annual Directory of the City of Chicago. Chicago: The Chicago Directory Company, 1880–1917, and 1923.

Corporate Records

Information about male and female office workers came primarily from the Sears, Roebuck and Company corporate archives and the McCormick Collection at the Wisconsin State Historical Society Archives. The Sears archive contained an employee journal, employee manuals, photographs, and pamphlets about or oriented to office workers. The McCormick Collection had roll books with information about office employees. The one most helpful to me was from the Deering Harvester Company of Chicago and was listed as *(Deering) Record of Employees, 1896(?).* To supplement this, I used selected materials from the Archival Organization File at the Labor–Management Documentation Center,

Martin P. Catherwood Library, New York State School for Industrial and Labor Relations, Cornell University. This large, haphazardly catalogued collection contains pamphlets, booklets, and in-house organs from a variety of companies throughout the United States. I was able to find some information about Chicago companies within this collection, particularly Sears, Roebuck and Company, and Montgomery Ward and Company.

Cultural Materials

Images of clerical workers appeared in novels, short stories, and motion pictures. Most of the novels were easily available in a college or university library, although Sinclair Lewis's *The Job* has been out of print for half a century, making it harder to find. Most of the short stories that I used in the book appeared in *The Phonographic World* or in *Woman's Weekly*. I viewed as many of the films as I could, but, in many instances, I needed to resort to descriptions or scripts. I was able to see the early silent films at the Motion Picture, Broadcasting, and Recorded Sound Division of the Library of Congress. Summaries of these motion pictures and others appear in Kemp R. Niver's *Motion Pictures from the Library of Congress Paper Print Collection, 1894–1912* (Berkeley, Ca.: University of California Press, 1962), and Rita Horwitz and Harriet Harrison's *The George Kleine Collection of Early Motion Pictures in the Library of Congress: A Catalogue* (Washington, D.C.: Library of Congress, 1980). I also viewed talkies from the early 1930s at the film collection at the Wisconsin State Historical Society. Most films, however, were difficult, if not impossible, to see, making Kenneth W. Munden's *The American Film Institute Catalogue of Motion Pictures Produced in the United States, 1921–1930* (New York: R. R. Bowker Co., 1971), an extremely valuable resource. This reference book provides an index of the title and content of all the films. I needed only to look under "stenographer," "typist," "office worker," and other key words to find many appropriate films' titles and descriptions of their plots and characters. I then matched this list with reviews in *Variety* magazine to make sure the film was actually seen by the public and to gather any additional information about it. See *Variety Film Reviews*, vols. 1–4 (New York: Garland Publishing Co., 1983), and Max Joseph Alvaroz, *Index to Motion Pictures Reviewed in Variety* (Metuchen, N.J.: Scarecrow Press, 1982).

Organizational Records

The records of many of Chicago's philanthropic, religious, and public organizations are found in the Chicago Historical Society and the manuscript collection at the University of Illinois at Chicago, Chicago Circle Campus. The historical society houses the records of the Chicago branch of the American Association of University Women, the Chicago Women's Club papers, and the

entire Women's Trade Union League papers on microfilm. The regular library at
the historical society contained many important published works used throughout
this book. The Chicago Women's Aid Collection, the Scholarship and Guidance
Association records, the Women's City Club of Chicago papers, and the Young
Women's Christian Association of Chicago Collection are all part of the Midwest
Women's Collection at the University of Illinois at Chicago, Chicago Circle
Campus. I also consulted the Hull House Association Collection, now at Hull
House itself. The Board of Education of the City of Chicago has its own library,
and in addition to the annual reports and proceedings of the board, also has old
curricula, surveys, and other valuable information. The annex of the New York
Public Library is where the Beale Collection on Shorthand and Stenography is
stored. This eclectic collection contains helpful journals, books, pamphlets, and
leaflets about the unions and associations that shorthand reporters of the late
nineteenth century attempted to organize.

Some of the richest material in the book came from the Eleanor Association,
now called the Parkway Eleanor Association. Much of the material used came
from the association's journal, the *Eleanor Record,* but some came from files,
pamphlets, photographs, memorabilia, and unbound typed sheets that are still in
mountains of boxes in the basement of the last remaining residence at the corner
of Dearborn Parkway and North Avenue in Chicago. There is a wealth of
information there that will one day, I hope, be preserved and made available for
many more scholars to use.

Journals

Many different types of periodicals were examined for this book. Trade or
specialty journals such as *The Phonographic World* (which between 1885 and
1913 also appeared under the names *Illustrated Phonographic World, The Typewriter and Phonographic World,* and *The Phonographic World and Commercial
School Review), Gregg Writer* (1903–1916, and 1928–1929), *System* (1902–
1930), and *Chicago Commerce* (1911–1923) featured prominently in the text in
a variety of ways. Many of the short stories discussed in the book, for example,
appeared in *The Phonographic World.* Both *System* and *Gregg Writer* were
published for some of the time in Chicago and contained much useful information about both the private business scene and office work in general in the city.
Other journals used in the study are *Association Monthly* (1916–1918, 1922–
1923), *Chicago Daily News* (selected dates), *Chicago Daily Tribune* (selected
dates), *Chicago Tribune* (selected dates), *Chicago Principals' Club Reporter*
(1911–1927), *Chicago Record Herald* (selected dates), *Chicago Schools Journal*
(1918–1935), *The Educational Bi-Monthly* (1906–1911), *Eleanor Record*
(1915–1930), *Harvester World* (published by International Harvester from 1909
to 1918), *Journal of the Association of Collegiate Alumnae* (1898–1931), *Life
and Labor* (1911–1921), *National Shorthand Reporter* (1913–1917), *The Practical Phonographer* (1884), *The Skylight* (published by Sears, Roebuck, and

Company from August 20, 1901 to December 8, 1908), *The Stenographic World* (1892–1893), *Union Labor Advocate* (1904–1910), *The Woman's Press* (1923–1930), and *Woman's Weekly* (1917–1930).

Dissertations and Surveys

Chicago is a wonderful subject of study because of its rich Progressive legacy. Everyone, it seems, was examining the city. Much helpful information came from the doctoral dissertations and masters' theses produced by the graduate students in commerce and administration (later business), education, history, political science, and particularly sociology at the University of Chicago during the early twentieth century. These are all available at the Regenstein Library at the University of Chicago.

Some of the most helpful published local surveys found in the various repositories in Chicago are:

Vocational Guidance Bureau, *A Study of Beginning Office Positions for Young Women*. Chicago: Board of Education of the City of Chicago, 1925.

Breckinridge, Sophonisba, and Edith Abbott. *Finding Employment for Children Who Leave School to go to Work: Report of the Chicago Women's Club, the Chicago Association of Collegiate Alumnae, and the Women's City Club*. Chicago: Chicago School of Civics and Philanthropy, Department of Social Investigation, 1911.

Subcommittee of the Committee on Public Education. *A Report on Vocational Training in Chicago and Other Cities*. Chicago: City Club of Chicago, 1912.

Cavan, Ruth Shonle. *Business Girls: A Study of Their Interests and Problems*. Chicago: The Religious Education Association, 1929.

Comstock, Harriet Jane. *A Study of Girls' Work in Chicago*. Chicago: Chicago Council of Social Agencies, 1924.

National Industrial Conference Board. *Clerical Salaries in the United States, 1926*. New York: National Industrial Conference Board, Inc., 1926.

Trotter, Elizabeth Ann. *Housing for Non-Family Women in Chicago: A Survey*. Chicago: Chicago Community Trust, 1921.

Zorbaugh, Harvey W. *The Gold Coast and the Slum: A Sociological Study of Chicago's Near North Side*. Chicago: University of Chicago Press, 1929.

Index

Montgomery Ward and Company, 80, 94, 171–173
Morley, Christopher, 146–149
Murolo, Priscilla, 92
Myerhoff, Barbara, 157

National Industrial Conference Board, 96–101, 168
National Shorthand Reporters' Association, 133
National Union of Stenographers, 15
Nativity: females, 33–34, 38, 48, 49 (Table 12), 188; males, 8–9
New York City, 136
Nickelodeons, 73, 74
Northwestern University's School of Commerce, 91
Novels: depiction of female clerical workers in, 70–73, 146–151; use in history, 217–218 n.41

Occupational hierarchy, 92–103, 171–173, 187
Office, 12; in cultural depictions, 70, 140, 141; as male space, 10, 54, 105; sexual division of labor in, 92–103; and women's morality, 57–60
Office Employees Association, 134–135
Office machines, 89, 92, 170–171, 187
Office romance: in short stories, 68–69, 73
The Office Wife (1930), 143–144
Office wives, 141, 173
"Old maid parties," 157, 158, 159, 161, 163

Patriarchy, 92, 165; definition, 204 n.11; effects on occupational sex typing, xvii
Peiss, Kathy, 73, 74
Phillips, David Graham, 71
The Phonographic World, 9, 11, 51, 55, 57, 59–60, 62, 65–70, 94, 206 n.26
Phonography. *See* Stenography-typing
Private business colleges, 26, 62, 85,

119, 120; amanuensis courses in, 23; and collegiate schools of business, 23–24, 90, 121; curricula of, 22–24; female students in, 22–23, 24–25; male students in, 9–10
Progressive era, 119
Promotability in clerical work: of men, 93–94; of women, 93, 94–96, 171–173, 187
Prostitution, 118

Race. *See* Black women in clerical work
Rationalization of clerical work. *See* Degradation of clerical work
Reformers, 117–118, 131, 133, 136, 186; change in attitude toward working women, 179–186; of Eleanor Association, 152, 153
Religious Education Association, 168, 185
Residential clubs, 180–181. *See also* Eleanor residences
Retail clerks, 44
Rituals: analysis for history, 157–158; at Eleanor residences, 157–164
Robertson, Ina Law, 18, 41, 152
Room registries, 181
Rooming-houses, 118, 180–181
Roosevelt, Theodore, 94
Rosing, Astrid, 88
Rotella, Elyce J., 47
Routinization of clerical work. *See* Degradation of clerical work
Rury, John, 127

Scientific management, xvii, 77, 78, 89, 90, 102, 140, 171, 173, 187
Sears, Roebuck and Company, 80, 88, 173; clerical work at, 86–87
Secretary, 187; appearance of, 173
Segmented labor force, 78
Sennett, Richard, 8–9
Separate spheres, 17, 19, 52, 53–54, 60, 74

248

INDEX